Australian & New Zealand Edition

Success *Online* *Start-Ups*

FOR

DUMMIES®

by Stefan Korn

WILEY

Wiley Publishing Australia Pty Ltd

Successful Online Start-Ups For Dummies®, Australian and New Zealand Edition

Published by
Wiley Publishing Australia Pty Ltd
42 McDougall Street
Milton, Qld 4064
www.dummies.com

Copyright © 2012 Wiley Publishing Australia Pty Ltd

The moral rights of the author have been asserted.

National Library of Australia
Cataloguing-in-Publication data:

Author:	Korn, Stefan.
Title:	Successful Online Start-Ups For Dummies/Stefan Korn.
Edition:	Australian & New Zealand ed.
ISBN:	978 1 11830 270 5 (pbk.)
Series:	For Dummies.
Notes:	Includes index.
Subjects:	New business enterprises — Management. Electronic commerce — Management.
Dewey Number:	658.11

Cover image: © iStock/Axaulya

Typeset by diacriTech, Chennai, India

Printed in China by
Printplus Limited

10 9 8 7 6 5 4 3 2 1

About the Author

Stefan Korn is a New Zealand–based internet entrepreneur who is passionate about online technology and enjoys the challenge of getting new businesses off the ground. Stefan has a PhD in artificial intelligence and machine learning, an MBA in international business and an honours degree in computer engineering. Before becoming an entrepreneur, Stefan held senior management roles for large international corporations in the IT, telecommunication and hospitality sectors. In 2007, Stefan set up WebFund, a private incubator, to provide a vehicle for investments into online start-ups. Over the last five years, Stefan and his business partners at WebFund have worked with hundreds of entrepreneurs, helping them get started on their start-up journey and, for many of them, avoid financial failure with their ventures. In addition to running WebFund and serving his board duties for WebFund's investments, he is also actively engaged in community education — and enjoys producing trance music tracks with his son, Noah.

Author's Acknowledgements

First and foremost I would like to thank my wife, Raquel, and my son, Noah, for letting me write this book (and thus forgoing some family time with me). I'd also like to thank my business partners, Dave Moskovitz and Campbell Means, for their help and support over the years.

A special thank you goes to Lincoln Gasking who has inspired us all with his innovative ideas and projects, and for his help in reviewing the manuscript for this book.

Many thanks also to the wonderful team at Wiley — Charlotte, Clare and Dani — who helped tremendously with turning my raw thoughts into readable and structured content. Special thanks also to Rebecca Crisp, who believed in this book from day one.

And last but not least I'd like to thank all the individuals and organisations who have worked with me over the last 15 years to provide many of the experiences I have covered in this book.

Thank you and best wishes for all your start-up ventures!

Publisher's Acknowledgements

We're proud of this book; please send us your comments through our online registration form located at http://dummies.custhelp.com.

Some of the people who helped bring this book to market include the following:

Acquisitions, Editorial and Media Development

Project Editor: Charlotte Duff

Acquisitions Editors: Rebecca Crisp, Clare Weber

Editorial Manager: Dani Karvess

Production

Cartoons: Glenn Lumsden

Proofreader: Catherine Spedding

Technical Reviewer: Lincoln Gasking

Indexer: Don Jordan, Antipodes Indexing

Every effort has been made to trace the ownership of copyright material. Information that enables the publisher to rectify any error or omission in subsequent editions is welcome. In such cases, please contact the Permissions Section of John Wiley & Sons Australia, Ltd.

Contents at a Glance

Table of Contents

Introduction

● ●

*S*uccessful Online Start-Ups For Dummies is the first book
written for entrepreneurs of technology start-ups in
Australia and New Zealand. The content represents a summary
of the last ten years of my life working in e-commerce and
helping entrepreneurs get their businesses off the ground.

In 2007, I started WebFund, a private incubator for web-based
start-ups, to formalise my efforts to help local ventures become
wildly successful. Despite building up a portfolio of investments
quickly, the experience of running an incubator is somewhat
challenging because I get many more requests to help companies
and entrepreneurs than I can accommodate with our resources.
Unfortunately, many entrepreneurs approach me at WebFund
at a point in their start-up journey when they've already made
many common mistakes and have basically run out of resources
or energy. At that point, I can really only help them realise
the 'lessons learnt' and motivate them to keep going as an
entrepreneur — potentially with a different venture.

With this book I hope to help entrepreneurs avoid some of these
mistakes, and to either get off to the right start or never start
the new venture in the first place. Fortunately, many tools now
exist that make starting up far less expensive and risky than
it used to be. Obviously, the start-up landscape is also more
competitive but the rewards are greater than ever. As I finish
writing this book, Facebook just bought Instagram for around
$950 million after only 18 months in business. What an amazing
start-up journey for Instagram and what a fantastic motivation
to get going with your own start-up.

If you've been thinking about starting your own online venture,
don't procrastinate — get going! There's nothing like running
your own start-up and, no matter what happens, the experience
beats working in a nine-to-five job, hands down. I truly believe
that start-ups offer the fastest and most direct method for
personal and professional growth. If you follow the suggestions
in this book, you can also gain this experience without taking
huge risks or potentially losing a lot of money.

About This Book

In this book I share my experiences at WebFund and what I have learnt about starting new ventures successfully. The book also contains case studies, templates and lots of tips on what to do (and what not to do) when you're starting your own tech start-up. Sometimes you may find that there isn't really a clear path available for you to take your business forward. This book describes the shortest paths I've found to be most useful in my career. These might prove useful for you to find out where you currently stand, or where your next step might lead if you've already begun the journey.

So, why this book? Because

- ✔ Entrepreneurs still keep making the same mistakes when starting new companies and as a result experience unnecessary financial or personal crises.

- ✔ Starting your own company is one of the most exciting things you can do in your career and professional development — and it's so much easier if you do it right from the beginning.

- ✔ Australia and New Zealand need entrepreneurs and start-ups. Most of the truly life-changing technologies originate from start-ups. Wouldn't it be great if Australia and New Zealand had global start-up success stories like Pinterest and Instagram?

- ✔ You may be missing out on 'the time of your life' if you keep thinking about starting an online venture but never actually do it.

The tips and advice offered in this book can help you quickly move through the initial stages of evaluating your idea (and perhaps ditching it early if the fundamentals don't stack up), and then testing and validating your assumptions. By closely following the concepts and techniques in this book and avoiding the common mistakes I outline, you may even be able to have your concept investment ready in as little as three months.

(**Note:** Getting your concept 'investment ready' in three months is the aim of specialised accelerator programs for entrepreneurs, and I briefly cover these programs in this book. If you want to ensure your concept is ready for investors in this time frame, an accelerator program may be a good option for you — in which case, *Successful Online Start-Ups For Dummies* is the perfect companion text!)

What You Don't Have to Read

Although I hope you read every paragraph I've included in this book, I understand your life is busy and you want to read only the need-to-know info. You can safely skip the sidebars, which are shaded grey boxes and mostly contain case studies. These provide supporting or entertaining information that isn't critical to your understanding of the topic.

Throughout this book, I provide website addresses of a number of useful start-up related websites where you can find more information on some of the topics I discuss in the book. Although you don't have to go to these websites, it's well worth your while having a browse through them.

Foolish Assumptions

I assume that you're reading this book because you've just heard of an amazing start-up success story that inspired you or because you've been thinking about a groundbreaking idea for a new website for a while and just don't know where to start. Perhaps you have already started a company and you're experiencing some challenges, such as attracting funding, defining a sustainable business model or gaining traction with your products and services. I assume that you're somewhat overwhelmed by the demands of running your own start-up.

This book is for you if you're

✔ Concerned about your lack of knowledge and experience around all legal- and governance-related issues of being in business

✔ Confused about how your start-up journey has unfolded so far and looking for a structure to make sense of where you've got to with your business

✔ Deciding whether to enter a structured start-up program like an accelerator or incubator

✔ Depressed about a recent venture you were involved in that went belly up and keen to figure out what you can do differently next time round

✔ Excited about a web-based or mobile-based business idea but freaked out by the thought of actually running your own online business

✔ In business with a number of entrepreneurs and want to skill up on managing and growing a rapidly growing venture

How This Book Is Organised

This book is divided into five major parts with numerous chapters. You have everything at your fingertips to help you on your start-up journey — all the way to selling your business or listing on the stock exchange. While this book is organised in a chronological order, from preparing a start-up to a successful exit, I fully understand that start-up life is typically quite chaotic, if not messy. So don't be discouraged if your own start-up experience doesn't line up with the textbook-like structure I present in here — that's just life. However, the chapters are written in a way that you can 'pick and choose' — so you don't need to read the book from the beginning to benefit from techniques or advice I provide in later chapters.

Part I: Following Your Dream

Part I of the book covers all aspects of the start of your start-up journey. Before you dive into the nitty gritty of setting up a start-up, I begin by dispelling a number of common myths around tech start-ups and entrepreneurship. I also outline all the preparations that need to happen before you actually start your start-up.

Part II: Getting Your Start-Up Started

This part is where things get serious and I sketch out what you need to do to start a company. I provide an overview of useful techniques to define products and services, how to identify suitable business models and how to get to grips with basic company finances. I also share some secrets about increasing your chances to succeed with your start-up before discussing the launch of your product or service. Finally, I cover what you need to do to ramp up operations and scale your business quickly.

Part III: Growing Up

In this part, I provide some guidelines on managing the next stage of your start-up journey — the transition from cash strapped start-up to profitable and established business. I look at what you can do to increase the value of your company strategically, how to expand your operations (without killing your company) and what to do when your business is under threat.

Part IV: Chasing the Pot of Gold: The Reason Your Start-Up Exists

This part covers the final part of your start-up journey, where you're preparing for a potential sale of your business or a listing on the stock exchange. I discuss the various preparations you need to do to achieve a successful 'exit' or equity event. And I take a closer look at the steps involved in selling or listing your business.

Part V: The Part of Tens

The Part of Tens is a standard in all For Dummies books. This part is a great place to summarise many aspects of the start-up journey in a nutshell. Here you can find out about common mistakes that cause start-ups to fail, what you can do to boost the resources available to you in your start-up and what investors want to see when investing in start-ups.

Icons Used in This Book

Icons are those little pictures you see sprinkled in the margins throughout this book. Here's what they mean.

When you see this icon you can read about what happened to other entrepreneurs or organisations in the situation I'm discussing in a particular section of the book. Case studies provide a great way to learn from others; however, bear in mind that hindsight is a wonderful thing and seemingly obvious mistakes were probably difficult to spot at the time.

This icon denotes critical information that you really need to take away with you. Considering the state of my own overcrowded memory, I wouldn't ask you to remember anything unless it was really important.

This bullseye alerts you to on-target advice, insights or recommendations that I've picked up over the years.

This icon serves as a warning — telling you to avoid something that's potentially harmful. Take heed!

Where to Go from Here

You choose what happens next. This book is packed with information to help you at whatever state or stage you are on your start-up journey. You can go directly to the topics of most interest to you, or you can start at to the beginning and take it from there. With the information in *Successful Online Start-Ups For Dummies*, I'm confident that you're going to be able to master most challenges start-up life throws at you.

Part I
Following Your Dream

Glenn Lumsden

'That's the 6000th pre-purchase on
my new app in the last 24 hours ...
I quit! The next time you'll see me will
be on the cover of "Time" magazine!'

In this part . . .

Some people go through university, job after job and perhaps most of our lives feeling like Neo at the beginning of the film *The Matrix* — they're part of a life that's not for them. Perhaps you feel that you need to do something important and that the missing piece may well be executing a business idea that's been bubbling in your head. Typically, that feeling doesn't go away (whether you're 17 or 70) and so you might as well explore it further — but not blindly! The media generally only reports spectacular business failures or successes but it's hard to find out what to do (and what not to do) when starting out.

This part is all about starting an online business the right way (without ruining your life). I cover the essential ingredients you need for a business, how to define and research a successful product or service that customers want, and how to start approaching investors and securing funding.

Chapter 1

Understanding the Start-Up Journey

● ●

In This Chapter

▶ Getting real about your start-up and the work that lies ahead

▶ Understanding success or failure can come quickly

▶ Finding help and information

▶ Looking towards becoming profitable and expanding

● ●

So you've picked up a book on start-ups — great! Perhaps one of the following relates to you:

✔ You've just seen *The Social Network* on DVD and think you're the next Mark Zuckerberg (if you believe you're the next Jesse Eisenberg, please check out *Breaking Into Acting For Dummies*).

✔ You've just read about an amazing trade sale, IPO or exit of a local businessperson you went to school with (and remembered that you were better at everything back then).

✔ You're a second-year Bachelor of Business student and think your course is pointless and that you already know everything there is to know, and that you just want to get your start-up going.

✔ You've had an idea for a website that is going to be bigger than Twitter.

✔ You're 20 and you just inherited a lot of money on the condition that you do something 'useful' with your life.

The list goes on but, whatever your situation, you've come to the right place.

Creating a successful online start-up is not just about having a great idea. You also need to work really hard and, as well as being exciting, the journey can be stressful. But, when it comes to successfully navigating this journey, knowledge truly is power (especially knowledge of what not to do).

In this chapter, I cover the reality of the work and stress involved with online start-ups. I also provide some insight into the speed at which everything happens — including succeeding or failing. I outline who you can turn to for support and advice, and look at what happens if you're lucky enough to get further in your journey — to perhaps making a significant profit and looking to expand or exit your company.

So You've Seen 'The Social Network'

Start-up life seen from an incubator's or investor's perspective is filled with funny patterns. A natural ebb and flow of 'booms' and 'busts' tends to come round at least once a decade. Little predictable spikes of activity are usually triggered by local events (such as a big 'exit' of a start-up), the sudden popularity of a new start-up or something in popular culture — as happened in 2010 with the movie *The Social Network*. Suddenly lots of people are thinking, 'Wait a minute — I can do that!'

Unfortunately, in many cases, these bursts of activity lead to frustration. A number of persistent myths about start-ups exist, and these myths present an inaccurate picture of start-up life. So I'm going to tell it like it is — sorry to burst some bubbles!

In the following sections, I dispel some common myths on start-up life to help give you a more realistic idea of what to expect. I also provide some guidelines on finding out whether you've got what it takes to be an entrepreneur (and be your own boss) and a general description of the start-up journey.

Dispelling common myths about start-ups

At my investment firm, I frequently hear the same misconceptions from the entrepreneurs I meet with. The following is a list of the common start-up myths I've heard over the years. *Note:* The list is not meant to be comprehensive — it's just a summary of the most popular myths. Do any of the following sound familiar or valid?

Common start-up myths, along with how they stack up against reality, include the following:

- ✓ **'My start-up will make me billions.'** This may be true, and, of course, people like me are keen to help you achieve this, but the odds are against you making billions, especially with your first start-up. Investors generally work on a basis that out of every 10 ventures they invest in, seven will fold, two will return the investment and one will become financially viable and generate a return on investment (ROI).

  Many successful start-ups don't make their founders millionaires (or billionaires); these start-ups do, however, turn into viable companies that result in a comfortable lifestyle for founders. Investors refer to them as 'lifestyle' businesses as they don't offer a useful return on investment to anyone other than the founder.

- ✓ **'Start-ups are all about having a great idea and keeping it secret.'** Wrong — from an investor's perspective ideas are essentially worthless. All of the value of a business is generated through the unique execution of an idea (that is, through such factors as product definition, good timing and market positioning) rather than as a result of the idea itself. More about this in Chapter 2.

- ✓ **'Working in my own start-up is easy as — I can do whatever I want and be my own boss.'** Wrong — starting a business is hard work. Even as your own boss in a young and dynamic, informal start-up, you still need to produce something that's of value to other people who are prepared to use it and, ideally, pay for it. See Chapter 5 for more about start-up culture.

- ✓ **'I only need to capture 10 per cent of my target market.'** This myth is partly correct — the part that's wrong is the word 'only' because it implies that capturing 10 per cent market share is relatively easy to achieve. Not so. Capturing this percentage of your market is usually incredibly hard. See Chapter 2 for more on this.

↗ **'My business idea is completely unique — nobody has ever done this.'** Competitors are always out there and few ideas are unique. Even if you really do seem to be the first with the idea, chances are that someone with the same idea is working on their venture right now. And even if you actually are the first to launch a completely new service, you may find that the idea isn't viable or that your business draws a competitive response from other parties with deep pockets. See Chapter 5 for more on being noticed by competitors.

You need to be realistic about the time and effort required to make your start-up a success, but nothing is wrong with being enthusiastic and passionate about your idea. You need to retain that enthusiasm and passion when the going gets tough.

Looking at the pros and cons of being your own boss

Does it feel good to say 'I'm my own boss' or 'I've got my own business' at dinner parties? Absolutely! But a few challenges also come with being your boss. Table 1-1 gives you an overview of what to expect when you're your own boss, showing you the pros and cons.

Table 1-1	Pros and cons of being your own boss
Pros	**Cons**
Following your own rhythm. If you're very productive at night, you can work from 5 pm to 9 am (especially beneficial if your venture is servicing a market on the other side of the world).	**Having no-one to blame.** You are it. As Spiderman was once told, 'With great power comes great responsibility'.
Setting your own dress code. Not having to wear a suit may give you a sense of incredible freedom. You may have your own style that becomes a trademark outfit like Steve Jobs' turtle neck sweater (although the fashion police might have a word to say about that).	**Risking valuable assets in your life.** Typically, you put your career, relationships and personal assets on the line for your venture.

Pros	Cons
Avoiding direct superiors. That means nobody to report to, nobody to suck up to and nobody to avoid at the water cooler.	**Putting up with some constraints.** You need others to help plug your skill gaps or simply get tasks done. You may also have to share some of the equity in your business. And you need to please customers. So you can't really do whatever you want — you still need to compromise.
Controlling the vision. You're in charge and you can implement your vision exactly the way you want.	
Being the decision-maker. You get to define your brand, pick the company premises, present to investors, run an annual general meeting and much more.	

Being your own boss is really about accepting and embracing the challenges — and I believe the upsides far outweigh the challenges.

A really great way to find out what it's actually like to run a business or be involved in a start-up is to talk to others who are doing this already. If you don't happen to know anyone who is in that position go along to the many meetings, conferences and gatherings of start-up communities in most cities in Australia and New Zealand. Check out startupweekend.org for a list of start-up weekends around the world and see Chapter 4 for more on networking.

Getting to know the start-up journey

Many of us hear about start-ups when they appear in the mainstream media (for example, the first time the company is covered on Twitter or in the news) or when an established player buys them for mega bucks (for example, when Facebook bought Instagram for $950 million). However, most people never hear about the numerous start-ups that failed or never got off the ground. As a result many first-time entrepreneurs have a slightly skewed image of the start-up journey.

The following is a more typical breakdown of the start-up journey experienced by most new ventures these days:

- ✔ **Inception:** After coming up with an idea, doing a bit of research, creating something and perhaps even putting some sort of business plan on paper, the new venture is conceptualised. At this stage, founders often gather together with other like-minded people to get the business off the ground. (In my experience, one entrepreneur going it alone is somewhat unusual.) See Chapter 2 for information on determining whether your idea is feasible and who you should have on your team in the very early stages.

- ✔ **Deliberation and contemplation:** During this part of the journey, the founder(s) consider how to put the idea into practice, looking at funding and time commitment required. A lot of start-ups actually never make it past this stage because the founders keep waiting for something to happen — such as inheriting money, getting a meeting with Google, waiting for a government grant, or for legwarmers to become fashionable again (let's face it — that's never going to happen!). Sheer determination, courage and risk appetite among founders decides whether the concept gets to the next stage. See Chapter 3 for more on the research and validation required during this phase.

- ✔ **Implementation:** At this point the venture generally moves from concept to realisation. Some founders aren't afraid to take huge risks at this stage and mortgage their houses. Others are trying to get their business off the ground by moonlighting or working part-time. Others still outsource everything and carry on working in their day jobs. Often, the main goal during this stage is to create a presentable prototype, develop a pitch to investors, or get agreement from potential customers or suppliers to try the new product or service. I cover this phase in more detail in Chapters 3 and 4.

- ✔ **Formalisation:** After much deliberation, perhaps some frustration and for sure a lot of hard work, the new venture launches the products or services and publishes a media release. At this stage, most entrepreneurs formalise arrangements by forming a company, which creates its own special challenges — see Chapter 3 for more on these. See Chapter 4 for more on launching your company's products or services, what to focus on immediately after the launch, and dealing with potential post-launch blues.

✔ **Operation:** The start-up is 'in business' — it's a real company with real products and services, customers or users (hopefully), staff, cash flow (typically negative) and investors, shareholders or creditors. Start-up life during this stage is mostly about growth and survival (both of which tend to be hard at first). See Chapter 5 for more.

✔ **Validation:** This part of the start-up journey is where the wheat is separated from the chaff. Many start-ups are truly 'on to something' and have discovered a product or service that is well loved by the target market. Others are struggling to get traction with their ventures and either collapse or give up, change direction (usually called *pivoting*) or carry on regardless. I cover this phase in Chapters 5 and 6.

✔ **Evolution:** For those start-ups who have enjoyed initial success, this phase is about growth, expansion and creating strategic value. Many changes are happening inside the start-up venture as the rapid scale and growth requires new resources (human and others), funds and space (virtual or actual). I cover this phase in Chapters 6 and 7.

✔ **Completion:** Once a start-up has hit the mainstream, the company generally shows up on the radar of big corporates, is followed in the general media and analysed by investors. If the venture is able to sustain high growth rates or continues to attract large numbers of customers or users, typically a significant equity event soon happens. Most commonly this takes the form of an acquisition by a large company, a large financing round with venture capitalists, or a public listing. While the venture continues, this generally completes the 'start-up' journey because the company can no longer be considered a start-up — it becomes an established player. I cover this phase in Chapters 8 and 9.

The average time from inception to completion is around seven to eight years.

The breakdown shown in the preceding list is merely an outline of what many entrepreneurs encounter during their start-up experience — most importantly, it illustrates all the various things that have usually happened in a start-up by the time people hear about it in the media. Of course, the actual process may be different for specific start-ups, and many other journeys can lead to successful start-ups — such as university research commercialisation programs, corporate spin-off companies, inventions based on patents or legislation changes that prompt a new product or service.

It is very unusual that new entrepreneurs hit 'the jackpot' (that is, completion of the start-up journey with huge financial rewards) with their first venture. More often than not, entrepreneurs tend to become serial entrepreneurs who work on one idea after another. Many entrepreneurs keep 'producing' bigger and bigger start-ups until they eventually create one that becomes extremely well known. Skype is a good example for eventual commercial success of serial entrepreneurs — the company's founders Zennström and Friis were involved in several other start-ups before launching Skype (including get2net, everyday.com and Kazaa). Facebook, on the other hand, is considered Mark Zuckerberg's first real venture (after the college experiment with 'hot or not', which wasn't done as a commercial enterprise).

Looking at becoming a lean start-up

The Lean Start-up Method is a structured approach for starting a venture based on a number of principles. The method has been developed by Eric Ries and had its origins in Eric's own experience with start-ups and his Startup Lessons Learned blog. After receiving a lot of positive feedback about the concepts and principles he proposed for starting ventures, Eric finally wrote a book called *The Lean Startup*, which provides the basis for his method. Some of the techniques covered by Eric's method are well known in established businesses, such as the continuous improvement process, process waste and process optimisation, and split testing. However, he has also developed new techniques particularly relevant for start-ups, such as:

✔ **Hypothesis validation:** This refers to a theory (hypothesis) of the need for a product in a particular target market and its validation.

✔ **Minimum viable product (MVP):** This refers to a prototype that has the minimum amount of features to validate a product or market hypotheses.

See Chapter 3 for more on hypothesis validation and MVPs.

Succeeding or Failing Fast

You may have heard this mantra from start-up gurus around the planet as a general rule for creating start-up success: Succeed or fail fast. However, all the words in that sentence are quite fluid (okay — the word 'or' is probably sufficiently clear). 'Success' and 'failure' mean different things to everyone — and just how fast is fast? Once you look at these words in a bit more detail, you realise that they're not that easy to define.

In the following sections, I suggest a way to help you define success for yourself, and provide an overview of information and techniques you can use for 'pacing' your start-up and to help you with the constant evaluation of which idea you should focus on and for how long.

Defining success

A standard question I ask when I first meet with entrepreneurs wanting to work with me is, 'How do you define success for yourself and for your venture?' Until you really start thinking about how to answer that question, the answer seems obvious — success means lots of money and recognition.

However, many of the descriptions we often hear are only symptoms of success (or a bank robbery for that matter). To get a better handle on answering this question you need to figure out what success means to you — that is, what does life look like when you're successful and what measures exist that indicate whether you're getting close to your success?

The following list is a suggestion of questions to ask yourself when trying to define success:

- ✔ 'Where do I see myself living?' Do you see yourself living in the same house, city or country that you live in at the moment?

- ✔ 'What does my average day look like?' Do you see yourself working from home, having a fancy office, spending the whole day in front of the computer or in meetings? What are the things you want to do on a regular basis?

✔ 'How many hours a week do I work?' Does success mean working 40 or 80 hours per week, or two (or none)? *Note:* 'Work' in this context is defined as the time you spend doing something when you'd rather do something else.

✔ 'How do I contribute to the world at large?' That is, how do you see yourself making your 'mark' on history? Do you want to build a school named after you in a developing country, become famous for burning $10 million cash on YouTube, be on the cover of *Time* magazine or find a cure for cancer?

✔ 'What are my personal circumstances?' Do you want to have a family, kids, or be in a same-sex marriage? Think about how many friends you want to have and how often you want to be able to catch up with them. How do you want to keep well — physically, mentally and spiritually?

Defining what success means to you is important because doing so allows you to compare your definitions with those of other key people in your start-up. Getting an understanding of how each of you defines success is imperative for aligning interests, making strategic decisions and agreeing goals for the company. A definition of success also makes for a neat poster in your workspace to constantly remind yourself why you're working hard on your start-up and to help you recognise when you have achieved success (which many entrepreneurs tend to forget over the years).

In this book, I use the terms *success, successful* and *failure* in terms of the financial viability of the start-up. That is, a successful start-up is one that sustainably creates profits for its founders and investors. A failed start-up is one that is forced to cease operations or never reaches profitability.

Understanding why start-ups succeed or fail

Understanding why some start-ups fail and others succeed is the ultimate goal for every entrepreneur and, of course, no complete answer exists. However, over the last three decades, typical reasons for the success or failure of start-ups have been identified, and are covered in the following sections.

Common factors for start-up success

Here's a list of some of the factors that can help in the success of your start-up:

- ✔ **Excellent team:** You may have heard the statement that investors typically *back the jockey not the horse* (they believe in the ability of the founders rather than the strength of the concept). The ability to execute well and create something from nothing is key and so assembling a strong team (ideally with a track record of successful start-ups) increases your chances of success tremendously. See Chapter 2 for more.

- ✔ **Expertise or exclusivity:** The *value add* that every company must demonstrate to its customers has to come from somewhere. Two prominent areas of value add for start-ups are knowledge (talent) and exclusivity (access). See Chapter 2 for more on developing your idea.

- ✔ **Favourable pre-conditions:** Some entrepreneurs have access to a range of assets that increase their chances of success before they even start their venture. Examples include a PhD thesis that can be readily commercialised, patented inventions or a significant existing network (such as thousands of Twitter followers).

- ✔ **Good advisors and influential board members:** If, in addition to a good team, you can also attract good board members and external advisors (for example, in the form of an advisory board — see Chapter 3) your chances of success increase dramatically. See Chapter 5 for more information on the value of advisors and boards.

- ✔ **Killer product or service:** These are products or services that represent a completely new way of approaching an existing problem, or offer far superior qualities or design compared to a current offering. Many consumer products or online services you use every day started out this way.

- ✔ **Right time, right place:** Sometimes, a critical success factor is recognising that you happen to be at the right place at the right time. A very popular example of someone realising this and making the most of it is Bill Gates, when he managed to convince IBM to allow his unknown company Microsoft to provide operating systems for a new category of IBM computers (the PC).

✔ **'Skin in the game':** You may have come across investors referring to their preference for entrepreneurs to have *skin in the game*. This refers to the personal (financial) situation of the founders, their level of ownership of the venture and the risk they are prepared to take — for example, investors like to see entrepreneurs take on personal debt to help finance their venture. The debt obviously creates a certain level of pressure that tends to act as a key motivator and driver for many entrepreneurs.

Factors that can contribute to start-up failure

Factors that commonly bring about the fall of start-ups include the following:

✔ **Concept not strong enough:** This mostly relates to the product or service created, but other conceptual problems include lack of a viable market, legal risk or inability to monetise the concept.

✔ **Customer acquisition cost (CAC) exceeds lifetime value (LTV) of a customer.** Businesses sometimes realise that the cost of attracting a customer exceeds the amount of money the business is ever able to extract from that customer. See Chapter 4 for more information about customer acquisition cost and customer lifetime value.

✔ **Ignoring customers:** This is a mistake that can happen all along the start-up journey. Often, it happens when entrepreneurs have experienced initial successes and are becoming too confident about how to run their business. See Chapters 4 and 8 for more on listening to your customers at different stages in the start-up journey.

✔ **Managing growth:** Allocating efforts and resources in a rapidly growing business is difficult. Many entrepreneurs end up focusing on the wrong area of their business (for example, product development instead of sales or capital raising) and consequently find themselves with no money, no customers or no staff. See Chapters 5 and 6 for managing rapid business growth.

✔ **No sustainable competitive advantage:** You can only sustain a competitive advantage in a few ways: Legal protection (such as patents, copyrights and contracts), outgrowing competition, constant innovation, *cost leadership* (being able to produce a product at much less cost than any other competitor), or by making use of existing barriers (such as jurisdiction and legislation, location and insider knowledge). Many start-ups don't have any of these sustainable competitive advantages. See Chapter 2 for more on competitive advantage.

✔ **Not enough resources:** Many start-ups are undercapitalised, understaffed or lack focus. Chapters 2 and 11 explain how to raise capital and find investors.

✔ **Poor execution.** When a venture is not run well in a number of disciplines (such as product and service design, sales and marketing, operations, finance or human resources), failure is on the cards. You might be too naive, or have a lack of skills, dedication or knowledge. See Chapter 8 for more on recognising when you can't do everything in your start-up.

In particular the ability (or inability) to sell is a common issue — that is, nobody in the team actually has any sales skills. Selling is a lot harder than most people think. However, in order to have a viable company the business must sell something (even if it is shares to an investor).

✔ **Ownership issues:** Entrepreneurs are typically required to negotiate the ownership structure of their start-up (usually to raise capital) at various stages of the start-up journey. Some founders are reluctant to give up equity or control (known as the *founder syndrome*) even when the venture has clearly outgrown their skills, expertise or ability to take advantage of growth opportunities. Also, founders disagreeing among themselves over equity stakes or contributions to the company is not uncommon. See Chapter 8 for more on this.

✔ **Running out of steam or giving up.** Many start-ups simply run out of motivation after a short time, and other priorities appear or health issues arise. Some entrepreneurs simply give up halfway. Creating a successful start-up typically takes many years and some founders simply don't have the patience, commitment or tenacity to go the distance required.

You're forgiven if you're thinking, 'Hang on — the list of failure factors is much longer than the list of success factors'. That's true, but this is simply because failure factors are easier to identify and tend to be commonly experienced across many start-ups (that ended up failing). Success factors, on the other hand, are more difficult to pinpoint and tend to be more specific to a particular start-up. However, the good news is that throughout this book I cover many ways to avoid the failures and increase your chance of success.

One element of your start-up is essential to almost any commercial undertaking: Providing something that's valued, treasured, appreciated and cherished by someone else. When a company stops creating value for its customers (as judged by the customers themselves) the business is in trouble sooner or later. However, what's valuable to one person may not be to another, and so the importance of testing your product on your target market can't be understated. In Chapter 3, I describe in detail how validations for products and services, customers and markets work.

Knowing what it takes to be a successful entrepreneur

A lot has been written about what it takes to be successful in business, and Steven Covey's 20-year-old book *The Seven Habits of Highly Effective People* is still celebrated by many MBA lecturers as a landmark study on success in business. In addition to the various skills, techniques and habits that help entrepreneurs succeed outlined in Covey's book, I believe three essential attitudes or mindsets exist that radically successful entrepreneurs exhibit:

✔ **Unshakable optimism and determination:** Or, as Donald Trump would put it, 'never give up'.

✔ **Uncanny observation skills:** The ability to notice key pain points, opportunities or pick up on hidden preferences that others miss. Some entrepreneurs have become known for having a sixth sense for business deals or opportunities. Typically, this ability to sense a beneficial outcome for your business is based on skilful observation (of such aspects as customer behaviour, consumer or technology trends and human nature).

✔ **Passion and charisma:** The ability to continuously motivate others and convince staff, clients or investors to get behind a new concept or venture. One way or another, as an entrepreneur you're always selling — whether it's selling a concept to investors, a new product or service to customers or a proposition to (potential) staff. Your ability to make an impact and convince others makes all the difference between getting a yay or a nay.

Realising your dream might become a nightmare

Dreams are often used as an analogy for starting your own business — motivational speakers often say 'follow your dreams', 'do what you love' or 'if you can dream it, you can build it'. The analogy is perhaps quite fitting here — dreams can turn into nightmares and, unfortunately, start-ups can also end up in disaster.

A huge part of what determines the success or failure of a start-up is determined during the inception phase and whether or not the founders decide to go ahead with an idea. In a way, you can compare a start-up to a living organism — what happens at the beginning represents the DNA or genetic code of your start-up. Just like in real life, the genetic code — to a certain extent — determines the developmental potential of your business.

Essentially, three main components need to make up the initial *screening* of ideas (figuring out whether you should spend more effort on a business idea). These components are the feasibility of the idea itself, timing and the market that the idea aims to serve. I cover these components in the following sections, as well as how to recognise the potential risks and rewards involved with an idea.

Understanding that business ideas are a dime a dozen

A business idea in itself is worth nothing without the right team, connections, support and various other things to turn a good idea into a successful business. In order to decide whether an idea is worth pursuing, ask yourself the following questions:

- **What do you know about the industry or market that the idea aims to address?** If you have worked in that industry for several years, great; if you know nothing about it, that's bad.

- **How easy is it to create the first sellable (usable) product or service?** If you require significant upfront capital to just get your first product out, the concept may be a tricky one (unless, of course, you already have that capital).

- **How sure are you that the idea addresses an actual need?** If you have ever heard the saying 'a solution looking for a problem', that's what we are talking about here.

A good example of creating a product that doesn't meet an actual need is Motorola's immense investment into satellite mobile phones in the 1990s. The company spent billions of dollars creating the necessary infrastructure and when they finally launched the service, they realised that only a handful of people on the entire planet actually really need a satellite phone (everyone else can use existing technology).

✔ **Will someone actually pay for your product or service?** While starting free services (especially online) to try to replicate the story of YouTube or Twitter is exciting, you need to keep in mind that while you're working on your free service, you and your staff still need to eat and pay the bills. So the money has to come from somewhere. If you have proof that others are willing to pay for what you want to offer, that's great.

✔ **What else is available?** After you've had an idea, the most important activity is to check what else is available in that space. Search engines are fantastic for this because you can generally get a good understanding very quickly of how your idea relates to other existing products and services.

In Chapter 2 we elaborate on the importance of testing and validating your idea as early as possible.

Finding out whether the time and the market is right

The timing of an idea is probably one of the aspects most commonly overlooked. The reality is that the timing has to be right for an idea to really take off. Understand that being too late with an idea is just as bad as being too early.

Many big name brands that you use today (especially those operating online) were not the first ones to launch their product or service. For example, many video-sharing services existed before YouTube, but the idea of such a service only became viable when broadband internet penetration in key markets (especially the United States) had reached critical mass.

However, knowing when the time is right for an idea is perhaps one of the hardest aspects to ascertain. Some entrepreneurs, like Steve Jobs and Richard Branson, have been known to purely go with their 'gut feel' — Apple launched the iPad despite direct advice from analysts who said the device wasn't needed and didn't offer any value-add over existing technology.

Learning from those who have gone before

Another successful strategy for upskilling and learning about start-ups is to find out how other successful entrepreneurs did it. A number of autobiographies and biographies are certainly worth a read, each providing insight into the personal and professional story of the world's best known entrepreneurs. Here's my top 10 of biographies worth reading:

✔ Scott Adams, *The Dilbert Principle*

✔ Richard Branson, *Losing My Virginity*

✔ Walt Disney, *The Man Behind the Myth*

✔ Larry Ellison, *The Difference between God and Larry Ellison*

✔ Bill Gates, *Up Close*

✔ Jody Hoffer Gittell, *The Southwest Airlines Way*

✔ Walter Isaacson, *Steve Jobs*

✔ Anita Roddick, *Business as Unusual*

✔ Jack Stack, *A Stake in the Outcome*

✔ David A. Vise and Mark Malseed, *The Google Story*

To find or validate business opportunities, most entrepreneurs rely on

✔ Industry trends

✔ Information from focus groups or online surveys

✔ Talking to known influencers in a particular market

If the opportunity is based on other external events (such as a legislation change), timing is typically just a matter of validating the need for a new product or service and synchronising the launch with the external event having an effect on mainstream customers. If the idea is truly innovative and represents a new way of doing things, I encourage entrepreneurs to follow the techniques for market validation and creating a sustainable product–market fit. You can find more about these techniques in Chapter 3.

Sharing music online — the Napster story

Remember Napster? How would you have categorised this service at the outset, in terms of its risks and rewards? Without the benefit of hindsight, most entrepreneurs would have probably recognised the huge potential for creating an online file-sharing service for a new music format (MP3). Many would have perhaps worried about the legality of the service — it clearly provides a platform to conduct an illegal activity of copyright infringement.

However, entrepreneurs with significant risk appetite may have argued that this situation isn't unique and, given the right agreements, a deal may be struck between copyright owners and online distributors.

As it turns out, the service did become hugely popular, which forced a response from the recording industry — to have the service eventually shut down. Ironically, the recording industry had to give in to allow distribution through a much more powerful player (Apple) with presumably less favourable terms than had they agreed on a deal with Napster.

Recognising risks and rewards

Understanding the risks and potential rewards of an idea is really important before spending a significant amount on developing the idea further. Here are the top three aspects you must check about every idea you are exploring:

 ✔ **Expertise:** Unless you happen to have significant (and I mean years) experience in the market you're trying to target, you need to spend some time with an industry expert to check or validate your assumptions. In fact, even if you're the expert, running something by another expert to get another view on the opportunity generally doesn't hurt.

 ✔ **Legality:** Speak to a lawyer or someone with legal training who has at least some knowledge of the field you are looking at. For example, if your idea is in the music industry, speak to a lawyer who has done work in that space.

Even a cost of $1,000 for an opinion is small fry compared to the potential legal cost later on or the opportunity cost of pursuing an idea for months if the idea isn't actually legal (or has significant legal risk).

You may also have to consider international law if you are planning to offer your services outside your domestic market. See Chapter 5 for internal expansion strategies.

✔ **Technology:** Get with a developer or technician (if you need to manufacture something) to understand how easily your product or system can be developed. Also find out how easy it is to scale and what's involved to offer your product or service to (potentially) millions of customers.

Serial entrepreneurs

Successful entrepreneurs work hard on quickly validating assumptions and the feasibility of a viable business. If that's not possible they move on to the next idea.

As a result, successful entrepreneurs tend to become *serial entrepreneurs* — they move from one idea to the next (typically, regardless of the success or failure of their previous idea). For most serial entrepreneurs, starting a company or developing an idea is a mindset and something that defines them — it's not just a job or a way to make money. Most wildly successful entrepreneurs (such as the likes of Richard Branson) are serial entrepreneurs.

Some founders leave the start-up world after their first failure, returning to the corporate world. Others become *parallel entrepreneurs* (working on several different concepts at the same time). Statistically speaking, your first start-up is unlikely to succeed and starting lots of companies in parallel is equally unlikely to succeed. However, the chance of success increases with every venture and so does the ability to fully focus on one particular concept (and execute it well). So my advice for aspiring entrepreneurs is to become a serial entrepreneur and to focus on one idea at the time. Your first start-up may not be a raging success, but the third of fifth one might.

Remember the words of Sir Winston Churchill that are quite relevant for serial entrepreneurs: 'Success is the ability to go from one failure to another with no loss of enthusiasm.'

See Chapter 2 for help with analysing your initial concept and working out whether to continue with it or move on to the next idea.

Help, I'm an Entrepreneur!

The good news for aspiring entrepreneurs is that a lot of useful information is available. A whole range of organisations and individuals are also interested in helping young entrepreneurs succeed with their start-ups. This includes private enterprises like business incubators, accelerator programs, angel investment firms, co-working spaces, venture capitalists and business hubs. Typically, the government also takes an interest in helping entrepreneurs in the form of seed capital grants, business mentoring and coaching programs, regional development agencies and education programs for small- to medium-sized enterprises (SMEs).

In Chapter 3, I discuss the various options for assistance available to entrepreneurs in more detail. In the following sections, I cover some basic aspects of getting help as an entrepreneur.

Asking for help

While you're working on your idea or concept and you're pondering whether to set up a business or not, you can do a number of great activities that are likely to come in really handy once you've got your start-up up and running. Here's a list of suggestions:

- **Ask your friends and family:** Sometimes asking your friends or even family members what they think of an idea is worthwhile. This is called the *common sense test*. The feedback you get from people who aren't experts or in your target market can still be really valuable because they often see things that are easy to overlook when you're very close to your concept.

- **Attract a mentor:** Personal mentors can be tremendously helpful throughout the start-up journey. (I use the term *personal mentors* here because you can also use business mentors or advisors, who are often in paid positions, whose focus is on helping with your business.) A personal mentor provides input into your career and life choices over a longer period (typically years). If you have a personal mentor whom you've worked with for a while, discussing your concepts and ideas before you start a venture can be really useful. Mentors often challenge your thinking, test your assumptions and provide a different perspective — which is exactly what you need during the early stages of developing a concept.

✔ **Build your network:** Use networking sites such as LinkedIn, Facebook or Twitter to connect with other entrepreneurs or experts in the field you are targeting with your idea. The networks you're building are invaluable for testing concepts or getting feedback from others. Most people are willing to help free of charge — especially if they've known you for a while and you've helped them at some point.

The 'Golden Rule' is particularly relevant in the start-up world. So if you would like to get help, make sure you also provide help to others. What goes around comes around and the easiest way to build a network initially is to simply help others who are looking for advice, feedback or a tester. At some point it will be your turn to ask for help and others are more likely to respond if you have helped them before or have established a relationship with them.

Finding trusted sources of information

An abundance of information is available on any topic these days, including the subject of starting a business — so much so that getting lost or sidetracked when looking for reliable information can be easy. However, reading up on key aspects of entrepreneurship is really useful, especially during the early stages of running a start-up or even before starting a venture.

Here's my list of trusted online sources of information for entrepreneurs:

✔ **Eric Ries:** startuplessonslearned.com

✔ GetElastic.com

✔ **Guy Kawasaki:** blog.guykawasaki.com

✔ Inc.com

✔ **Malcolm Gladwell:** gladwell.com

✔ Mashable.com

✔ **Paul Graham (YCombinator):** paulgraham.com

✔ ReadWriteWeb.com

✔ **Seth Godin:** sethgodin.typepad.com

✔ Ted.com

Connecting with the people in the preceding list is actually not as hard as you may think. If you follow some general principles of online etiquette (such as being brief, polite and to the point, and offering something as well when asking for help) when contacting people, you may get a response or even an email from some of them. Even if you don't succeed in getting a direct response, you can certainly follow most of these people on Twitter, which still provides you with a stream of relevant advice and suggestions for your start-up.

You may find that you get 'sucked in' to reading about start-ups every day without progressing your concept or idea. If you don't have an idea just now, great — read as much as you can and build up a knowledge base of articles and material. However, if you're actively working on an idea, set yourself a time limit (such as 30 minutes per day to catch up with all the blogs and tweets) to make sure you've got enough time to actually progress your own idea.

Learning About What Comes Next

After your initial decision to start your venture begins the curious journey of turning an idea that only exists in your head into a real business.

The following sections provide a summary of what you need to do to gain traction, grow your business and expand strategically. I also provide an overview of working towards a trade sale, acquisition or public listing on a stock exchange, and take a quick look at the 'endgame' of all start-ups — cashing out and achieving your dream.

Turning an idea into a real business

The best way to create a successful start-up is to eliminate as many as possible potential ways the business can fail *before* you even start. This is where prototyping and testing comes in. Refer to 'Succeeding or Failing Fast' earlier in this chapter for an overview, and Chapter 3 for much more extensive detail.

Once you've performed your research and validation on your product or service and proposed market and you're getting ready to launch, you need to decide on a suitable launch strategy. Perhaps the most important aspect of launching a business is planning, and you need to pay particular attention to setting targets and deciding how to measure progress. Online start-ups have a fantastic advantage in that practically all information about customers and transactions are readily available from the website logs and access data that are collected for every site. This data can be used to plan your launch. Chapter 4 discusses the various launch options in more detail.

As soon as an online business is *live* (launched) you need to spend a lot of time tracking, analysing and adjusting your online platforms based on the information and intelligence you can glean from the website statistics. Responding quickly to customer preferences and requests provides the objectives for further growth. In addition, entrepreneurs during this stage need to find ways to fuel the business growth — typically by attracting additional resources (in the form of money, staff or business partners). Chapter 5 is dedicated to discussing details of what you need to do to ramp up your business.

Growing and accelerating

Successful start-ups tend to grow at least 100 per cent year on year — in other words, the volume of business (as measured in revenue, sales, traffic or number of customers) doubles every year. If growth isn't happening you need to understand why.

In some cases, a simple adjustment of your approach and a sharpened focus on understanding your customers' needs and preferences may be all that's needed. Sometimes, however, the lack of growth may be caused by a fundamental flaw in the business — caused by incorrect assumptions, fundamental problems with the product or service, or sudden (and powerful) competition. If this is the case, you need to decide whether to persevere, pivot or part with your business. Chapters 5 and 6 provide detailed guidelines on how to overcome growth hurdles, when to change direction or how to recognise when it's time to move on to your next idea.

At some point while your business is expanding, you may experience rapid growth, which can be tricky to manage. Handling significant increases in traffic of customer numbers often isn't easy because most of your core business functions are under stress — including technology, operations and finance. Chapters 6 and 7 provide details on how to get through this phase of your start-up journey. You may also need (or want) to boost your business by expanding the customers you service, perhaps through branching out into other geographies or markets. Chapter 7 outlines some common expansion strategies.

Rapid growth usually also results in a need for additional resources — most importantly, capital (because money can be used to solve most growth issues). Raising capital is almost always an interesting part of the start-up journey and many entrepreneurs have to go through several funding rounds (seed capital, growth investment and acceleration investment) to fuel the rapid growth of their businesses. So you need to know how and when to attract capital. Chapter 7 discusses all aspects of attracting funding, with helpful tips on what to do and what not to do.

Making your business the best it can be

I emphasise the importance of creating or adding value to a business throughout this book because it's such an essential task for entrepreneurs. The importance of this task doesn't change even when the business is (highly) profitable — at that stage of a start-up, the task is still important because you're likely preparing the business for a potential acquisition, sale or public listing. The venture is turning from a start-up into a mature business that creates certain expectations in customers, business partners and investors.

During the early stages of a start-up you can generally get away with many aspects of the business being somewhat 'unrefined'. People tolerate and sometimes like the 'unpolishedness' of start-ups — after all, that's part of the excitement when trying something new (even as a customer). However, once the start-up generates substantial revenue and has a certain size (in terms of staff, revenue and number of customers), the sympathy for start-ups tends to vanish and all stakeholders of the venture expect a professional service all round.

Turning your start-up into an established and respected company generally comes down to establishing standards (for example, for business processes), guidelines and policies as well as tidying up the public image (the brand) and tying up any legal lose ends (such as registering or enforcing trademarks and patents).

All of these activities add further value to the company because they make the business a more attractive and complete 'package' for a potential buyer — even if the buyer is represented by the share market at large. Chapters 7 and 8 provide details on how to mature a business and prepare it for a major equity event.

Accomplishing your dream

The last part of the traditional start-up journey is when the company is sold or *floated* (listed on a stock exchange). At that point, the founders and investors receive the financial rewards on their initial investment, and the venture has become an established company (or part of one) — so from here on in, it's 'business as usual' and the same rules of doing business apply as exist for all other established businesses in the world.

Sometimes an acquisition or trade sale doesn't just happen but is the result of careful positioning and planning by entrepreneurs — Chapter 9 discusses how to do this. In Chapter 9, I also outline the process of listing a company on the stock exchange and touch on what's left to do at the end of this process — reflect on the journey and enjoy life with the sweet scent of success (as you have defined it for yourself), knowing that you have achieved your dream.

Chapter 2

Starting as You Mean to Go On

In This Chapter

▶ Checking your idea is something that customers need

▶ Completing in-depth market analysis and validating your assumptions

▶ Working out who should be part of your team

▶ Finding out how to improve the lives of your key stakeholders

▶ Understanding your options for funding your venture

*T*he beginning of your start-up journey can feel like a roller-coaster ride — you're likely to feel enthusiastic about a new idea and then depressed as you realise the idea's been done before or you can't make it work for some reason.

Most entrepreneurs go through many of these idea–discovery cycles before they settle on an idea to spend more time on. The roller-coaster experience during this period is actually a pretty good exercise, because it helps you understand what the future is likely to hold for your start-up journey. Often, running a start-up can feel very much like a crazy ride, where something as basic as a phone call can mean the difference between feeling ecstatic about the venture or down in the dumps. Well, my advice is simple — enjoy the ride!

To get you started on your 'ride', this chapter covers what you can do to assess the merits and risks of your business ideas. Doing this homework before you register a company or set up a business saves a lot of potential frustration down the line. Assembling the right team around you from the start is also important, so I cover the key areas you should look at. I outline how to validate key assumptions in your idea or business plan and why this is so important. I also reveal what investors are really looking for when you pitch your business to them and discuss the most common funding options available to you when you want to get serious about your start-up.

Preventing a False Start: Assessing Your Idea's Potential

At WebFund, we often tell entrepreneurs who approach us for funding that starting a business is a bit like dating someone — starting a relationship can be easy but ending one can be complicated, embarrassing or just plain hard. And so, just like with dating, you need to recognise the signs of a potential breakdown before you get involved in a venture. In business terms, getting involved usually means incurring debt, being subject to compliance and legal requirements or signing agreements with business partners (such as a shareholder agreement). Once you have done one or more of these, things tend to get complicated if you no longer wish to continue with an idea or venture.

The easiest business to get out of is the one you never started in the first place. Your aim should be to avoid false starts — and you can do this by learning to recognise key weaknesses of a concept or business plan before making any serious commitments.

In the following sections, I break down the task of doing a pre-assessment of your idea or concept.

Looking for game-changing ideas

One of the most common start-up myths (which I discuss in Chapter 1) is that starting a business is all about having a great idea. While your idea may be great (I'm sure it is!), you need to understand the nature of the idea and its potential when deciding whether to further investigate its execution. You need to consider to what extent potential customers for the idea are likely to need or desire the product or service. (See the sidebar 'Knowing your antibiotics from your vitamins' for an analogy that illustrates this concept.)

Knowing your antibiotics
from your vitamins

When analysing the need or desire that ideas create around particular problems, the start-up industry divides ideas into two groups: Antibiotics and vitamins.

Antibiotics, as their name suggests, are ideas for products or services that are so compelling that people 'must have' them (that is, they're potentially life-saving or life-changing).

Vitamins, on the other hand, are completely optional. Vitamin-type products or services generally make people feel better but don't provide a compelling need to keep using them.

Here's list of powerful attributes for products or services — ideally, your idea ticks all the boxes:

✔ **'Think different'**: An element in your idea involves you taking an

existing concept and flipping it on its head. For example, DIYFather.com is a parenting site for dads (not mums); Twitter allows users to send short messages to many people at once (not just one person).

✔ **'Lock in'**: Once consumers choose your product, is a cost or significant effort involved with them changing later? For example, how easy would it be to stop using Facebook now but still keep in touch with friends?

✔ **'Network effect'**: Does your idea become more and more valuable the more people use it? For example, the usefulness of exchange websites like eBay increases with the number of people using them.

Whether or not customers feel a compelling need to buy a product or service typically determines the speed of adoption and the associated marketing cost. In simple terms, the more compelling a product or service, the higher the adoption rate and the cheaper the marketing cost.

At the most fundamental level, successful businesses offer something of great value to their customers. Great value means different things to different people, so 'great value' needs to be qualified by adding 'as perceived by the customer'. Unfortunately, this qualification is something that many entrepreneurs forget — they create products and services that are of great (or sometimes average) value to them, but not to their customers.

To get a better handle on value (as perceived by customers), consider the concept of a *value equation*. This is where you compare what customers give you (for example, money, time or knowledge) with what they get in return (typically your product or service). You want to design your products and services in a way that customers feel they're getting way more in return than they have to give. You need to convince your customers that they're getting a bargain or that what they're receiving from you is of such great value that even a high price (or effort) is justified.

To illustrate the concept of a value equation, consider a chat service that aims to connect like-minded people. In order to work out whether people have similar interests, new users are required to fill in a questionnaire that takes at least 25 minutes to complete. This means new users have to invest at least 25 minutes of their time before they can even find out whether the chat service is of any value to them. In contrast, consider Twitter where an account can be set up in less than a minute and other Twitter users with potentially interesting information can be followed instantly. Which business has the better immediate value equation from a customer perspective?

For products or services that are used repeatedly over time (or that realise their value over time, such as newsletter subscriptions), the value equation is constantly changing and your product or service needs to demonstrate great value at any point. Otherwise, if customers believe the product or service is no longer of value to them, they're likely to stop buying or using it.

Considering the timing of when value is created is absolutely crucial for start-ups because many new ideas rely on a 'critical mass' of other customers also using the product or service. Take eBay, for example — the marketplace only becomes valuable with a significant number of sellers, buyers and possible transactions. Typically, you can overcome this 'getting started' problem with marketing and promotional activities but they're expensive, so you need to be sure that the potential value of your marketplace is realised and customers benefit from it (before your marketing budget is all used up).

Ideally, you want to make sure that customers can at least see great value or, even better, benefit from your product or service the first time they use it — and quickly. Everyone is time poor and impatient these days, and 10 minutes can be a long time to demonstrate value to an audience with busy lives. Considering all aspects of what your customers need to do to use your product is crucial — for example, do they need to perform tasks such as register or create a profile, enter information, provide comments, upload documents, or go through an online payment transaction before they actually access your product or service? All of the activities the customer must perform are part of their side of the value equation.

Unfortunately, when the value equation isn't right for your customers (that is, they don't perceive great value in return for what they're giving you), it typically doesn't matter how many resources you throw at promoting your product or service. Your venture is destined to fail unless you change the value equation. (See the sidebar 'Looking at Ferrit's value equation' for a case study that clearly shows this.)

Looking at Ferrit's value equation

One of the best examples of a case where the founders didn't adequately consider their idea's value equation was the NZ online start-up 'Ferrit', which was funded by NZ Telecom. The company set out to create a second (in addition to TradeMe) national marketplace for Kiwis to buy consumer goods online. The rationale of the founders was that if TradeMe was the marketplace for used goods, Ferrit could become the marketplace for new goods. So far, so good.

Unfortunately, the value equation didn't work for customers because the website wasn't very user-friendly, customers often took a long time to find products, no price comparison was available, many retailers were missing from the marketplace and customers couldn't actually make purchases on Ferrit (initially they were instead redirected to other websites).

Uptake was very slow and the company spent vast amounts of money on high-profile TV and print ad campaigns (to the tune of several millions of dollars) to promote the site. Yet, the usage pattern of the site remained the same — traffic would increase during ad campaigns and then go back to more or less the same level the site experienced before the campaigns. After about three years of ad campaigns, Telecom finally pulled the plug and shut down the site (after having sunk significant resources and effort into it).

So, how do you assess the potential value of an idea? Useful factors to consider when evaluating an idea are as follows:

- ✔ Can the idea make money in some way, either through selling a product or service, or running advertising on the site (for free products)? (See the following section for help with deciding whether or not to charge for your product or service.)

- ✔ Is the idea based on deep industry knowledge and so can be validated and applied easily? (For example, online travel bookings require a detailed understanding of the travel industry's global distribution systems.)

- ✔ Is the idea based on substantial research in a particularly field and, therefore, difficult to copy?

- ✔ Does the idea address structural inefficiencies in a particular business process and, therefore, offer substantial advantages such as time saving, convenience or cost over the current process? (An example of this kind of idea would be online banking.)

- ✔ Is the idea essentially a discovery or invention that can be protected through trade secrets, patents or copyrights (such as computer software or video games)?

- ✔ Does the idea use a concept that's already very successful in another industry or market (such as groupon.com.au)?

If your idea doesn't fit into any of the categories listed in the preceding list, it may be what's usually referred to as a 'nice to have' — that is, the product or service within the idea doesn't address an important need in customers to provide sustainable value. In other words the products or services are completely optional and customers' lives will be exactly the same whether or not they use the product or service.

Unfortunately, most start-up ideas fall into the 'nice to have' category and are based on observations of minor annoyances of daily life or based on unrealistic assumptions (as a result of inadequate knowledge of the industry or market).

Some ideas in the 'nice to have' category may end up in highly entertaining 'hits'. A great example is Instagram, which provides photo-sharing and photo-enhancing features for smartphones. The company is not life-saving by any standard, although it did achieve extraordinary, unsupported growth rates within its first year, and was acquired by Facebook after 18 months of operation.

Checking that you can make money from your idea

Once you have performed a basic assessment of your idea (see preceding section), you then need to broadly look at how you can use your idea to make money.

The way you estimate how much money you can potentially make from your idea depends on whether you're planning to offer your product or service for a price or free of charge, as follows:

- ✔ **Offering your product or service for a price:** If you're aiming to sell your product or service at a certain price to a certain target segment, you need to determine (or estimate, at this early stage) the total number of people who can benefit from the product or service and who could theoretically buy it (per year), multiplied by the price for your product or service; this is the *total addressable market (TAM)* of your idea.

Typically at this early stage you need to make a lot of assumptions to calculate your TAM. The more you know about your product and potential market and customers, the easier it is to more accurately calculate the TAM. If you do decide to take your idea further, a really important process in these calculations is validating your assumptions, which I discuss in the section 'Validating everything' later in this chapter.

- ✔ **Offering your product or service for free:** If your idea is to offer a free product or service online, you need to identify other sources of income to sustain your company. The most common model is to use advertising (as demonstrated by YouTube or Twitter); other models include sponsorship or voluntary donations.

If offering your product or service for free, the TAM calculation is less useful so you may find it easier to estimate the potential advertising revenue based on website traffic. A simple way to estimate the advertising income of an online service is to assume $1 revenue for every 100 unique visitors to your site per month. So, if your site has 100,000 unique visitors per month, you can expect to generate about $1,000 in advertising revenue — but bear in mind that reaching this level of website traffic often takes years.

Discovering the 'penny gap'

Chris Anderson, in his book *Free: The Future of a Radical Price*, describes a phenomenon called the *penny gap*. His theory is that for every product or service two markets exist: 'Free of charge' and everything else. So, charging even a minute amount of money (that is, one penny or one cent) forces consumers to decide whether or not to open up their wallets. If the product or service is free, no decision needs to be made.

The wide availability of free products and services on the internet has created a mindset in many consumers that many things can be found online that don't cost a thing. Many online businesses have failed catastrophically when they started charging for a popular product or service that used to be free (such as online newspaper subscriptions, stock quotes and games).

What does this mean for you as an entrepreneur? You need to think carefully about your product pricing strategy. Never assume a popular free product or service can easily be converted into a paid-for product or service. On the flip side, pricing can be more flexible once the penny gap has been crossed — once you've demonstrated that consumers are willing to pay at least some money for a product or service. As such it may not make a big difference to consumers whether you charge $2.99 or $3.99 — however, the $1 extra may make a huge difference to the profitability of your company.

Even when based on a lot of untested assumptions, a TAM calculation or an estimation of website traffic can quickly make it obvious that executing a particular idea is just not worth it. The main reason is that even the most successful businesses take years to capture *market share* (that is, a substantial portion of the available customers) of their TAM or attract a high level of website traffic.

Typically, market share for a new business ranges from 5 to 25 per cent after five years. Often, the cost to run the business for five years and acquire significant market share outweighs the total financial gain that can be made from the business.

Another reason a quick TAM calculation can show your idea isn't worthwhile is because it can indicate whether investors are likely to be interested in your idea. If your TAM calculation comes out at less than $1 billion, investors may not be that keen on investing. This is because investors understand that a lot of hard work is required to capture a relatively small percentage of the TAM (even as low as 1 per cent). If the TAM is less than $1 billion, the venture simply doesn't offer enough reward for the risk associated with investing in new businesses.

For information on the kind of in-depth analysis you should perform once you're confident your idea has potential, see the section 'Doing Your Homework' later in this chapter.

TIP

Non-disclosure agreements

When entrepreneurs approach my incubator and accelerator programs, many tell me that they've got a 'killer idea' and that we need to sign a 'non-disclosure agreement' (NDA) so they can tell me and my team about it.

I never sign these forms, mainly because we may already be working on a similar concept and the NDA would then conflict us. But these entrepreneurs really have nothing to worry about. Ideas are literally a dime a dozen and a business idea in itself is worth nothing without the right team, connections, support and the various other things required to turn a good idea into a successful business.

So, my tip for you is this: When you approach investors or people who can help you with implementing your idea, never ask for an NDA. Asking investors to sign a non-disclosure automatically puts you in the group of naïve entrepreneurs who think that the success of a business is mostly determined by the idea.

Instead, I encourage entrepreneurs to openly share their ideas with others, seek feedback and be open to suggestions. For someone to steal your idea from you and out-execute you on your own idea is extremely unlikely — the chances of you winning the lottery are higher. (Any stories you have heard about ideas being stolen and others making a fortune are most likely urban myths.) Certainly no professional investor, incubator or venture capitalist would ever be interested in taking an idea from an entrepreneur and executing it.

Doing Your Homework

Unlike in school (where you do your homework after class), the homework required in the start-up world ideally happens long before you actually start a company — before you consider spending serious time on your idea or quitting your day job. The more you know about your idea, your target market and your target customer segment, the better your chances for succeeding with your start-up.

The good news is that this 'knowledge gathering' phase can be done while you're still busy doing something else (for example, finishing a degree or working full-time).

Any idea needs to pass a pre-assessment stage to ensure it's even worth pursuing, which usually involves you making some assumptions. (Refer to the section 'Preventing a False Start: Assessing Your Idea's Potential' earlier in the chapter for more on this.) Once you're sure your idea has potential, you need to test and validate these assumptions. The following sections cover how to do this.

Finding out more about your target market and customers

This seems like such an obvious point to make but do you fully understand the customers who are most likely to buy your product or service and your target market? I'm constantly surprised by the number of entrepreneurs who approach me with a concept that applies to an area of business they know little about.

Knowing your consumers and target market is really important. For example, if you want to sell an online game on Facebook, you really need to be a gamer yourself and have spent years in that space.

A good example of people coming up with ideas outside their area of expertise comes from the recent popularity of 'smart appliances' solutions — these are home appliances that can switch on and off, depending on the electricity prices. Many entrepreneurs who have developed concepts around this idea have no background in the electricity industry and don't understand the challenges and opportunities of the industry. (Unfortunately, having smart home appliances isn't particularly interesting to the electricity industry and doesn't address a big enough pain point for consumers.) I've also had entrepreneurs approach me who wanted to develop a smartphone app for toddlers but didn't actually have children.

The timing of an idea is crucial — being too early with an idea is just as bad (for business) as being late. The textbooks of MBA students are filled with numerous examples of companies that were ahead of their time, which ultimately caused the business to go under. The same goes for ideas that arrived too late — in other words, when the underlying value proposition has become obsolete as a result of changes in technology or legislation, or because of the widespread availability of a superior competitive product. Low-cost digital cameras are a prime example of 'late' ideas. For the last few years, (low-cost) digital cameras have offered very little advantage over built-in cameras in smartphones but have a significant disadvantage in that they need to be carried around (in addition to the smartphone that most people always carry with them anyway).

If you hear yourself saying 'I can't believe no-one else has thought of this before' alarm bells should go off and you should stop right there. Usually, a reason exists for why something has not been done before and this reason is usually to do with specific knowledge of the market or industry that has prevented that solution. That's not to say that industry outsiders can't discover a solution or opportunity that industry insiders haven't yet spotted, but it is quite rare.

Sometimes an industry outsider can come up with an idea that revolutionises an industry. Anita Roddick and the Body Shop is a good example of this — she repeatedly stated that she had no idea about the cosmetics industry when she started her business. But if you're intent on pursuing an idea you're developing in an area outside of your expertise, you better be prepared to be a very fast learner. Better still, speak to an industry insider before you commit serious time or funds. Many ideas look perfectly feasible from the outside until you understand the nature of an industry or market with its unique set of challenges, rules, peculiarities, legacy issues and so on.

Validating everything

The current era is a great one for entrepreneurs, and most people in Australia and New Zealand have access to an immensely powerful tool that hasn't been available to most entrepreneurs in the past. This tool is the internet and more specifically the search engines available online.

Using a search engine like Google is one of the simplest first steps when validating key assumptions around your idea or concept. Once you have an idea about your target market and the value your idea offers this market (see preceding sections), you can easily and quickly find out how popular your idea is likely going to be.

Let's say you have an idea for a smartphone app that helps train spotters identify a particular train. A search using the terms 'train spotting hobby' on Google yields about 1.5 million search results. (That may seem like a lot but is small compared to search terms like 'lose weight' or 'stop smoking', which yield hundreds of millions of search results.) You can find out a lot more about your idea (such as geographical variations in popularity and related keywords) by using advanced search options and refining your search terms.

Using the web as your main source of information initially is perfectly acceptable (from an investor's perspective) and easily achieved. Here's what you want to confirm or refine about your idea, and how to conduct this research, when aiming to validate your assumptions online:

- ✔ **Your target market:** Sometimes it's not immediately obvious how your idea can be applied commercially and which specific market it addresses. Online research can help: Search for websites using a number of words associated with your idea and you're likely to come across websites that cover a similar (or identical) field. You can pick up some common terminology or expressions from these websites that in turn can lead to more information when entered in a search engine.

  Make a list of the search terms that provide the most relevant search results for your idea. Over time, you generally get a sense of what problems and solutions exist in a given market. If you have identified a particular opportunity that your idea addresses, you can find out about the corresponding target market for it.

- ✔ **The size of your target market:** In the section 'Checking that you can make money from your idea', I further discuss the concept of the total addressable market.

  In most cases, you can find out more information about your TAM online — from such sources as industry-specific websites and publications, online newspapers or magazines, and specialist reports by research organisations (for example, Gartner Technology Research, a company specialising in providing research on global technology trends). Chances are, something already exists online that provides you with a reference to refine your assumptions on the TAM.

✔ **The relevance of your idea in the current market:** Trend research is another important area for validating assumptions. Things come and go (especially online) and the pace of change is accelerating constantly. Ideally, you want to get in on a major trend early so you have enough time to fully develop your concept and then capitalise on it when the trend is in full swing. Use your list of relevant search terms (refer to the first bullet in this list for more on this) and pay close attention to the 'update dates' on websites and articles. If most of the highly relevant articles or web pages are three or four years old, you may have caught the trend on its way out. You can also use Google Trends or Google News Search, as well as Twitter, to get a better idea of how 'current' a particular topic is.

Both Google Trends and Twitter display a list of trending topics for a given period. Google Trends even allows you to check trends over time for particular keywords (allowing you to check how many searches have occurred for particular words). Check `google.com.au/trends` for more.

✔ **The existing products or solutions already available and major competitors:** Spending a significant amount of time (at least a full day) on a thorough competitor analysis is absolutely essential at this stage. Use your list of relevant keywords (refer to the first bullet in this list) and dig around on websites to find out who is active in the space you're targeting. Researching your competitors is one of the key activities investors expect you to have completed before you approach them. You also benefit from it — you don't want to waste a lot of time and energy on something that has been done already.

Once you've compiled a good list of competitors in your target market, keep an eye on their websites and set up News Alerts with a search engine such as Google for relevant keywords. To set up a News Alert in Google, simply go to `google.com/alerts` and enter a keyword to trigger the alert (for example, the name of a competitor). This means you then receive an email every time someone publishes information that contains the keyword you specified.

The time you spend on this fact-finding and validating mission is well worth the effort because it may save you from a whole lot of frustration later on — for example, finding out that major competitors exist in your market or that your actual TAM is just too small.

If during your validation process your research seems to show your idea may not work, don't lose heart immediately. Sometimes, several options exist — you may be able to address a number of different markets or produce a set of more distinct products or services. Capture the three most popular product–market combinations with the highest TAMs and clearly define those. Forget about all other possible combinations and application areas for the time being — focus on just a few options initially. Otherwise, you can easily get lost and end up with products and services that aim to be all things to all people, but don't provide a required solution to any particular market.

Looking at the People Around You

Most investors would agree that start-ups run by a good team are more likely to succeed than start-ups run by an individual entrepreneur. Many reasons exist for this, but at the most fundamental level it comes down to strength in numbers and strength from diversity. Picking business partners is actually quite difficult and assembling a winning team (rather than just a bunch of also rans) is perhaps one of the trickiest tasks along your start-up journey.

Finding the right people to be in business with is not something you only need to do at the beginning of a venture — it's a constant task that eventually you need to trust someone else to do (most likely your HR manager). Still, the task of building the right team at the start of your venture remains absolutely crucial because unfortunate team compositions have killed many a promising companies.

In the following sections, I cover how you can identify who you need in your team, and what sort of agreement you should have in place with your team members, even in the early stages of your start-up.

Assembling a winning team

The task of assembling a team may look pretty simple at the outset. Often, a bunch of you are at university or form a group of friends (or even relatives) and it seems obvious to start the business together. However, when you consider that the start-up journey typically lasts for several years and that you may encounter many bumps along the road, checking whether the most obvious choices for members of your team are also the most useful is worthwhile.

Here's a list of things to consider when picking business partners and co-founders:

- ✔ **Talent:** What are other team members bringing to the table? Ideally, the people you want to be in business with have a unique talent that's different from yours. They should be overachievers in their field and, in a perfect world, you should have already worked together for at least a few months.

  Working with people is very different from knowing them socially.

- ✔ **Diversity:** Do you have sufficient diversity on your team? Investors are very interested in team composition and they want to see a good mix of skills, experience, personality styles, risk appetite and focus (such as a focus on detail versus big picture thinking). Ideally, you don't want people who behave and think like you and have the same experience or knowledge.

- ✔ **Relationship:** Where do you know your team members from? Being in business with a family member can be a real blessing — or a disaster. If you're related to someone in your team, consider what is likely to happen to that relationship when the start-up goes through a tough period or goes under. The same principle applies to couples in a team or being in business with a 'best mate'. On the other hand, starting a business with someone you hardly know can present its own set of difficulties because, ultimately, you only really get to know people once you've worked with them for several months or you have mastered a crisis together.

When you realise that you don't have all the skills you need to get your start-up off the ground (which is usually the case), consider whether you need to add a new team member or find a contractor or employee to fill your skills gap. For example, many entrepreneurs team up with developers who can build a website, game or app. This can work well if you've got the right person and if the development skill is absolutely essential to the business. It usually doesn't work well when the website is only a small part of the business. Ideally, you add people to your team when their skill set is business critical and complementary to your talents. If you need help in a specialist area that only has a minor impact on the overall business, using contractors, freelancers or employees is usually the better option. Why? Because it's very easy to stop working with a contractor but very hard to get rid of a business partner you aren't happy with.

Formalising your business arrangements

The start of a venture isn't always a clearly defined date — sometimes you start working on an idea with some friends and, before you know it, the idea generates revenue or a major customer is interested. That's great, but making sure some ground rules are in place before things get more serious is also really important. You need to start thinking about formalising business relationships before spending serious amounts of time or money on a new concept.

At a bare minimum, you should consider drafting and signing a *memorandum of understanding* (MOU), which captures the key aspects of what you're doing.

In the early days of planning a start-up, things can get out of hand really easily and expectations can run wild. To avoid a major distraction of having to deal with frustrated business partners before you even get to the starting line with your business, use clear agreements between everyone involved. Often a few clear statements, a minuted meeting and a signed MOU can help you ensure that all your team members are on the same page when it comes to working on an idea or concept.

The MOU should cover the following aspects (all of these can be one-liners in the MOU):

✓ **Names of those involved with the project or idea.**

This could be something as simple as 'This MOU captures an agreement between the following parties [list of names] to work on a business concept'.

✓ **Nature of the project or idea that you're working on.**

I suggest using one sentence that summarises the essence of the business well, such as 'Develop a smartphone application that helps people lose weight'.

✓ **The role or contribution of each party.**

For example: 'Under this agreement, party A is responsible for website development, Party B is responsible for sales and marketing, and Party C is responsible for business operations and finance'.

✓ **Agreed ownership of a resulting commercial entity.**

For example: 'The ownership of the concept/idea is split as follows: (list of names and percentages)'. If no split has been agreed, write down that the ownership is split equally between all parties listed on the MOU (so, if four parties are listed, each party ends up with 25 per cent equity of a resulting venture).

✓ **How the concept or idea will be developed.**

I suggest you list particular steps and dates.

✓ **Validity period of the MOU.**

I recommend a maximum of six months, but a minimum of three.

✓ **Signatures.**

Make sure all listed parties sign and date the MOU.

See Appendix B for a sample MOU template.

If the founding team members are keen to continue with the venture at the end of the validity period for the MOU, I recommend registering a company and signing a *shareholder agreement.* This agreement is a legal document that captures the way in which you want to work together with your business partners, sets out the ownership structure of the company and provides guidelines for management. See Chapter 3 for more information about shareholder agreements.

For more information about working out whether you're ready to start a company (and perhaps quit your day job), see the section 'Getting Serious' later in this chapter.

Developing a Good Story

Everyone loves a good story, which is why fiction titles usually top the overall bestseller lists. Customers, investors and business people in general are no different — they all want a good story. So an important task at this early stage is to think about how you want to put your story together and how it should be told.

When you're pitching to investors (or to partners or customers), your story must answer the all-important question: What makes you unique in your market or line of business?

When thinking about your response to this main question, try to incorporate answers to the following:

- What is it that you know, own, have or make that's different to everyone else? That is, what do you have that nobody else has?

- Why should other businesses work with you? Why should investors invest in you?

- Why should customers buy or use your products or services?

As well as what makes you unique, people always want to know who's behind a particular product or service. The background of the story teller is part of the story. For example, if you were interested in buying an eBook on how to make lots of money on the stock market, wouldn't you want to know that the person who wrote the book actually did make lots of money trading stocks? Same goes for start-ups — you need to demonstrate your credibility to customers, business partners (such as those providing distribution channels) and investors.

In the following sections, I look at what investors want to see in your business before they hand over the cheque and how you can make the most out of unfair advantages you have.

Understanding what investors want

Professional early stage investors look for certain things when you tell your story, so consider which part of your story appeals to investors or how to tell your story so investors are interested. You need to get into the mindset of investors to truly 'hit their buttons' with your story.

Here's my list of what your story needs to offer investors:

- **A chance to make money:** Okay, this seems like an obvious point but it's surprising how many entrepreneurs don't do the maths to work out how much potential gain an investor stands to make from a deal. In order to work that out, you need to prepare a capitalisation table (see Chapter 7). Most early stage investors want to see a return on their investment in the range of at least ten to one (that is, they give you $1 million and expect $10 million back within a given time frame). The ratio of return to investment is usually indicated by the letter x — so if investors tell you they're looking for a 10 x return on investment, this means they want ten times the amount of money back.

  Seed-stage investors (investors who provide capital to set up or launch a business) often expect a return of up to 30x. So if you present to them and show a 3x return, they're probably not going to be very interested in the deal.

- **A de-risked investment opportunity:** Investors understand managing risk pretty well. So, if you want to impress them, you need to show that you also understand how to manage the risk of your venture. Ideally, you should be able to show investors what risks you have identified and how you have 'de-risked' (that is, eliminated) the key risks in your venture. An example of de-risking is if you have identified potential sales as a key risk in your venture and you can present investors with a signed sales agreement for your products with a major reseller.

- **Your unfair advantage:** You need to identify and promote your unfair advantage (see the following section for more on this). When you pitch to investors, ideally have a slide titled 'Our unfair advantage' (or similar).

- **Details about the potential size of your business:** Investors aren't interested in *lifestyle* businesses — those businesses that allow a comfortable lifestyle for the business' principals but don't generate a lot of returns for shareholders. So if you're pitching to investors and the overall size of the opportunity is less than a million dollars (where the opportunity equals the potential gain in a best-case scenario), you may not get much interest. Make sure your venture targets a major market ($1 billion TAM — refer to the section 'Checking that you can make money from your idea') and you can demonstrate how your company is going to be valued at over $10 million within the next five years.

✔ **Information that shows why you're a good entrepreneur:** Investors trust in people rather than ideas — they trust the jockey, not the horse. The reason for this is, even if the initial idea turns out to not be feasible, a good entrepreneur can change direction and do whatever it takes to turn the venture into a successful business. So, if you can demonstrate that you've assembled a star team and that you have a proven track record of successful business activities, you're off to a good start. In particular, investors look for a good team composition with a wide range of skills, focusing not only solid technology and business skills but also excellent sales skills — because, one way or another, every company has to sell something to make money.

✔ **An exciting opportunity:** At the end of the day, investors are just ordinary people with a bit of money. They are human (yes — despite what you may have heard) and as such they get excited about certain things. Some investors are known for only investing in a particular niche (such as within biotech or gaming). If you can find out what gets the investors you're pitching to excited, all the better. Play to their interests and get them excited. Investors often refer to this as *selling the sizzle not just the steak* — which means you have to elicit an emotive response in your audience in addition to providing sound reasoning. So show potential investors fancy screenshots, let them play with a mock-up or give them exclusive access to your test platform.

Engineering your unfair advantage

Investors often get several teams pitching the same idea and, if the idea is a good one, may have to determine which team they should invest in. To work out the best option, investors often use the concept of an *unfair advantage*. Investors want to be convinced that the team they invest in has something that gives them an edge over other teams.

This unfair advantage can be a number of things, including the following:

- An established network and existing relationships (for example, with buyers in a given industry)

- An existing (and exclusive) contract with a distribution partner, retailer or other sales outlet

- Insider knowledge (such as extensive knowledge of a new technology)

- A large existing customer base (for example, 1 million newsletter subscribers)

- A patent or trade secret

This concept of an unfair advantage works equally well when trying to convince other businesses to partner with you or when attracting customers to try your product or service. If you can present them with a convincing argument why you're in the perfect (and unique) position to execute a business plan or deliver your product or service, you stand a good chance of getting some interest from others.

Getting Serious

You've worked hard on your idea and have decided that it's time to kick off for real and start your venture. Well done!

Don't get ahead of yourself and start your venture before you've completed the required research and validation. You need to have identified your target market and your TAM, worked out your value equation and determined who you need on your team to ensure all areas are covered — and found people to fill these gaps — among other essential steps. Refer to the preceding sections in this chapter if you have any doubts about whether you're ready to start your venture.

A good indication you have what it takes to ensure your start-up is successful is if you're still as excited about your idea as you were on the day you first thought of it. Ideally, your level of enthusiasm should just keep going up.

If you can voice a resounding 'Yes' to having completed all your research and still being enthusiastic about your idea, good on ya! Let's do it!

The following sections provide some recommendations on what to do next, such as working out whether you're ready to devote yourself full-time to your start-up and looking at funding options to cover your costs through the initial period of getting things up and running.

Completing the prep work for your start-up, such as researching your target market and establishing your team, can all be done at minimal cost and effort. From now on, things get serious and typically require some funds and more significant effort.

Working out if you can quit your day job

Should you quit your day job? The answer is — it depends. Let's be very clear. Working full-time (as in around 80 hours per week) on your start-up is a key success factor. Few entrepreneurs who work part-time on their start-up (or, even worse, moonlight on it) end up with a venture that's a huge success story.

Your start-up needs total focus, utter commitment and the ability for founders to go the extra mile constantly. That's not possible when you have to worry about doing a nine to five work day or working for someone else.

However, just like with everything else, timing is key when it comes to quitting your day job. Ideally, you want to put yourself in a situation where you know exactly how long you can sustain yourself for when working on your start-up. You need to consider your cost of living as well as all general expenses (including health care and unexpected expenditure — like when your washing machine or car breaks down). Entrepreneurs commonly work out what their minimum cost of living is and factor this into the financing plans for the venture.

We recommend a *runway* time (the time until your business runs out of funds) for your business of about 18 months from when you start out. This means you need to work out how you can sustain yourself and your business for a year and a half. By the end of that period, you need to have given up, attracted funding, generated revenue or worked out another way to continue with your venture. (The following section outlines options available to get yourself into a financial position that allows an 18-month runway to execute your concept.)

When putting together a budget for your venture, work out a justifiable 'minimum cost of living' for yourself and all team members. No investor wants to see money being spent on top salaries. In 2012, most investors would probably consider a salary of $2,000 per month per entrepreneur acceptable.

Once you've worked out your minimum living cost and a plan of attack to finance your business, you can think about the timing of quitting your day job. Consider a number of factors when deciding on a time to quit, such as notice periods, potential issues or opportunities around major holiday periods (for example, Christmas and New Year) or annual leave you're still owed.

You can easily accomplish a number of important tasks for your venture before you quit, including the following:

- ✔ **Formalise agreements with your co-founders:** Turn an existing MOU (refer to the section 'Formalising your business arrangements') or other agreement into standard documentation for companies. Generally, you need a shareholder agreement and a constitution for your business. See Chapter 3 for more information on these.

- ✔ **Register your company:** In Australia and New Zealand, the easiest commercial vehicle for your company is to register a limited liability company. This process is extremely straightforward and you can do it yourself online (the whole process should take you about 30 minutes, at most). Go to www.asic.gov.au or business.govt.nz. In New Zealand, you can register for a tax number (IRD number) at the same time as when you register you company (doing so saves time and hassle, so is highly advisable). In Australia, you're issued an Australian Business Number when you register your company. You can then register with the Australian Tax Office later.

- ✔ **Sort out the basics:** Have a think about where you're going to locate your business and where you can work (yes, garages are a favourite). If you realise you need an office, start looking around for a suitable space (as well as equipment). Ask around if someone knows a good accountant, lawyer or business advisor. Organise a meeting with these people to find out what they can offer and how much they charge.

You don't need to use an accountant, tax agent or other professional service to register your company. People offering these options generally charge additional fees for providing the service and the process is really very straightforward.

You can read a number of how-to guides on government websites (asic.com.au in Australia and companies.govt.nz in New Zealand) and you can't really make any serious mistakes by completing the registration process yourself. For more information about setting up your business, check out *Small Business For Dummies*, 4th Australian and New Zealand Edition, by Veechi Curtis (published by Wiley Publishing Australia).

I've come across a number of entrepreneurs who didn't bother registering their company or formalising agreements with co-founders or team members to save money (or because they didn't think these steps were important). Unfortunately for the entrepreneurs I met with, skipping these steps ended up ruining their business or personal finance because they had to fight bitter and expensive legal battles with former business partners over shareholdings, dividends or intellectual property rights. While spending up to around $5,000 may seem like a lot of money, the expense is absolutely worth it (and pretty much a pre-requisite for creating a successful company). Setting up a limited liability company protects your personal assets and shareholder agreements clearly define shareholdings as well as relationships with your business partners. You're planning to create a multi-million dollar company, right? (Say Yes!) So start as you mean to continue and do things properly right from the beginning.

Quitting your day job is a big deal and a big step. Considering the timing of this move wisely can work in your favour — rather than create all sorts of problems when you quit too early or too late.

Reviewing your funding options

If you've decided to get serious about your venture and worked through the timing for quitting your job (refer to the preceding section), the next issue you're typically faced with is funding. That is, you know that focusing completely on your new business is the best (really the only) route to success, but you just don't have the funds to sustain yourself and pump money into the business. The majority of first-time entrepreneurs (and most other entrepreneurs) are generally in this situation, so you're part of a large group. Welcome to the club of keen but somewhat poor entrepreneurs!

Apart from capital, you may also be slightly daunted by the tasks ahead. So, as well as capital, you may also want some advice on running your start-up. You may have heard the terms *smart money* (funds provided by investors who also bring significant experience, networks or other resources to your start-up — in addition to the capital!) and *dumb money* (funds from investors who only give you cash, and have no other input in your business).

Fortunately, a number of options are available for entrepreneurs that provide a range of services in addition to capital. The following sections cover the most common options for start-up assistance, including going it alone, private investors (including family and friends), incubators, accelerators, angel investors and venture capitalists.

Going it alone

Funding your venture yourself is your baseline option for launching your start-up. When you 'go it alone', you need to make sure you have a reliable source of funding to finance your business for (at least) the first 18 months (refer to the section 'Working out if you can quit your day job' earlier in the chapter). If you're lucky enough to have inherited money or you just have the funds anyway, great!

Having to pitch for money is a full-on job in itself and by not having to do this task you free up a lot of time to focus on your business. Going it alone also means you don't have to give away any *equity* (a share of your business) to investors. The downside is that you may not get input from investors — but you can easily work with business mentors, an external advisory board or incubators (see the section 'Incubators') to get some input from experienced business people.

 Going it alone is a good option if you have enough money to self-finance, but not having the funds and thinking that you can just get by somehow is a recipe for disaster. This typically ends in huge personal debt or abandonment of the venture (because you run out of money and have to go back to your day job).

The only other scenario for successfully going it alone is if your venture makes money from Day 1. This isn't impossible and actually puts you in a very strong position for all other options as well. See Chapter 3 for more on starting cashflow-positive ventures.

The three Fs and private investors

An extension of the 'going it alone' option (refer to the preceding section) is to raise funds from private networks. The most common source of funding for first-time entrepreneurs is friends, family and fools — also known as the *three Fs*. Asking others for money doesn't come easy for many people, especially when dealing with non-professional investors bears a lot of risks. While raising money from options within your three Fs may seem easier, doing so also comes with a lot of baggage.

Consider the following aspects before approaching friends and family for funding:

- **Full disclosure:** Make sure your private investors understand your idea and what type of deal you're offering. If you're using a return on investment, ensure that the investors know what level of return, what time period you're looking at, and how their financial interest in your venture is going to be registered (for example, they could become shareholders). Also be very clear with your investors how you want them to participate in your venture. If you just want their money but no input, be upfront about their involvement. If you want them to take up the role of an advisor or director, make sure they understand the rights and responsibilities associated with the position you have in mind for them.

- **Potential risk:** Provide details on the risk involved in investing in your business. If you suspect the business includes even a slim chance of the investors losing all their money, you need to be clear about that.

- **Financial situation of your private investors:** In the worst-case scenario where your venture goes under, is this likely to create dire consequences for your investors, such as your investors losing their house? Make sure your investors can easily afford their investment in your business.

- **Long-term ramifications:** Make sure you understand how your relationship with the investors is likely to be affected by their investment. In particular, you need to be clear about how you're going to inform them of progress with your company and the likely outcomes of their investment. If you don't set this out upfront, you may find yourself in the midst of some uncomfortable conversations next time you meet over dinner or coffee.

As well as family and friends, another option is to approach professional investors or high-net-worth individuals directly. This is often a feasible option when you know someone in that category well. Most people in this category are open to looking at business propositions and making private investments. Again, you need to understand who you're dealing with, what they expect in return and how the investment is structured.

You should formally document any investment deal, even if it's your mum and dad who are investing — which does mean you need to involve lawyers. See Chapter 3 for details on shareholder agreements and Chapter 7 for details on investment agreements.

Incubators

Business incubators typically help early stage businesses get off the ground and provide a conducive environment for new ventures to grow and gain momentum.

Many flavours of incubators are available in Australia and New Zealand, with options being provided by state-owned entities, city councils, development agencies or private companies. Examples from Australia and New Zealand include CreativeHQ, Pollinizer and WebFund.

Incubators typically provide a mix of the following:

- ✔ Assistance with applying for grants or attracting investment
- ✔ Business mentoring (e.g. two hours per week)
- ✔ Capital (usually very small amounts — perhaps up to $25,000)
- ✔ Networking opportunities with other entrepreneurs and experts
- ✔ Serviced office space

In return for the help provided, incubators take an equity stake in your company (commonly between 5 and 25 per cent, dependent on the level of services and capital provided). Some incubators also charge a small monthly fee on top of the equity stake.

Incubators represent a useful option to get started for first-time entrepreneurs, but shop around before deciding on a particular incubator. Speak to people who are already enrolled in the program and check contractual conditions before enrolling (and ask a lawyer to look over the contract as well). Some incubators have a limited 'incubation period', such as three years, after which your venture is expected to 'graduate' and leave the program.

Accelerators

Accelerators are somewhat similar to incubators (refer to preceding section) but are typically highly structured. The idea of *accelerators* is to condense the incubation period into a short time frame to assist entrepreneurs with making a decision on the viability of their concept — after the program, the venture is either able to attract funding, sustainable in its own right or not viable (meaning it should be shut down).

Accelerators typically

- ✔ Use a strict process of a defined intake period (for example, once or twice per year) combined with a screening and admission procedure followed by the acceleration program and graduation.

- ✔ Run for anywhere between six weeks and three months, during which entrepreneurs need to commit to a full-time schedule of lectures, presentations, mentoring and business development. You're usually required to attend any presentations or events for the duration of the program (which may mean you have to move to wherever the program is run and live there for the length of the program).

- ✔ Provide a small amount of funding for successful applicants (usually between $5,000 and $25,000) to cover living expenses during the program.

- ✔ Provide frequent opportunities for you to pitch to potential investors.

After being involved in start-ups for about 10 years I consider accelerators among the most successful programs for start-ups, because they typically create the highest ratios of successful companies from applications. This means the screening process to be accepted by an accelerator is usually rigorous and typically you're competing with thousands of other entrepreneurs just to get admitted to the program.

The most well known accelerator programs are YCombinator and TechStars (both from the US), but recently accelerators have also become available in Australia and

New Zealand. Options in New Zealand include HyperStart in Wellington (www.hyperstart.co.nz). In Australia, check out AngelCube in Melbourne (www.angelcube.com) or PushStart in Sydney (www.pushstart.com.au).

Angel investors

Business angels are early stage investors who typically provide 'smart money' up to around $250,000 (depending on country and market). However, unlike biblical angels, who are typically purely selfless, beautiful and spiritual beings, business angels are business people who are interested in creating returns on their investment.

Angel investment is often facilitated through angel clubs (such as AngelHQ in New Zealand or AngelCube in Australia), which screen ideas and prepare investment for their membership of high-net-worth individuals. Check out Appendix A for a list of angel networks.

Angels are investors and they're looking for results just like any other investors.

Angel investment tends to take place during the very early stages of a business and, therefore, attracts individuals who also have an interest in helping young entrepreneurs and seeing others succeed. As a result, angels often contribute more substantially to the ventures they invest in than other types of investors.

Angel investment is almost always conducted within a formal investment deal involving lawyers and contracts. The investment process itself typically involves the following steps:

1. **Submit a business plan.**

   You can create your own business plan or fill out a template (usually provided by the angel investment group), describing your venture.

2. **Work through a screening process.**

   You're invited to pitch to the investors only after getting through the screening process.

3. **Provide definition of the investment deal.**

   Most importantly, you need to confirm how many shares the angel investor receives and at what share price.

Note: Often the angel club facilitator assists with putting this information together.

4. Pitch to an investor audience.

The pitch usually takes place at an investment evening, where you pitch your idea along with three to five other entrepreneurs in front of an assembly of angels (a bit like the TV show *Dragon's Den*, but with more dragons in the room — often 20 to 50 angels are present at these events).

5. Receive a subscription.

Angels decide individually whether or not to invest in your venture.

6. Perform the due diligence and receive final commitment (or rejection).

If enough angels have agreed to invest in the investment deal you presented, a due diligence team is established to work with you through details of the investment.

Sometimes a *term sheet* is used to summarise the investment deal offered; expect to negotiate on the terms of the deal.

The due diligence team provides a recommendation back to the angels who signalled interest and confirms the final details of the investment deal. At this point, angel investors have to commit to the amount of money they're willing to invest, based on the conditions of the investment deal. If the desired investment capital can be achieved through these commitments, the investment round is considered 'closed' and the parties move on to preparing legal documentation.

7. Prepare legal documentation.

This usually involves drafting a new shareholder agreement and constitution for your company (see Chapter 3). Again, expect some lengthy negotiations at this point.

8. Execute the investment agreement on the due date.

This involves signing the shareholder agreements and executing its provisions (such as appointing directors). It usually also coincides with the investment capital being provided to the venture.

Venture capitalists

Venture capitalists (VCs) are professional investment firms and typically represent the most sophisticated group of investors with the highest levels of capital resources.

Many VCs don't invest in early-stage businesses directly — VCs are typically interested in investment deals of $500,000 to $1 million (of investment capital) and upwards. So, if you're looking for $100,000 in seed capital, VCs may simply ignore you because you're outside of their investment range. Make sure to check their website for information about what kind of deals the company is interested in and what range of capital they generally provide.

However, VCs have been known to invest in particularly promising early stage start-ups and some VCs have decided to provide 'blanket' investment for all graduates of a particular accelerator program (for example, the YCombinator and Start Fund in the US and HyperStart and HyperFund in NZ). Finding out if a VC does invest in start-ups (before you even approach them) is easy — again, just check the company website.

The process of securing investment from VCs is similar to angel investment (refer to the preceding section), although the parameters vary because VCs generally invest through a company or fund (not as individual investors). VCs typically take equity stakes of between 10 and 50 per cent of your company and expect representation on the board (through a VC-appointed director).

Naturally, VCs expect a good return on their investment (typically a return of at least 10 x investment) and drive entrepreneurs hard to deliver results. This option is probably the most difficult to pursue for early stage businesses and entrepreneurs — but it's not impossible. Many successful companies started out with an investment from a well-known VC, where the investment itself became a cornerstone of the success (because investments from well-known VCs are seen as validation that the venture must be on to something big). An example of this is when well-known VC Peter Thiel invested in Facebook — and the venture immediately attracted a lot of attention.

Part II

Getting Your Start-Up Started

Glenn Lumsden

'He used to work for NASA.'

In this part ...

*A*fter a decent amount of preparation and doing your homework on your business concept, you're now ready to start your business, right? Yes — but not before you do an essential round of testing and validating your assumptions. In this part I outline the essential process for verifying your idea and turning your dream into a viable business.

Once you've done that, you're ready to get on with a few other important details of being in business, such as finance, compliance, paperwork and legal matters. Don't worry — it's a lot less boring and easier than it sounds!

This part also covers a particularly exciting phase of any business — the launch (online businesses launch whereas traditional businesses start trading). Find out what happens after the launch and the early days of running a business.

Chapter 3

Setting Up Shop: Products, Paperwork and More

● ●

In This Chapter

▶ Defining products that customers want to buy

▶ Thinking about your business model and preparing a business plan

▶ Sorting out the legal side of your business, and making technology decisions

▶ Understanding accounting and finance aspects

▶ Staying focused and working with an advisory board to really boost your chances of success

● ●

*H*ave you heard of the story of the chicken and the pig who want to open a restaurant? The chicken suggests calling the restaurant 'Ham 'n' Eggs', but the pig points out that with a name like that the pig would be committed whereas the chicken would only be involved.

When it comes to your start-up, you need to be the committed pig. Once you've decided to go for it, you really need to give the venture your all, and make serious choices about what you're going to sell and how you're going to run your business.

In this chapter, I discuss these serious choices, covering working out your business model and creating a one-page business plan, and making sure your product or service is viable for a large enough market. I also look at your legal obligations, finding the right location for your company and what to consider when making technology decisions. I offer tips on staying on top of your accounting and finances, and I provide some guidance on selecting suitable members for your advisory board.

Running a start-up can be a truly exciting and wild time in your life. It's easy to forget that any start-up is first and foremost a company that comes with a number of responsibilities. Don't forget — the pig.

Making Sure Your Idea is Viable

At the centre of every business is a product or service that needs to be sold in order to generate income for the company. However, when you start from scratch, how do you decide on the features and characteristics of your product or service? You may have done some initial research and validations on your idea (refer to Chapter 2) but in order to build a viable (profitable) business, you need to define and test your product or service, and your assumptions about how vital it is for your target market, a lot more. Shaping your initial product or service is the most important and most crucial step of every business.

You need to decide which features or functions you consider absolutely essential for your customers, and test them first. At this stage, your set of assumptions about essential features is also sometimes called a *customer hypothesis*. This hypothesis is untested until you can demonstrate a corresponding prototype to customers to get their feedback.

This is where a technique called the *minimum viable product,* or MVP, comes in. An MVP is essentially an early stage prototype that allows potential customers to experience the set of key features of your product, and provide useful feedback. The trick is to create an MVP that demonstrates the features in a meaningful way (to people who typically experience the product for the first time), but not to spend too much time and resources on development.

Behind the term MVP is a whole philosophy of constantly defining, validating and adapting your product or service based on customer feedback. The MVP process addresses the main dilemma that start-ups face — namely, defining new products or services based on undefined or not-well-known customer needs and market needs. The MVP process allows you to determine these needs, and change your product or service accordingly; however, at the same time, you also need to monitor your overall target market, and ensure you're not tailoring your product or service too specifically to a small segment within this market (and as a result losing out on sales to the larger mainstream segments).

In the following sections, I outline the MVP process and offer some guidance in monitoring your overall market alongside any potential changes you make.

Testing customer preferences

So here's the million dollar trick in this book — the MVP process means you don't actually need to build anything to validate customer hypotheses and your assumptions of what features are essential for your product or service. With online commerce, selling a product or service that doesn't exist (yet) is entirely possible. All you need is a way to drive online traffic to a landing page (such as through using a Google AdWords account or equivalent) and some basic graphic design and copywriting skills, and then you're ready to test. In this section, I cover driving traffic to a particular page and using feedback from this traffic to make (virtual) changes to your product or service.

Creating an account to drive traffic to your page

Many popular websites offer a way to send traffic to your website by purchasing ads or specific keywords (which in turn trigger an ad display). Visitors then click on these ads and end up on your website. A popular and simple way to do this is using Google AdWords (adwords.google.com). You can create a free account by going to the Adwords website. Once you have set up the necessary account information (including payment, which you can do through a standard credit card) you're ready to start an ad campaign that drives traffic to your website. Having this account ready to go is essential for testing your virtual product using the process outlined in the following section.

Creating an account to analyse your website traffic

In addition to creating a way to drive traffic to your website (refer to preceding section), you also need a tool to help you analyse what people do when they get to your site. Google Analytics is one of the most common freely available tools and you can create an account by going to analytics.google.com. After providing some general information, Google Analytics asks you to verify that the site you'd like to analyse is actually your site. A number of methods are provided to verify that you own the site. Once you have completed this verification process you're all set. After a few hours, you should see statistical information come through on your analytics account. Make sure you test the account and settings by visiting your site and clicking on specific links, which you can then check in Google Analytics.

While I mainly use Google AdWords and Google Analytics as examples in this book, other sites offer similar options for testing products and services, such as Facebook, Yahoo, YouTube, Bing, StumbleUpon (to name but a few).

Putting the MVP process to work

Once you've created an account to drive traffic to a particular page and analyse the traffic on your website (refer to preceding section), you can use the following step-by-step process to refine your online business idea, without spending one minute on creating a prototype:

1. **Visualise a potential product or service that has all the features you defined in your customer hypothesis.**

   Imagine the finished product and picture how future customers would use it. Now describe what you have visualised in a document — use brainstorming techniques, scribbles, drawings sketches or whatever works for you. Describe the product or service and its features as a customer would see it. Also think of what customers would tell others about the product. Capture all of these thoughts (concepts or drawings) in a document.

2. **Turn the vague descriptions and designs from Step 1 into a product brochure.**

   Think of the product brochure as being like a leaflet or flyer you could hand out. Ideally, you should keep it to one A4 page. Include visual materials like a screenshot, mock-up sketch or 3D model, or design drawing. Highlight key benefits customers would experience when using the product.

3. **Pick a price point for your product or service.**

   You can use the testing technique to try out different price points (for example, change the price point after a certain amount of visitors to see whether you get better results with a higher or lower price). Make sure to also test a free version against a paid for version of your product or service. The data you gather when testing the price point (including the $0 price tag) is extremely useful when deciding on your business model later on.

4. **Create a web page from your one-pager and host it online.**

   You can use a free web hosting or blogging site, or a website or web server you may already have to present the product brochure as a real product. Make sure the page includes a Buy Now or Sign Up button as well as a Contact Us button (all should lead to a simple form where people can leave their contact details, which are then sent to you by email). Make sure each feature of your product and each benefit are hyperlinked to an empty link (such as an anchor on your page). This is absolutely crucial for tracking customer interest (see Step 6).

5. **Use Google AdWords (or equivalent) to create keyword campaigns for your virtual product.**

   Think of keywords that reflect the nature of what you're selling and write your online ads (triggered by people searching for your keywords) in a way that attracts an *early adopter* crowd (people willing to try out new products or services). Use the website address for the page you created in Step 4 to send the keyword advertising traffic to.

   If you're using Google, make sure you link your AdWords account to a Google Analytics account — so you can track which keywords worked for potential customers and what they clicked on when looking at your site. (For more on Google AdWords, see *Google AdWords For Dummies*, 2nd Edition, by Howie Jacobson and published by Wiley Publishing, Inc.)

6. **Analyse traffic to your product page.**

   If using Google Analytics, pay particular attention to the *heat maps*. These analytics show which areas of your page have received the most clicks (hence the need for hyperlinking, outlined in Step 4). This means you can work out whether customers respond particularly strongly to certain features or product benefits.

Don't lose customers before you really even have them! Keep an eye on your email account to see how many enquiries or purchases you receive. Make sure to respond to all enquiries or purchases and explain that the product or service is sold out or no longer available. Alternatively, you can choose to tell the potential customers that you were only testing an idea. Either way, thank them profusely and ask them whether they'd be interested in being contacted once the final product is available.

You can use this method to pretty much test most potential products or services, as well as individual product configurations, features or price points.

To get useful results on what people like or don't like, you need to attract at least 500 to 1,000 unique visitors to your MVP test website. If you've had 1,000 visitors through your site and nobody clicked on anything or even read the content (time on site is less than 5 seconds), this indicates that what you're offering on the page is probably not particularly interesting to people.

Getting valid results for most products and services tested this way should cost you less than $1,000, and almost the entire budget is typically spent on keyword advertising. That's still a lot cheaper than having to develop the product and asking customers once the product is built.

Keeping an eye on your target market

At the same time as you're testing your customer hypothesis and refining your product (refer to preceding section), you also need to keep an eye on your potential target market and total addressable market (TAM). (Refer to Chapter 2 for more on identifying your TAM.)

As you modify the features of a product or service based on feedback from particular potential customers, you may end up affecting the overall customer segment your idea predominately appeals to. So you need to continually test your market hypothesis in parallel with your customer hypothesis tests.

To test your market hypothesis, you need to first clearly describe the overall market and each market segment within it. For example, if you're developing a parenting app, you would define the market and segments as follows:

- ✔ **Overall market:** Parents with smartphones.

- ✔ **Segment characteristics:** Gender (mums and dads), age of child (such as pre-birth, babies, toddlers or teens,), age of parents, household income, work status (stay at home, part-time or working parent), marital status and location.

To get your TAM of the overall market, start with the number of smartphones (globally or per territory) and make some assumption on how many of those smartphone users would have children (or be pregnant). Then assume an average app price of $2.99 (or whatever price you believe is most relevant).

You can then apply your latest set of validated features (those tested through the MVP process — see preceding section) to the market segment characteristics to create a market hypothesis. Continuing with the parenting app example, you now may have reason to believe that your latest product configuration appeals most to suburban single mums with a toddler (child aged between two and three years) and a household income of over $100,000.

You now need to calculate the market size of the segment you believe your product appeals most to — in this example, calculate what percentage of the TAM is represented by suburban single mums with a toddler and a household income of over $100,000.

If the market size gets too small because of the specialisation of your product (that is, it only appeals to a very small niche segment of the overall market), the warning bells should go off and you need to rethink your validated feature set.

Assuming that your market hypothesis still results in a significant potential market you can now test this hypothesis by specifically targeting customers in the market size you have defined. As with testing your customer hypothesis, the easiest way to test your market hypothesis is to use Google AdWords. Driving traffic to your test website allows you to validate your hypotheses on a significant scale — for example, by getting 1,000 (or several thousand) people to look at your test website. Anything over 1,000 unique visitors is a large enough test group to be able to say with a degree of confidence that any results from this test group would also be true for the entire market segment you're testing. An offline version of this is having to ask 1,000 people on the street (what many bricks and mortar business have to do), which takes a long time. So pay close attention to the traffic analytics for ads and your sales page to fully understand whether your market hypothesis is correct and the product indeed appeals to the segment you want to target.

Some sites let you select which users see a particular app — for example, Facebook allows you to select users based on aspects such as gender, location or status. Alternatively, you can simply test your market hypothesis through writing your ad copy accordingly (such as putting 'Single Mums' in the title) or by displaying the ads only on websites that specifically target your segment (like a 'richsinglemums.com' site).

Show Me the Money: Business Models and Plans

Once you have found a great product–market fit through the testing process (refer to the preceding section), you can start thinking about your business model. In the following sections I outline how to go about defining your business model and how to write up a meaningful (and short) business plan that helps you grow your company successfully.

Working out your business model

Given that our world has millions of companies in business, you may think that millions of ways to make money are possible. Not so. Only about a dozen ways to generate revenue are used and yet fewer ways to make money exist online.

The following is a list of the most common business models (listed in order of their robustness in revenue generation):

- **Selling your product or service:** This is the most common model in business — you create a product or service and you sell it. A key aspect of this revenue model is that you're producing the product or service yourself (you're not just reselling products made by other companies). This is a very strong business in the online world because electronic products tend to scale really well and are typically high margin.

- **Retailing products or onselling services:** This is where you sell products that other companies make. Typically, you sell a wide range of different products and the revenue is generated as a result of a mark-up between the wholesale price (what you pay) and the retail price (what your customers pay). This revenue model is quite powerful, as has been demonstrated by Apple iTunes and Amazon.

- **Selling subscriptions and memberships:** This revenue generation is based on providing access to something of value in return for a (recurring) fee. *Software as a service* businesses (such as SalesForce or XERO) are in this category, as are subscription-based content providers (such as adult-only websites) or online clubs (like Club Penguin).

✔ **Licensing:** This model involves you selling the rights to something — for example, the right to use a patent, a logo or proprietary algorithm for a specific purpose. In order to follow this model successfully and legally, you need to own the rights to whatever you're licensing in the first place. In the online world, this revenue model is mostly used by license holders for a specific purpose (such as Google's Site Search, which is a licensed version of Google Search specifically for your website).

✔ **Earning commissions and fees:** This model is also known as *clipping the ticket* and applies to a range of commercial activities where you get paid a certain percentage of a product or service sale. Common examples are affiliate commissions, sales commissions, and transactions fees — Commission Junction or Paypal use this model.

✔ **Attracting advertising, donations and sponsorship:** These revenue models rely on selling advertising (for example, banners on a website), asking for user donations or attracting sponsorship deals (such as providing funds, products or services in return for association or exposure). This is the weakest of all revenue models because it highly depends on the disposable income of others. Whenever times are tough, companies reduce their marketing spend and people stop donating or sponsoring.

Investors generally consider revenue models purely based on advertising (or sponsorships or donations) as weak businesses. The revenue generated from these models is highly unreliable and fluctuates significantly depending on the available marketing dollars companies are prepared to spend on your product/service. So if you're planning to use this revenue model, you better have other impressive aspects of your business to show investors.

One way or another, you always have to sell something. The important part about the business model is working out what you can sell and how you are going to sell it. Ultimately, people only buy something that is of value to them — so your job is to work out how to create this value, communicate the value and deliver the value to your end customers. Once you have worked out that magic money-making formula, you need to capture it (in your business plan — see following section), validate the revenue generating component with customers and tweak it if need be until you find a sustainable revenue stream for your venture.

If you believe the best way to create value is by offering your products and service free of charge to build a massive user base (which can then be monetised through advertising), you need to demonstrate massive growth to justify this strategy. Many famous online start-ups have used this approach (such as Instagram, Pinterest and Twitter) and all of these demonstrated growth rates of several 100 per cent month on month to attract capital from investors. In this situation, investment is the only source of income for your company, so you really need impressive statistics to convince others to put money into your business.

The one-page business plan

One thing that pretty much every business needs is a *business plan*. A business plan is just that — an outline for what you intend to do. You might have heard about banks and investors asking for business plans (when you're hoping to get a loan or attract capital), or you may have even come across or have participated in a business plan competition. Great — you're way ahead!

Unfortunately, business plans have earned a bit of a bad reputation because traditional investors and lenders (especially banks) tended to ask for business plans that were the size of *War and Peace*. When you've written a 100-page business plan, you realise that it's actually not a very useful document and most entrepreneurs (if they even have the patience to finish a large business plan in the first place) never revisit their business plans once they're finished. That's not what a business plan is for — a business plan needs to be a working document that outlines where you're heading with your business, captures what you know about your business and defines how you're intending to make money with your company.

At my investment company WebFund, I use a somewhat radical approach for business plans: We only use one-page business plans that we can print out on a single A3 sheet. One-page business plans are ideal for start-ups because the document is easy to update, can be printed out to put up in the office or can be easily shared with potential investors. Creating a one-page business plan also doesn't feel like an arduous task to complete.

Here's a list of what should be contained in your one-page business plan:

- ✔ A one-line statement of the vision and purpose of your company

- ✔ A very short description of what products and services the company offers

- ✔ A definition of each customer segment the products or services target

- ✔ Assumptions and hypothesis (including those that were found invalid)

- ✔ A list of key performance indicators per month, quarter and financial year (for the current financial year)

- ✔ A list of financial and performance targets for the next three years

- ✔ A list of the company's strengths, weaknesses, opportunities and threats

See Appendix B for a one-page business plan template.

The most important thing about the business plan is that it needs to be looked at and updated at least every three months. Start-up life is fast paced and a lot can change in three months. Forgetting about some principles or previous lessons learnt is also easy, so by revisiting your business plan frequently you and your team can remind yourself of important aspects and plan how to drive the business forward.

Understanding That a Start-Up is a Business

Forgetting that you're actually 'in business' during the initial stages of your start-up is easy, especially when you start out with a simple idea that can be implemented on the internet or as an app. However, when your site goes live or you sit down and start to actually develop your product, you realise that you're the one in charge — and you're the one who has to make decisions.

Businesses of all sizes have to make decisions about legal matters, location and technology. And since you're in business, well, that means you, too.

A large part of running your start-up as a business is ensuring you have the right people around you. I cover picking a winning team in the very early days of a start-up in Chapter 2, and adding more staff as your business ramps up (or if you secure a substantial amount of funding early on) in Chapter 7. For much more detail on staffing issues, see *Small Business For Dummies*, 4th Australian and New Zealand Edition, by Veechi Curtis (published by Wiley Publishing Australia).

Making sure everything is legal

One of the first requirements of running a business is making sure it's legal. 'Ah ... it's just a website' is a common expression I get to hear when talking to first-time entrepreneurs. But in Australia and New Zealand when you carry out any commercial activity (for example, buying and selling of goods and services that are not for your own use), you're automatically in business and the corresponding legislation (commercial law and the Companies Act) applies to your activities. Whether you have a registered company or an ABN doesn't matter — the various government agencies tasked with overseeing commercial activity treat you as a commercial entity.

Registering a company

As an entrepreneur, you have a choice in selecting a particular entity type for your business — such as sole trader, partnership or limited liability company.

By default, a person who doesn't have a registered company but carries out commercial activity is usually considered a sole trader. The problem with this classification is that you're liable for any liability incurred with all your personal assets. To avoid this liability, you need to register a limited liability company.

Because I believe registering as a company is the best option for online start-ups, I only cover this process here. For more information on the pros and cons of other business structures, see *Small Business For Dummies*, 4th Australian and New Zealand Edition, by Veechi Curtis (published by Wiley Publishing Australia).

Registering a company in Australia and New Zealand is very simple and can be done in less than 30 minutes. All you need to do is go to the ASIC website in Australia (www.asic.gov.au) and the Companies Office website in New Zealand (www.business.govt.nz). On these websites you can find the necessary online forms to register a company name and incorporate the business. In Australia, you need to go through a separate registration with the Australian Tax Office to get your tax number. In New Zealand, you can apply for a tax number (GST number) as part of your company registration process (which I highly recommend because you're going to need it eventually anyway).

Once you have registered your company you need to follow standard compliance practices to ensure you don't get into trouble with the government. In Australia and New Zealand this typically comes down to the following:

- ✔ **Filing annual returns:** In New Zealand, this can be done online at the Companies Office website (www.business.govt.nz) and, in Australia, at the ASIC website (www.asic.gov.au).

- ✔ **Following governance requirements:** See the following sections for more on this.

- ✔ **Paying taxes:** At a minimum your company, needs to pay GST and income taxes. However, income tax only applies to the profit a company makes. If your company doesn't make a profit, you may not have to pay tax but you still need to submit your accounts to IRD in NZ and the ATO in Australia. If you employ staff, you also have to organise tax payments for your employees. Speak to your accountant to understand your tax responsibilities.

Following governance requirements and managing your company

Governance usually refers to the way you manage your company and, in particular, setting and monitoring the company's strategy and ensuring compliance and legality of business operations. The Companies Act in New Zealand and Australia specifies what companies and directors have to do and must not do when running their companies. The things you have to do include keeping a share register and holding an annual general meeting. The things you must not do include trading recklessly. Details of your basic responsibilities under the Companies Act can be found on the Companies Office website (www.business.govt.nz) and ASIC website (www.asic.gov.au).

Governance is typically the role of the board of directors. You may think your start-up is too small for a board of directors, but even if just two of you make up the company, you can still have a board. In small companies, the board may be exactly the same as the management team but the law distinguishes between these roles. As a director of a company, you're legally required to do certain things (as outlined by the Companies Office or ASIC — see their websites for more details) that are different to the responsibilities of employees (and the management team).

No matter what size your company is, I highly recommend defining the composition of the board of directors (typically specified in the shareholder agreement — see following section) and holding regular board meetings. Board meetings are a key governance instrument that allows directors to formalise and document strategic business decisions. Any information or decision that materially affects the business is typically captured in board papers and board minutes.

Here is a suggested agenda for a board meeting that helps you cover the bare minimum governance requirements for your company:

- ✔ Review of previous board minutes
- ✔ Matters arising
- ✔ Board resolutions
- ✔ Financials
- ✔ Legal and compliance
- ✔ Strategic decisions or issues
- ✔ Other business
- ✔ Time and date of next meeting

By going through an agenda like the one in the preceding list, all members of the board are reminded of core responsibilities and can take necessary action or make decisions.

Whenever you approach investors for your company, they typically want to see minutes of all previous board meetings. So while it may seem weird to take notes and minutes to document board meetings when it's just you and, say, one other person, doing so can benefit you tremendously.

Preparing a constitution or shareholder agreement

In addition to complying with your legal requirements when running a company, you also need to sort out how the internal relationship between directors and shareholders is organised.

In Australia, limited liability companies are required to have a constitution that needs to be filed with ASIC. A constitution sets out the rights, powers and duties of the company, the board of directors, each director and each shareholder. In New Zealand, constitutions are optional and most companies use shareholder agreements to define the relationships between directors and shareholders.

Aside from the legal requirements, most companies in Australia and New Zealand prefer to define details of shareholdings and company procedures in the company's shareholder agreement because this document can be kept private, whereas constitutions need to be filed and are available publicly. Speak to your lawyer if you want to get specific information about how to structure a constitution or shareholder agreement.

At a high level, a shareholder agreement typically includes the following items:

- ✔ Name and role of each director
- ✔ Name and shareholding of each shareholder
- ✔ Definition of the nature of the business and intellectual property belonging to the company
- ✔ Definitions of terms used in business and the shareholder agreement
- ✔ Appointment procedure for directors (and removal of directors)
- ✔ Trading of shares
- ✔ Special provisions for directors (such as agreements not to compete after leaving the company)
- ✔ Dispute resolution procedures

Making sure you don't get sued

When you're busy trying to get your start-up off the ground, you really need to focus as much time and energy on the business itself — refining your offering, attracting customers or potential partners and talking to investors. Typically, you never have enough time to do everything so the last thing you need is other distractions that can seriously threaten your business. Getting sued by another organisation is in that category.

The best approach to avoid this kind of distraction is to make sure your company's business activities are 100 per cent legal in the jurisdiction you operate in (the place where your company is registered and does most of its business). The nature of what start-ups do (innovate and disrupt) means that sometimes whether a particular business activity is 100 per cent legal and doesn't infringe on copyrights or other laws may not be immediately obvious. So if you have any doubt over legality or potential infringements, you need to check with someone who is legally trained.

Here's a list of things to check with your lawyer or someone who is legally trained before you start trading:

- ✔ All agreements and contracts you issue or sign to ensure these are legal and cover all important aspects.

- ✔ Any intellectual property (IP) you think you may have to see to check if you might benefit from applying for copyrights or patents.

- ✔ The terms and conditions (T&Cs) on your website to make sure these are valid and meaningful.

Make sure you check the legality and potential tax liability of your commercial activities in every market you operate in. Commercial law and taxation varies significantly around the world and you need to understand what local laws apply to you. Clearly state which law applies in all of your agreements and T&Cs so that if someone wants to challenge you on those they have to do this in your preferred (local) jurisdiction rather than theirs. This is particularly relevant for online businesses because most websites are accessed globally.

Picking the right location

Most entrepreneurs start their businesses in the place where they live. This seems obvious and makes sense because their business and support networks are typically around to help make things happen quickly. However, each online business needs to consider location factors that affect the ease of doing business and attracting suitable partners and investors.

Ask yourself the following when trying to work out where you should locate your company:

✔ Where is the largest customer segment you're targeting located? The United States is the largest single marketplace in the English-speaking world, so many industries have their largest customer segments there.

✔ If your business involves physical products, where are these sourced from and where do they need to be shipped to?

✔ Do you have access to skilled staff in your business location?

✔ What is the start-up ecosystem like? Do many start-ups exist and is it easy to get access to investors?

The most common business development path for start-ups is to capture their local market and use the income generated from the local market to expand internationally. Starting a company in your local economy of Australia and New Zealand has its advantages and disadvantages, as shown in Table 3-1.

Table 3-1   Advantages and Disadvantages of Starting a Company in Australia or New Zealand

Advantages	Disadvantages
Simple regulatory framework for business	No direct access to the world's major economies such as the US, Japan, China and Europe, which are all a long haul flight away
Supportive culture when approaching other established businesses or industry leaders	Lack of cultural understanding when servicing major economies without being based there
Easy to get media coverage	
Great for 'flying under the radar' — testing products without drawing attention from major competitors	

The location of your business in relation to your key markets is also an incredibly important factor when pitching your idea to others. At WebFund, I frequently hear pitches of entrepreneurs who base a large percentage of revenue generation on the US market, but have never been abroad and have no clear plan how to access this market. Make sure you can credibly demonstrate how you want to address a particular target market — usually partnering or locating your business in the market geography are the only credible strategies.

ReadWriteWeb.com is one company that successfully overcame a location disadvantage. This start-up became one of the world's most influential technology blogs, but was run from the Hutt Valley in New Zealand. This success was mostly possible due to incredible talent and a decision not to follow consumer trends, industry news and the usual marketing calendar, but to provide content based on deep analysis (of technology products and services).

For more on expanding into other territories, see Chapter 7.

Making good technology decisions

Many start-ups originate from a technology-based innovation or are started by a team with a strong technology background. For those start-ups, making the right technology choices isn't usually a major problem — at least initially.

However, a large number of start-up ventures are created by individuals without a technology background. These start-ups typically have to rely on advice from third parties when making choices about how to develop web-based or mobile web-based products and services.

In this section, I cover some considerations to keep in mind when you're considering general office and online technology choices, especially as your business starts to expand.

Pay particular attention to the licensing cost for your software. Inside the office, if you go for a fully licensed system while you only need three licences, that may seem relatively cheap; however, make sure you work out how much the solution would cost you when you've got something like 50 staff. Online, if your technology platform requires the purchase of software licences, don't forget to do the maths and figure out how much the solution is going to cost you when you've got over 100,000 (or over 1 million) users.

General office technology considerations

Unless your start-up is based on highly specialised proprietary technology (in which case you would almost certainly have someone on board who understands this technology), you're faced with a number of standard technology choices. Here's a list of the most common or most important technology typically used by start-ups:

- ✔ **Accounting, finance and banking software:** When you run a business, you need to account for your sales and expenses (among other things) and for that you typically use an accounting package or finance software. In Australia and New Zealand, MYOB used to be a common choice (see www.myob.com.au for more). However, alternative options such as XERO.com have now become available. 'Software as a service' solutions such as XERO are really useful because they typically allow multiple users and direct bank transactions feeds, and you can access them from anywhere because they're web-based. Check with your accountant because they might have a preference for a particular package.

- ✔ **Collaboration tools and project management software:** Start-up life often requires teams and individuals to work together on tasks while being geographically dispersed or on a business trip. Think about how you want to organise work and keep working on your task when team members aren't all at the same place and you need to manage projects and share deliverables. For example smartsheet.com is a collaborative project management tool and many start-ups use Google Docs to collaboratively write and share business-related documents.

- ✔ **Communication technology:** Over the last decade, many low-cost communication solutions have become available to start-ups that help avoid significant infrastructure cost in the early days. Free tools such as Skype, Google Talk or Messenger have made long distance telephony, video conferencing and online collaboration very affordable and highly usable. In Australia and New Zealand, Voice of IP (VOIP) technology is also widely available — many systems provide the same functionality as traditional telephony for a fraction of the price. If your business is highly reliant on significant telephony (such as for customer enquiries, sales or support), check out VOIP solutions as an alternative to standard communication technology.

- ✔ **Graphic design and desktop publishing software:** If someone in your team has the skills to create designs, branding collateral or advertising material, chances are that person already has a preferred package. One thing you should have is a PDF creator, converter and editor (several commercial and open source products are available, such as Adobe Creator and the open source product suite Ghostscript, as well as Open Office). PDF documents are the best format when sending information to external parties (and investors in particular). PDF can also be used for contracts (because documents generally can't be changed once generated).

✔ **Information and communication technology hardware:** The cost for things like laptops, office computers, phones (mobile and desktop) and faxes, photocopiers and any other office communication equipment has come down considerably over the last 10 years. Buying a reasonable PC for $500 is now entirely possible. However, you need to think a little bit about how all of your various devices work together and how you can share services (like printing, back-ups, calendar and email synchronisation, voicemail and other communication services). If you make unfortunate choices and need to purchase more gear, your business is unlikely to be threatened, but it's an unnecessary expense especially when money is tight at the beginning.

✔ **Office automation software:** This kind of software usually includes word processing, spreadsheets, slide show or presentation, and email and calendar software. You basically have three choices these days — licensed proprietary software such as Microsoft Office, open source software (which is essentially free) such as Star Office and Thunderbird, or hosted software such as Google Docs/ Spreadsheets and Google Mail/Calendar. Fortunately, your choices here aren't crucial and pretty much depend on personal preferences. Practically all common office automation solutions provide conversions between the various file formats.

Online technology considerations

The importance of technology to an online business can't be understated. Unfortunately, seemingly trivial technology choices can end up determining the fate of start-ups because the technology ends up restricting the business to a point where it can no longer operate.

Note: Attempting to provide advice on the specific technology that works best for your business is impossible. In this section, I list some of the general requirements most start-ups need, before covering some of the factors that should be considered when choosing online technology. For information on some of the basic technology that can get you started online and general information on website hosting and tools, see *Starting an Online Business For Dummies*, Australian and New Zealand Edition, by Melissa Norfolk and Greg Holden (published by Wiley Publishing Australia). For advice specific to your business, consider speaking to one of your business advisors (someone from the advisory board or a business mentor) who was involved in making similar technology decisions.

General questions most start-ups need to answer when deciding on their online technology include the following:

- ✔ Who supports the system (are you planning to do this internally or rely on assistance from a hosting provider or third party)?

- ✔ What security protocols and tools are in place and who is in charge of ensuring the system is secure (especially if personal user data or payment data is involved)?

- ✔ How is the system backed up and what failover mechanisms are available?

- ✔ How popular is your chosen technology? (Do a Google Search with corresponding technology keywords and compare the result count for several options.)

I recommend keeping in mind the following as a matter of priority when deciding on web technology:

- ✔ **Ability to integrate with other solutions:** Integration with other systems is often the biggest headache and not easy to foresee, but if you already know that you're going to have to integrate with another solution at some point, make sure you use technology that offers a recognised path for integration.

The switching cost with web technology is extremely high (hence the significant risk to your business). Prototype solutions can cost $100,000 or more. If you have to replace the technology during the early stages of your business, you may simply run out of money.

- ✔ **Scalability and storage capabilities:** Fortunately, hosting and storage technology has come a long way so that you can easily find hosting providers that offer entry-level packages that can seamlessly scale to enterprise-level performance. Just make sure you check with your hosting provider how easy it is to massively increase the key parameters of your hosting package (traffic, storage and

CPU usage). Other than using a free webhosting for specific products (such as blogger.com, wordpress.com among others) expect to pay for hosting — entry-level packages for hosting start from about $10 per month.

Many start-ups have failed because they simply couldn't provide a reliable enough service once they started attracting significant website traffic or customers. Most growth patterns in start-up businesses are not linear (you may have heard of the hockey stick, when the shape of website traffic graphs end up looking a bit like a hockey stick as a result of exponential growth rates). When rapid growth occurs, it usually happens exponentially, and you rarely have time to fix things when the business is heating up. So you need to have a scaling out plan in place — consider how your technology and services can respond to a 100-fold increase of transactions, sales volume or website traffic.

✔ **Total cost of ownership of the IT solution:** A common path for start-ups is to base their initial technology solution on open source technology (because it's free) and then move to licensed technology once the concept is proven. Scalability and storage factors are related to this issue; that is, how much does having a very large user base using your system cost? However, costs typically also depend on your web-hosting contract. Make sure you do the maths based on massive increases of your user base (that's what you want anyway, right?).

Make everything mobile

The reason I keep referring to mobile and the mobile web in this book is that mobile computing is in the process of replacing (or assimilating) web-based computing. If you're thinking of starting a venture, you must consider mobile computing and how your product or service can deliver through mobile platforms.

Customers love the simplicity and availability of smartphone apps and no start-up should ignore this market (in 2012, over 1 billion smartphones were in use worldwide). Even if your product or service isn't immediately applicable to the app market, you should consider how you could use an app as a marketing tool or potential sales channel.

Finally, another good reason to consider the app market is that investors have already accepted mobile computing as a megatrend and as such are more likely to consider investing in start-ups that are based around mobile computing technology.

Staying in the Black: Keeping on Top of Your Finances

In Chapter 2, I cover aspects to consider when pricing your product or service (such as looking at the value equation and understanding the penny gap). However, once you've worked out how to generate revenue with your business, understanding the rest of your company's finances is important.

Many entrepreneurs don't have a background in business administration or finance and as a result struggle with business finance a little bit. While the world of finance and accounting certainly has its complexities, the underlying principles are actually quite simple. At a fundamental level, all activities are split into those that are bringing money into the company (such as sales) and those that require the company to pay money out (such as salaries). Accounting and finance tools provide mechanisms and a discipline to organise the various activities and the status of your company (in terms of what it owns or owes). That's it — not that hard, eh?

In the following sections, I provide an overview of the key aspects of accounting and finance.

Note: The information I provide in the following sections is an overview only. For more in-depth information about accounting and bookkeeping, see *Small Business For Dummies*, 4th Australian and New Zealand Edition, by Veechi Curtis. For information on the basics of online commerce, such as financial transactions, credit card payments and setting up merchant accounts, see *Starting an Online Business For Dummies*, Australian and New Zealand Edition, by Melissa Norfolk and Greg Holden. (Both books published by Wiley Publishing Australia.)

Revenue and profit — a crash course in finance

A very important component of the financial world to understand properly is the difference between revenue and profit (this difference, sadly, has tripped up a lot of fantastic inventors throughout the history of the world). *Revenue* refers to your company's income (any money that comes into your business), typically as a result of commercial activity. *Profit* refers to money that's left in your company after all the bills have been paid. If not enough money is available to pay the bills, your company is making a loss. Yes — you can run a company that generates millions of dollars of revenue but makes a loss.

When your company makes a loss, you need to find the money from somewhere to make up for the loss (such as through investment, loans or through selling something the company owns).

Investors tend to categorise companies they are interested in into *pre-revenue*, *pre-profit* and *profitable*. You need to understand these terms because your company is going to be judged according to these categories when you pitch to investors.

Here's the categories investors use when assessing start-ups in terms of the money coming in, and what these categories mean:

- ✔ **Pre-revenue:** The initial period in a company's life cycle when no sales have happened yet. Sometimes this period can be very long — for example, despite having millions of users, Facebook and Twitter had no company income until they started switching on advertising.

- ✔ **Pre-profit or post-revenue:** A period where the company has had some sales but the revenue generated from the sales isn't enough to cover the company's costs. This is a very critical phase because you still have to cover the loss somehow to avoid bankruptcy (which is when a company can no longer pay bills or repay debts).

- ✔ **Post-profit or profitable:** The stage where a company's revenues exceed the cost of running the company. Sometimes this is further split into *operationally profitable*, which means the company generates a profit from its operations but not enough profit to cover debt repayment and other liabilities, versus fully profitable, where all costs are covered.

Understanding cash flow

You may have heard that cash flow is the biggest business killer for small businesses. That may be true but cash flow itself isn't actually what kills companies — what can be fatal is the lack of readily available cash.

Even when you're generating more revenue than the total cost of running your business, your business still may not be financially viable. The problem with running a business is that typically you need to pay your bills before your customers pay you. This is a particular problem for retailers, who often have to pay for the stock they're selling in their shop before they're able to sell it to customers. Sometimes the period between having to pay for goods and being able to collect revenue is significant (up to several months). So your company can run out of money before more money can be collected.

If your company has a positive cash flow, this means that at any one point money is available — the company's bank account shows a positive balance. A negative cash flow means for certain periods not enough cash is available to make a particular payment and the company's bank account goes into overdraft. This may not be a problem if the period is relatively short and your bank has granted an overdraft facility, but it can become problematic when the planned payment (money coming in) doesn't arrive. Expected payments not coming through can be especially problematic for small companies, because they usually have limited company funds.

Use cash flow projections to work out the timing of payments (both payments you have to make and payments you're going to receive). In this sense, *cash* refers to the money that's available in the company's bank account for immediate use.

You can create a cash flow forecast by making a spreadsheet that shows payments (to be made and to be received) over time and keeping a balance. Your bank does this for you (in retrospect) when it sends out bank statements, but you need to do this looking into the future and projecting a future bank balance. Your accountant, if you have one, can also prepare a cash flow statement for you. See Appendix B for a cash flow template.

Once you have a basic cash flow for the next three months, you can see how sensitive your cash flow is to missed payments or unexpected expenses. Ideally, your business has a cash buffer (such as $20,000) that it doesn't use. So if you have the odd supplier who doesn't pay or receive an unexpected invoice, you can use your buffer to cover these costs without having to ask the bank for an overdraft (or risk going out of business because no cash is available to pay the bills).

Accounting in a minute

Accounting typically refers to the discipline of keeping an eye on your company's finances both in terms of its commercial activity as well as its financial position. Every company must keep a record of transactions as a result of commercial activity and that's usually done by keeping a ledger where all transactions are recorded. In addition to transactions, the company also has *assets* (things it owns such as equipment or intellectual property) and debts. Companies must also keep a record of their financial status in terms of assets and debts.

That's why accountants have come up with a clever system that shows the status of a company with two key documents — the profit and loss statement (income statement) and the balance sheet:

- ✔ A profit and loss statement (also referred to as P&L) describes the company's financial performance — that is, whether the company has made a profit or loss over a given period (such as a month, a quarter or a year).

- ✔ The balance sheet provides information about the company's financial position — that is, the financial value of what a company owns (such as assets and claims) and the value of what the company owes to others (such as investors, banks and creditors).

Entrepreneurs can benefit hugely from understanding the P&L statement and balance sheet. By looking at these two documents, you can quickly gain a detailed insight into how a company is doing. The P&L and balance sheet are also absolutely essential for managing a business. As an entrepreneur, you need to know how your business is doing financially (at any one time) in order to make decisions that positively affect the financial performance and position of your company. You do not need to understand the details of book keeping and accounting — that's what accountants are for. But you do need to understand the output accountants generate (the P&L and balance sheet) in order to run your business well.

Work with a reliable accountant from the beginning. Accountants can save you a lot of trouble by pointing out what you need to do to run your business legally and typically also provide finance and tax advice. The best way to find a reliable accountant is to ask other small business owners who they use and how happy they are with the service provided. Don't be afraid to ask prospective accountants about how they work and what they provide you with. If they use lingo you don't understand, ask them to clarify. Every accountant should be able to explain accounting terminology and processes to you in plain English. If you're not happy with the way the accountant responds, keep looking for someone you can work with.

Increasing Your Chances of Success

In the early days of your start-up, two things can really put you ahead of other businesses — making sure you focus on the right things and putting together an advisory board.

Focusing on the right things

In the absence of a manager who allocates work, many people tend to work on things they're good at or like doing. This tendency is problematic in start-ups because many more things are always going to need doing than time is available. Start-up teams are typically also relatively small, so every member of the team has to cover many areas of business.

Unfortunately, many start-ups fail because founders focus on the wrong things. Not all activities (even when done extremely well and diligently) have the same impact on business outcome.

A good example of a neglected activity in early stage businesses is sales and related tasks (such as putting together sales collateral or assembling lists of people to call). Selling is a crucial activity without which no business can flourish — and even if you don't close a sale, you still generally learn something about your customers or your product. But selling is hard to do (whether in person, on the phone or online) and many entrepreneurs hate the sales process. Sales should always be a focus, however, and you should constantly ask yourself whether enough time and energy is spent on sales.

Other areas that you need to focus on early in the start-up process include the following:

- ✔ Customer service and getting direct feedback from your users (see Chapter 4)
- ✔ Website traffic generation and analysis (see Chapter 4)
- ✔ Product development using the MVP process (refer to the section 'Making Sure Your Idea is Viable', earlier in this chapter)

If you find that any of the following are happening constantly in your start-up, it may be time to put a 'time boxing' policy in place (that is, restricting the amount of time allowed to spend on certain activities): Online chats, social networking status updates and commenting, fixing something that's not broken, meetings with no agendas or objectives.

Understanding the value of advisory boards

Advisory boards are an incredibly useful (and powerful) tool for start-ups that few entrepreneurs know about. In contrast to the board of directors, where members of the board have a significant stake in the company (either shareholding or employment), advisory boards typically include individuals who are simply interested in helping a start-up without direct compensation. Many successful business people have a good-hearted and altruistic side, and want to see others do well too and so they agree to participate in advisory boards.

By establishing an advisory board, entrepreneurs can benefit from the expertise and networks of individuals who otherwise have no involvement in the company. Advisory boards can be invaluable for getting introductions to established companies, investors or industry bodies but can also provide valuable feedback on strategy or tactical initiatives (in addition to the board of directors).

Advisory boards are only valuable when you select suitable individuals, set expectations correctly and treat members of the board respectfully.

Here are a few tips for getting the best value out of an advisory board:

 ✔ **Select members carefully:** Find out who the movers and shakers of your target market and industry are. Find out what companies or organisations they're involved with and how you're potentially connected to them. Organise a meeting and see if you can get them on your advisory board — often you can simply suggest the board to them and see what they say.

✔ **Create a useful composition:** Make sure you've got a good mix of skills, expertise, networks, backgrounds and even age and gender in your advisory group. Advisory boards are most valuable when a wide range of viewpoints are represented in the group.

✔ **Set expectations:** Define the ground rules for your advisory board and be upfront about them with potential members. You need to be clear what kind of commitment you expect from members of the board (perhaps two hours per month) and to what extent reimbursement of expenses or compensation for time is available. (Usually offering reimbursement for expenses but no compensation for time is acceptable.)

✔ **Manage board meetings professionally:** Your advisory board should meet regularly (once a month or once a quarter) and you need to manage these meetings professionally. Any material relevant to the meeting should be distributed beforehand, minutes should be kept, and actions should be done and results recorded. By running your board well, you demonstrate your abilities to members of the board and honour the time they devote to helping you.

Chapter 4

Launching Your Start-Up: The Early Days

*E*very artificial structure, technology or system you use or experience in this world started out as a simple idea in someone's head. It's amazing to realise that massive buildings, established organisations and fantastic achievements were all just ideas at some point. Now you can show the world what started out in your head when you launch your product or service. It's a powerful moment — enjoy it! And then get ready to really work.

While you may have found that the research and preparation needed to get you to this point was hard work (refer to Chapters 2 and 3), once you launch your product or service you're typically in an operational pressure cooker because of the sometimes relentless demands of keeping your business going. Attracting customers and looking after your first few customers well is absolutely essential when launching a business. And promotion, marketing and sales typically consume significant resources (both time and cash). When sales aren't happening and you can see the bank balance going down rapidly, you can really start to feel the pressure.

This chapter covers what you can do to make sure the launch of your business gets off to a good start and how you can keep the momentum going once you've launched. I also provide key indicators you need to keep an eye on during the first few months, and tips for how you can overcome initial hurdles.

Preparing to Launch: Naming Conventions

When you're about to launch your product or service a few things suddenly become important. One of them is branding. Deciding on the right name for your product or service as well as your brand (company) is an important part of your launch. The good news is that the companies law in Australia and New Zealand allows businesses to have two different names — a legal name and a 'trading as' name. So you don't have to use your registered company name as your brand name.

You probably had some idea of what you were going to call your product or service and how you were going to brand it as you were performing all the preparations required to reach your launch date. However, these aspects can often change as you perform more market research, talk to more experts or receive funding from different sources. So you may not finalise names and branding until just before you launch, which is fine. Just make sure you're very comfortable with the name and branding for your company when you launch. Changing these aspects afterwards can be damaging to your business and your prospects as a good investment.

Entire books have been filled about the ins and outs of branding and product naming. I suggest you don't read these books initially but focus on a few branding guidelines, which I outline in the following list.

Your brand

> ✔ **Needs to be customer focused (even when your customers are other businesses).** This means your brand and name of the business needs to make sense to your customers. In other words, the brand needs to be meaningful in the context of the market you operate in. Salesforce.com (a software provider for customer relationship management systems) is a great example of a meaningful brand name for other businesses.

✔ **Needs to be easy to remember and, ideally, easy to spell.**
Customers often hear about a new product or service
over a coffee and then search for it online afterwards,
so they need to be able to find your product easily.
The news service Delicious used to have the domain name
`del.icio.us` and then changed to `delicious.com` as they
became more mainstream — a good example of a domain
name change that made it easier for people to remember
the URL.

✔ **Should avoid generic names (especially for online
brands).** For example, `books.com` is virtually unknown
whereas `barnesandnoble.com` is well known.

✔ **Shouldn't use a trendy buzzword.** This means you
shouldn't choose a name that relies on current trends or
fads, such as adding a 2.0 or 3.0 to your name.

Test a few names with friends and colleagues (or, even better,
with some target customers if you can). Some companies even
let users choose their product or brand names (although not
too many success stories have emerged from this strategy). Also
create a brand guideline to define your brand (logo, colours,
fonts, styles and other defining elements). Marketing agencies or
designers can help you with this task, but the brand definition
is usually just a simple document that summarises all aspects of
your brand. (Also see Appendix B for a sample brand definition
template.)

Make sure you have your branding collateral available in
common file formats (such as PDF, JPG or Photoshop format)
so you can make files available to media outlets on request.
Another useful technique when defining brands is to figure
out at where your brand stops — that is, identify what images,
colours, styles (and other defining elements) don't fit into your
brand. These boundaries help define and refine your brand. All
guidelines can be summarised in a company brand style guide.

Spend a good amount of time on branding and naming (usually
around 20 hours over a few days or weeks is sufficient) but make
sure you time box your branding and naming efforts and costs.
In other words, set a limit on the amount of time and money you
want to spend beforehand so you don't get carried away.

Getting a good URL is important but nowhere near as important
as it was during the dotcom boom in the late 1990s. Avoid
spending large sums of money on buying domains from *domain
squatters* (organisations who make money by registering domain

names and on-selling them to others at exorbitant prices). You can almost always find unregistered alternatives and if you have a good brand and name, the URL isn't that critical to the success of your start-up.

It's Alive

One of the most exciting days in the start-up journey is when, after months of preparation, you get to launch a product or service you've largely had in your head for a long time. To see something made manifest that started out as a (perhaps slightly crazy) idea in your head is truly rewarding. To get the most value out of your launch, you need to be well prepared — the following sections show you how.

Picking your launch date

Picking the right timing for the launch and a suitable launch strategy can be quite tricky. Here's a quick list of aspects to consider when you're getting ready to launch your product or service:

- **Process readiness:** Have you thought about how your customers are going to engage with your product or service? If your product or service isn't free, how do customers pay for it? What happens with the sales transaction — how is it recorded and what documents (such as an invoice or a sales record) are created? Have you got all the necessary terms and conditions in place to make sure you're protected if customers aren't happy or your product or services causes some damage? Finally, have you thought about how you can service customers — for example, through training and enquiries and complaints support? Have you decided who in your team can look after these aspects?

- **Product readiness:** How far along are you with your product development and refinement? You don't need to create the 'perfect' product but you do need to have a product that demonstrates the 'killer features' and creates instant value for someone using it (as perceived by customers). Depending on your launch strategy (see the section 'Launch strategy' later in this chapter) the level of refinement of your product can vary.

While you do have to make sure you properly display your T&Cs, working out what to include in the terms and conditions can be tricky. But you don't have to go through the drudgery of starting a T&C list from scratch. A good place to start is to look at the T&C page for popular online sites in your territory. Make a note of the things you think you need to include and work with a lawyer to create a version that can work with your company.

✔ **World readiness:** Consider the timing of your launch carefully. Can you synchronise your launch with another event that happens in your space? For example, conferences, trade shows or special days in the marketing calendar (such as Mothers Day) can provide a boost to your launch. Alternatively, you may pick a date when not much else is going on to stand a good chance of your media release getting picked up.

In addition to the factors outlined in the preceding list, you also need to have a number of deliverables in place before you launch (either because they must be done before launch or because you may not have the time to put them together properly after the launch). Here's a list of items to consider:

✔ **Brand definition and branding collateral:** Refer to the section 'Preparing to Launch: Naming Conventions' earlier in this chapter for more on this.

✔ **Media kit:** Have a media kit (or at least a short media statement or media release) ready for the launch of your product or service. Even if you pursue a soft launch strategy (see the following section), you may get asked by journalists for more information, and having something ready to go is useful — rather than not responding or making something up on the spot. (See Appendix B for a sample media release template.)

If you're trying to get coverage in print media, write an article or story for them. Include quotes, photos and other material that make the story more compelling. Most publications (including blogs and online news services) are thirsty for interesting content and the easier you make it for them, the better your chances of getting a story or announcement published.

✔ **Sales collateral:** Even if you offer a free product or service, you should still be selling one aspect or another (for example, you may want to sell advertising on your site). No matter what you're selling, make sure you clearly define your product or service in a document that you can send out to interested parties. Ideally, you want to make it look presentable too. A good example is a *rate card* or *sales pack* that you can send out as a PDF document if people are interested in your product or service but want to find out more in their own time. This saves invaluable time.

To help your launch run a bit more smoothly, you should also have a launch date in place — see the following section.

Don't underestimate the critical factor of time available to you after launch — this is when things typically get very hectic (and that's a good sign). The reason I recommend preparing marketing and sales collateral prior to your launch is that often you simply don't have the time to prepare these documents well afterwards. Because you want to run a professional business from day one, you need to be able to send out material that's well put together and makes your company look good.

Launch strategy

In preparing your launch, you need to think about a suitable launch strategy. Common options include

✔ **Soft Launch:** This is where you simply start offering your product or service without sending out media releases or organising launch promotions.

✔ **Beta launch:** These types of launches are typically announced and may include a special offer. However, the product or service is clearly positioned as a *beta* product (a product that isn't completely finished). A beta launch can be further distinguished into a *private beta* and *public beta*, depending on what customer group is allowed to access the new product.

✔ **Hard launch:** This is a traditional strategy, where all launch activities are done around a specific date. This date is fixed in advance and is usually not changed — no matter what. This means your product or service and business operations need to be geared up to go from no activity to full activity, as of the launch date.

What strategy is right for your business depends on how confident you are about the maturity of your product or service, your ability to deliver on customer expectations and your budget. Soft launches and beta launches typically give you more options to fix issues or challenges as they arise. However, the risk with soft or beta launches is that you may not get another chance to create a lot of excitement out of your launch — and you may allow competitors to check out your product and react with a competing offer.

Hard launches are often difficult to postpone or back out of altogether. So you need to be very certain that everything is ready before you set the launch date.

Put together a launch plan for your launch, especially if you're preparing a beta or hard launch, because the list of activities to organise can be quite long. For example, you may need to plan a teaser campaign and media release, advertising, your social media strategy and launch events. Also bear in mind that some marketing activities, such as public competitions, need to be registered in Australia and New Zealand, so you need to allow time to follow the correct procedure. A plan helps you stay on top of these activities and make sure they happen at the right time or in the right sequence for maximum impact.

Once everything is in place, the *go live* moment is just a simple action of making a website, or online or mobile service available to the public or the launch group (if it is a private beta launch). This usually simply involves the removal of a password protection or the change of a domain name record.

Discovering your 'firsts'

The period immediately following your launch is generally a hectic and exciting phase of your start-up journey. Often, you need to attend to hundreds of little things and you may struggle to find time to do them all between media interviews, enquiries or customer support. Being really busy during this period is a fantastic problem to have, though, because it means your launch was successful and has generated genuine interest in your product or service from media and customers. Hopefully, you haven't created headlines for the wrong reasons — but if you have, you need to be in damage control, which is also quite exciting. Either way, keep your cool during this period and focus on your strengths.

Once you've launched your product or service, you get to celebrate or acknowledge a few 'firsts'. Here's a list of what you may encounter and some suggestions on what to do:

- **Your first sale:** What a fantastic feeling to have achieved an actual sale. Print out the transaction record, put it up on an office wall and splash out on a bottle of bubbles for the whole team.

- **Your first 100/1,000/10,000 visitors:** Enjoy the attention and energy the launch generates. Make sure to follow up diligently with all customers and any interested parties who contact you.

- **Your first complaint:** A complaint is a particular type of feedback that should be welcome. Complaints present unique opportunities to learn where you can improve. You can also use complaints to demonstrate how good your customer service is and to turn annoyed customers into fanatic supporters.

- **Your first media interview:** Brilliant — enjoy every minute of it. Make sure you prepare for the interview by focusing on three key messages you want to get across (keep your key messages to three because most people can only remember three aspects of any new information they hear). Practice media interviews with someone who has had media training (especially if the interviews are broadcast live).

- **Your first bit of bad press:** Relax — remember the saying that there's no such thing as bad press which is mostly true. Resist the urge to reply or 'retaliate' online. No action is typically the best response to bad press.

Embrace your firsts and use your network if you encounter situations you're not sure how to handle. During this period, working with your mentors, an advisory board or non-executive directors can be really helpful. Use the experience and expertise of your advisors when dealing with firsts.

Making it up as you go

One aspect of start-up life that may take a bit of getting used to is the fact that often you have to 'make things up as you go'. You may get requests or offers from third parties that you don't know how to respond to. Your team or staff may go through situations you have no idea how to handle. A myriad of things

can occur in business life and if you don't know how to deal
with them you need to read up on them or skill up quickly
(for example, through doing courses or by researching online).

You may encounter situations you don't know how to handle
and you can't find a precedent that you can use or anybody
you know who has experienced a similar situation. In these
situations, you need to demonstrate leadership and confidence.
Trust your instincts and approach the situation or opportunity
as you have done since your start-up journey began. You have
mastered many challenges to get your company and product off
the ground — take some confidence from that and do the best
you can.

Being comfortable about 'making things up as you go', or not
having everything completely under your control, is a useful
mindset for entrepreneurs — after all, it's the excitement of
doing something new, of stepping outside of your comfort zone
that has (hopefully) attracted you to the world of start-ups in
the first place.

Critical Success Factors at the Start (and Beyond)

As you are working away on your start-up following the launch
(refer to the preceding section), you need to establish some
useful habits. The following sections outline some critical regular
tasks and good practices that can help ensure your company
grows and makes progress on its path to success.

Listening to your customers

An expression that's used frequently in the start-up world is
'turn your customers into fans'. To achieve this, constantly seek
feedback from your customers and respond to their comments.
Listening to your customers can't be emphasised enough as a
useful discipline for all businesses — and start-ups in particular.
Your customers typically know exactly what they want (and
what they don't want) and, if you ask them, they're also typically
more than happy to tell you what they like or dislike about your
product or service.

Many start-ups fail because they keep ignoring key messages from their customers. Paying attention to your customers not only provides you with relevant information on your business but, by acknowledging customer feedback and acting on it, you also create a fantastic rapport with your customer — which typically leads to loyalty and enthusiasm.

Successful entrepreneurs often report about the early days of their businesses and how they 'showered' their very first customers and early adopters with 'love'. While this sounds funny (if a bit cheesy), it's an accurate description of what you need to do during this phase. 'Love your customers' and respect their input by listening and acting on feedback.

A good way of remembering to listen to your customers is to have physical objects in your workspace that represent the customer's views — for example, print out emails, photos, complaints and feedback. Some companies even dedicate a chair or make a puppet and label them 'the customer' to constantly remind them of this important practice.

Listening to your customers isn't always easy because they also tell you things you don't want to hear. When this happens, don't dismiss feedback and think you know best. That's a dangerous assumption! And try to stay close to your customers. While keeping up the practice of listening attentively to your customers over months (and years) is hard, thinking you can always anticipate the needs of your customers following the first few signs of success is an easy trap to fall into.

Consumer and client behaviour is very fickle. Often, your customers have many alternatives to using your product and service and they may simply walk out on you (that is, use a competitor) if you lose touch with their needs and desires.

Losing customers is generally referred to as 'customer churn' and you need to watch the churn factor in your business closely. At no point should customer churn be more than 3 per cent of your entire customer base — in other words, if you have 100 customers and you're losing five customers every month, it's time to get active.

Iterating quickly

Staging a successful launch and getting attention from media and customers feels great. But this is only the beginning — you need to keep evolving your products and services (and quickly). Use the feedback you receive from customers to improve different aspects of your business.

Product development typically happens in a cyclical process: A product is launched, then improved based on internal and external feedback, and then launched as an updated version. Start-ups follow the same process but generally have to use much shorter development cycles to find a good 'product–customer fit' in order to keep the business going. A good product–customer fit is usually the basis for significant growth (through word of mouth and referrals) and thus allows start-ups to generate sufficient revenue from sales or raise capital on the back of impressive growth figures.

The technique of *split testing* is very useful during this phase. Work with your team to see how you can offer slight variations of your product to different customer groups to find out what they prefer. You can apply the same technique to your advertising campaigns — especially online, where split testing is very easy. For example, Google AdWords allows you to create different versions of the same ad. The click through statistics in Google Adwords tell you which ads appeal more (because certain versions of the ads have attracted more clicks). See www.google.com/adwords for more and also check out *Google AdWords For Dummies*, 2nd Edition, by Howie Jacobson (published by Wiley Publishing, Inc.).

Avoiding distractions

A major pitfall for start-ups during this period is getting distracted. A launch typically provides great focus — the whole team works towards a shared goal of making the company's product or service available to customers for the first time. After the launch, you and your team risk losing focus because now that single goal is gone.

The following is a list of common distractions during the early stages and what to do about them:

- ✔ **Government grants and competitions:** Applying for grants or participating in competitions may seem like a good strategy to get funding, resources or free advertising. However, these avenues often also turn into distractions because of the sheer effort involved in completing forms or participating in mandatory activities that aren't related to the core business of the company. Grants often involve detailed presentations, document preparation and reporting over long periods (especially after the grant is awarded). Consider the drain on available time and resources carefully before deciding to apply for grants or to enter competitions.

✔ **Office games:** Start-up office culture is often celebrated by having little games, gadgets and parties in the office. This is useful to energise the team and celebrate milestones. However, your start-up is a business that requires a lot of work during the early days. If the little games or celebrations get out of hand, you might struggle to maintain a professional work ethic and focus on tackling issues or opportunities that the company is facing.

✔ **Partnership offers:** A successful launch often attracts other businesses who want to partner with you. Unless the partnership offers a direct and significant benefit to your company, it may actually be more of a distraction. Business partnerships are based on a value exchange — check what you're expected to contribute and what you stand to gain from the partnership to work out whether the partnership is worth pursuing. Watch out for deals that can end up being too time consuming for you or your team.

✔ **Social media:** You can easily spend an entire day just replying to comments and posts about your company, or its product or service. Especially when your launch has gone well, lots of articles may appear online that spark discussions or commentary. While you need to be aware of the social media impact your company is having, you also need to make sure you don't spend an inappropriate amount of time on it. Time boxing is a useful technique to use when working on your social media related tasks — that is, have a dedicated member of your team who coordinates responses on a priority basis and only spends a given amount of time on this activity.

✔ **Sweating the small stuff:** In a vibrant and hectic start-up environment, a constant stream of little distractions tend to appear — for example, disagreements in the team, technology issues and quarrels over expenses. The best way to address these is to check whether the issues create a direct and significant impact on the company's finances, operations or reputation. If not, remind everyone of the bigger picture and their important tasks.

A good way to avoid distractions is to set clear daily, weekly and monthly goals during the early phase after launching your product or service. Tracking against these goals provides an excellent framework to help members of your team to work out how to spend their time in a way that has the biggest impact on achieving targets.

As well as helping you and your team avoid distractions, having a documented medium- and long-term strategy also helps evaluate business opportunities against the planned direction. Understand that a business can't be all things to all people. You should aim to do a few things well during this phase, rather than start lots of initiatives that inevitably fail because you have insufficient resources to work on them.

Networking

Early stage start-ups tend to be very resource hungry. The companies need customers and orders, good staff, funds and exposure. Taking care of every aspect of business with a small team is difficult. That's why successful entrepreneurs use every opportunity to find shortcuts to any specific challenge they're trying to overcome (such as getting free advertising or attracting investors).

Many things that a start-up needs can be helped by having a good network of resources to draw on. In the start-up world, people who can help you achieve things quickly are sometimes called *enablers*. Developing a good network of enablers requires some work, but you can actively grow the number of connections you have with other people or organisations to help your start-up.

Here are some suggestions for developing a useful network:

- ✔ **Attend conferences.** You should aim to attend at least two conferences per year but, ideally, you attend a range of events (not just events directly related to your industry or target market). Identify movers and shakers of a particular field that could be helpful to you (for example, in the area of technology or marketing) and follow them on Twitter and try to engineer a connection on LinkedIn.

- ✔ **Go along to parties.** Representing your start-up at parties and meet-ups is an important part of start-up life. You can spread around this 'chore' among the team — but don't forget to hold your own party periodically to make sure you get invited again.

✓ **Have coffee with people.** Similar to the party strategy (see preceding bullet) but more targeted. Get out of the office frequently and keep in touch with influential people like journalists, mentors or lecturers.

✓ **Join a business club.** Lots of business networks and clubs exist in Australia and New Zealand. Organisations like Lions, Rotary, Zion, Chamber of Commerce, Institute of Directors and many others offer excellent opportunities to find valuable contacts.

✓ **Organise a lunch meet up with other entrepreneurs.** Pick a central place with special lunch offers and invite other entrepreneurs to have a good chat about running start-ups.

✓ **Post vacancies for freelancers.** A great strategy to enhance your network is to use online job boards or sites like www.freelancer.com.au and thebigidea.co.nz to post vacancies for freelancers. These can be for little jobs that need doing in your start-up for which you don't have the skills or resources.

✓ **Support a good cause.** Get your team involved in an event to support a good cause that everyone feels strongly about. Charity challenges or volunteering events are excellent networking opportunities.

✓ **Use online business networks.** Pick an online business network (such as LinkedIn) and update your online profile regularly. Pick one network rather than having a presence on many of them.

Whatever you do to increase your network, make sure you've got a good system in place to remember people's contact details and their area of expertise. Use whatever tool works for you (whether a professional online contact management system, a Filofax or business card sorter). You need to be able to access your network quickly.

Dealing with Start-Up Blues

In the preceding sections of this chapter, I mostly cover successful launches and how to keep up the momentum after the launch. However, start-up life doesn't always start with a bang and rarely everything goes to plan. The following sections are all about how to deal with disappointment, frustration and setbacks during the early days.

So you've had three clicks

One of the most frustrating situations in start-up life is lack of interest. You've put on a fantastic launch but the phones aren't ringing and your website analytics report shows three visitors per day. This is hard to deal with after months of development, preparation and excitement.

In Chapter 1, I describe the essential habits of successful entrepreneurs — perseverance is one of them and this habit really comes into play when your business is quiet. In a situation where you're getting no or little interest from customers, you need to dig deep and check your assumptions, your offering and reach out to people. You need to find out which part of your offering is not working for people — it could be the product or service itself or just the way you promote or sell it.

Here's a list of things to check, in the order you should check them, when you're not getting any interest:

- ✓ **Statistics and tracking:** The first and easiest thing to check is to make sure that your tracking mechanisms are actually working. For example, if you use Google Analytics, is your unique tracking code embedded in each page and have you done a complete internal test to ensure that page visits are registered correctly? Same goes for any other tracking mechanism you have put in place — do an internal test to make sure they work correctly.

- ✓ **Media:** If nobody picked up your media release, you must get in touch with a professional journalist (if you haven't already done so for writing the media release). Getting media attention is an art form and it can be difficult to understand exactly what makes journalists decide to cover a particular story (or not). So you need to speak to someone who's familiar with the field to give you advice on how to change your current positioning to get some media exposure.

- ✓ **Advertising:** Online ads are among the easiest and most effective ways to advertise a new product or service. Online ads should receive minimum click-through rates of between 0.3 and 0.5 per cent. So if your online ads are getting click-through rates of less than 0.1 per cent (that is, less than one click for every 1,000 times an ad is displayed) something is wrong with your campaign. (Email ad rates are lower — these ads should receive minimum click-through rates of 0.07 per cent.) Things to check include the following:

- Are you displaying your ads to the right audience? Make sure you select your audience through suitable site demographics or keywords (see the sidebar 'Making sure your keywords are the customer's'). Also check the geography of where ads are displayed (for example, if you're selling to customers in Australia but your ads are showing on an international site that gets most of its traffic from the US, you won't get a lot of clicks). If your ads are displayed in emails, the email list may not be suitable or may be outdated.

- Are your ads providing a clear and short message that's easy to read? Also check your ads for spelling mistakes or other language problems that might put people off.

- Are you communicating key benefits to customers (rather than just features of your products)? Show your ads to people you know well (but who haven't seen the ads yet). Ask them what they believe the ads are about and what appeals to them or puts them off.

✔ **Timing:** How long has it been since you've had your launch? Typically, you need to wait for at least a couple of weeks to be able to get reliable statistics on your campaign. Sometimes people are suspicious about a new product or service and want to do some research first before contacting you. Also, if other big events (such as a natural catastrophe) coincided with your launch, this could be a reason you're not seeing the results you expected.

Many online advertising platforms have started helping advertisers with their online campaigns. So you can get in touch with the support teams of sites you want to advertise on and have your ads checked — the advertising support staff are typically able to give you hints and tips to improve the effectiveness of your campaign. These ad review services are sometimes available free of charge or may involve a small fee (such as $50). You can also ask specialist online marketing agencies or advertising professionals to check your ads and campaigns but they typically charge for this service (and the fee may be a lot higher).

Making sure your keywords are the customer's

When working with keyword-based advertising, you need to ensure that your keywords fit with the searches and content of your target segment. In other words, you need to understand which search terms or websites your target segment would use to find out about something they're interested in (that's relevant to your product or service). For example, if your website sells discounted first class airline tickets but the keyword-based ads also show up when people type in 'plane crash' or 'scary landings', the ads may not convert well. *See Search Engine Optimization For Dummies*, 4th Edition, by Peter Kent (published by Wiley Publishing, Inc.) for more.

If you used an agency to create the campaign, make sure you work them hard to deliver results. Their job is to create impactful campaigns — don't accept excuses or placating statements that the campaign is really quite successful. Whatever the agency says, 0.3 to 0.5 per cent is an average click-through rate for website ad campaigns, and 0.07 to 0.13 per cent is average for email ads.

When talking to customers (or potential customers, journalists and other industry experts) always ask what aspects they like and dislike about your product or service, or your campaign or company. The feedback from your initial customers is invaluable. Remove any aspects of your offering that put people off or give them reasons to be suspicious. Highlight any aspects that have proven to be integral to your customers' purchasing decision. In particular, make sure you speak to customers who end up buying from you or using your services — ask them what has made the biggest contribution to their positive purchasing decision. Use this information to shape your offering and advertising campaigns accordingly.

Many factors can influence the results of a campaign or how your business is tracking in the first days, weeks and months following a launch. Keeping going at this stage is very important — don't let the disappointment about results affect your work. Check your assumptions again, perhaps adjust your campaigns and keep at it. What you lack in numbers (sales, customers) you need to make up in enthusiasm. Investors often refer to this as the *momentum* of a start-up. Your job during the early days is to build and maintain momentum.

Failing successfully

As an entrepreneur, you need to recognise the value of failure. True entrepreneurs have a definition for failure that differs to most people's. To them, failure just means that a particular hypothesis turned out to be incorrect (at a given point in time). In other words, success (of finding a hypothesis that turns out to be correct) is only a matter of time and can be achieved by eliminating incorrect hypotheses. As such, getting feedback from a significant number of people that a product or service isn't of interest is very useful. When that happens, entrepreneurs must decide whether to continue with, modify or abandon their current offering.

The decision to continue with, modify or abandon a current offering isn't an easy one and mostly depends on the feedback you receive. Most importantly, the decision on how to proceed must be a conscious one — rather than you just carrying on regardless (which, unfortunately, happens a lot). In the early days of a start-up the decision to continue, modify or abandon should be made on a weekly basis. This requires a certain discipline, where feedback is constantly sought and evaluated.

Assign the task of evaluating the continue/modify/abandon question to a particular team member, who can then present the most recent results to the team and provide a recommendation.

A key indicator when determining whether or not to abandon a product or service is the ratio between 'customer acquisition cost' and 'customer lifetime value'. The customer acquisition cost (CAC) is the total cost including advertising, sales support and customer support to sign up one customer or make one sale. The customer lifetime value (LTV) represents the average (total) amount of revenue that can be generated from one customer over the entire period that they are a customer. Successful companies need products that have a much higher LTV than CAC. In other words, the cost of acquiring a customer should be far less than the revenue your company is able to extract from that customer. Otherwise the company makes a loss. So if you determine both CAC and LTV for your new product and the CAC is consistently higher than the LTV, it's probably time to reconsider.

In many cases, abandoning a product or service doesn't mean that the company is finished. It can simply mean that the team has to go back to the drawing board to create a different offering from the initial validation results or customer feedback. This step is sometimes referred to as *pivoting* (changing direction) and is very common in the start-up world. Many highly successful companies started out with products or services that were abandoned to focus on a different offering. A good example for a successful pivot is Instagram which started out as a bourbon appreciation app.

Start-ups have been known to pivot several times along their journey — the number of times a start-up can change direction when required simply depends on motivation and resources. Most start-ups run out of money if they don't find an attractive product or service within a certain period. So, when your company is pivoting, make sure you check the energy levels around your team, and how much money is left in the bank to cover the costs of creating another product or service and getting it to the validation and launch stages.

Running out of steam

Many start-ups end up going under because the founders realise that running a start-up is a lot harder than they thought. As a result, they lose motivation or simply can't deal with the sheer workload. This situation isn't necessarily tied to bad feedback or problems with getting interest in the company's products or services. Running out of steam can happen as a result of struggling to deal with the increased workload and responsibility, or because of financial pressure, or challenging customers or team members. Investors usually refer to this situation as 'the start-up blues'.

When you or your team gets the start-up blues, keep in mind that most issues are only temporary in nature. A simple phone call or email can make all the difference between feeling on top of the world or down in the dumps. Secondly, remember your strengths and what you have achieved so far. Giving up is not an option just because your start-up has had a couple of bad days. Finally, take a closer look at exactly what's bringing people down. Is it because of factors such as bad customer feedback, no uptake or product failure? An important learning opportunity may exist for you there. Do some due diligence on what exactly is causing the blues to see if an issue exists that can be addressed.

If you or your team are simply going through a bit of a rough patch, you can take action and re-energise the company. Here's a list of suggestions:

- ✔ **Book in a massage therapist.** When people are stressed, they tend to tense up and as a result end up not feeling that great. To address this you can get a physiotherapist or massage therapist to come in to your office and give people back rubs. It's usually not difficult (or expensive) to find a therapist who offers these services (for example, $250 for half a day is common).

- ✔ **Create a dream board.** Pick an area in your office that's highly visible and you pass by at least once per day (the coffee area is great). Get your team to put up images they associate with the success of your venture. Let the creative juices flow and pin up whatever people come up with. The board is a great motivator to remind everyone why you're doing all this hard work.

- ✔ **Create an incentive scheme.** This is a useful mechanism to improve motivation and align the team. Pick the most critical aspects of your business (for example, user sign up, sales or click-throughs) and display daily results somewhere highly visible in the office. Put targets next to your key measurements and create incentives when certain milestones are reached (use individual or team incentives as appropriate).

- ✔ **Get out as a team.** Sometimes when stress levels are high, simply going out for a drink or a meal can make a big difference.

- ✔ **Get some gadgets.** Ask the team to suggest and vote for the favourite office gadget — for example, RC indoor helicopters, flying fish or a fussball table. Set a budget and get whatever gadget the team agrees on. Organise a competition when the gadget arrives and get maximum use out of the new toy. (Just ensure the gadgets don't become too much of a distraction when spirits are lifting — refer to the section 'Avoiding distractions' earlier in this chapter.)

- ✔ **Take a day out.** Taking time off can be a really good way to re-energise. If things aren't going well for your start-up, taking an extra day off is probably not going to affect your business in a big way. Make sure team members take their minds off the business and do something completely unrelated. So working from home or checking emails is not allowed during the day off (you may need to enforce this by locking the doors and shutting down the email server).

✔ **Watch TED talks.** Have a look through TED (www.ted.org) to find inspiring talks from other entrepreneurs who the team admires (such as Steve Jobs or Steve Ballmer). Organise a pizza lunch where you watch the videos, eat pizza and be inspired.

Whatever gets you or your team down, your job as an entrepreneur is to pick yourself up and pull everyone along with you. Many iconic entrepreneurs are also really strong motivators who inspire their teams and pull people along when energy levels are low. Motivating others is yet another essential skill you need to master along your start-up journey. Fortunately you typically get plenty of opportunities to practise. So embrace every business crisis as a challenge to demonstrate your entrepreneurial talent.

Chapter 5

Gaining Traction: Ramping Up Your Start-Up

· ·

In This Chapter

▶ Managing rapid growth and building momentum in your company

▶ Understanding the importance of continued analysis and goal-setting

· ·

*A*fter many months (or sometimes years) of hard work, you finally find the golden nugget along your start-up journey. A number of your customer and market hypotheses have proven to be the magic formula that satisfies a vital customer need in a large market. This is another crucial period for your start-up because you now need to focus on keeping up the pace (or accelerating the pace) of how your business develops.

Many important operational and strategic decisions have to be made and it's crucial to keep a cool head to avoid unfortunate choices that end up costing the company dearly (or even kill the company altogether).

This chapter covers what to do when you feel your company is taking off and how to ensure your company keeps growing. I also provide a run-down of what management practices you need to put in place to track progress, review your business strategy and decide which aspects of your business need strengthening.

Wait! We're On to Something

At some point along your start-up journey (you may be looking at your website analytics, order book, financials or customer database) you suddenly find yourself thinking, 'Hang on a second ... this is actually looking pretty good!'

In the following sections, I outline how to recognise the signs of sustainable success, what to do when competitors start paying attention and how to build on your success.

Working out the signs of success

Some signs of initial success are very obvious, whereas others can be subtle. In case you're in any doubt about what to look for and whether or not you're really onto something, here's a selection of parameters that typically mean your company (or product or service) is showing potential:

- ✔ **Very high conversion rates.** You experience consistently high conversion rates on your advertising campaigns and sales pages — for example, online advertising click-through rates of over 5 per cent or conversion rates of over 10 per cent on your sales pages.

- ✔ **Cost of sale per transaction is far less than purchase price or product margin.** (This is a particularly good sign in a large market with significant potential for high transaction volume.) When this happens you have reached a point in your business development where your customer acquisition cost (CAC) is less than the customer lifetime value (LTV). (Refer to Chapter 4 for more on CAC and LTV, and see the sidebar 'Working out your cost of sale' for how to work out this cost per transaction.)

- ✔ **Interest in your offering grows at more than 100 per cent month on month (for more than 12 consecutive months).** Interest can be expressed in a number of ways, such as website traffic, enquiries, sign-ups or subscriptions, and sales. Sustained growth at this level usually means that what you're offering is attractive — and that growth isn't just based on a temporary trend or campaign.

- ✔ **Unsupported explosive growth.** In other words, you experience growth of transactions or interest in your company of several hundred or 1,000 per cent without running any campaigns or promotions. This typically indicates that your products or services receive strong word of mouth (or *viral referrals*) from existing customers.

- ✔ **A well-known or well-established company (competitor) shows interest in buying your business.**

- ✔ **A recognised industry leader or commentator writes about your company.** Such coverage of your company (or products or services) could appear in a well-known forum, blog or other form of publication.

Working out your cost of sale

Using an online advertising campaign and online sales transaction (for example, an eCommerce shopping cart system) provides a simple way to work out your cost of sales per transaction. Simply follow these steps:

1. Divide the total online advertising spend for a given campaign by the number of clicks you received. This gives you the cost per qualified lead.

2. Determine your conversion ratio by checking your results to see how many qualified leads (as identified in step 1) result in a successful transaction (that is, a sale). (*Note:* One successful transaction can require as many as several hundred qualified leads.) A conversion rate of 1 per cent means that for every 100 qualified leads visiting your sales page, you make one sale.

3. Divide your cost per qualified lead (determined in step 1) by the conversion rate determined in step 2. This gives you a net cost of sale. For example, if your cost per qualified lead is $2 and your conversion rate is 1 per cent, your net cost of sale is $200.

4. Factor in other indirect costs, such as operational and customer service costs that aren't passed on to customers. Work out a 'per transaction' amount of these costs and add to the cost determined in step 3 — this gives you your total cost of sales.

You can count on investors and potential partners being interested to join forces with you if you observe any of the preceding parameters in your company.

Getting noticed by competitors and supporters

With success comes attention (generally). Many established companies are actively scanning their field of commercial activities for new entrants, disruptive technologies or innovations, or potential competitive threats. Ideally, you can 'fly under the radar' (go unnoticed) with your company until you reach a stable financial position (that is, your company is either profitable or you've secured sufficient funding to keep you going for a long time). However, if you're doing something well in a particular market that has many established incumbents, you probably appear on their radar at some point, and they may try to take (or take back) some of your market share.

If your product or service is easy to copy by other companies, protecting the market share you've carved out for yourself may be difficult. Well-resourced competitors may simply undercut your price, copy your offering or launch advertising campaigns to lure customers away from you.

Growing your company quickly and reaching a critical mass of customers (or traffic and transaction volume) makes it harder for any potential competitor to threaten your market position or development potential.

Getting noticed in the media or wider field can be great for your company (because it usually represents free promotion and advertising) but it can also be challenging to deal with. When your company receives growing interest from media, investors and potential partners, you need to keep your feet on the ground and focus on running your start-up. Evaluate carefully how you spend your time — that is, whether it's best spent on opportunities to talk about your business or working in your business. Keep an eye on the time you spend on media and public relations activities and what you receive in return.

As your business success ramps up, I highly recommend you keep a log of what you and your team spend time on. You may be surprised to see just how much time is spent on various activities.

Building strategic value

As your start-up is becoming a real (and perhaps profitable) business, where you're building on your initial success, you need to make sure enough time and effort is spent on initiatives that build _strategic value_ — in other words, you need to pursue activities that result in your company being more valuable at a future point when you want to sell it or float it. You can easily get caught up in day-to-day operational tasks (such as fulfilling orders) without looking at strategic activities (such as developing a new market or sales channel).

The easiest way to understand what adds strategic value to a company is to look at how companies are valued prior to a private trade sale or public listing. Many valuation techniques are used in practice but the three most common approaches are based on one of the following:

- Establishing a value by comparing the company to established values of similar companies in the same market or industry
- Valuing the company's assets (net asset value)
- Valuing the company's income stream (net present value)

Sometimes the three methods in the preceding list are combined, or parameters from other valuation methods are used to establish a 'realistic' value of the company. However, most valuation methods recognise a set of *value drivers* (things that add to the value of a company). By focusing on optimising these value drivers, start-ups can build strategic value.

Here's a list of value drivers to focus on:

- **Automation:** Reducing the time spent on manual tasks or interventions typically leads to medium- and long-term cost savings — and so increases the value of a company. Automated processes are also much more scalable because they don't rely on the availability of qualified staff. A good example for this is a fully automated sales transaction process (for example, an online shopping cart system) that automatically completes all necessary tasks in a sales process (such as order taking, order processing, invoicing and shipping).

- **Brand:** Having a recognised brand adds value to a company because brands convey trust and distinction (which, in turn, is more likely to generate sales than unrecognised brands). The value of brands can be increased by protecting brand assets (for example, by registering trademarks for the brand name or logo), increasing brand awareness (such as through marketing) or by brand refinement (for example, by updating or clearly defining a vague brand).

- **Customer or user base:** Having a large number of registered users generates value because you can sell to existing customers more easily than the general public. A common example of this is email subscriber lists or the user database of a free service. Generally, the more registered users a company has the more valuable it is.

✔ **Exclusivity:** Any aspect of the business that can be used to generate and protect exclusive access creates value. This can include exclusive partnerships, supply, sales or delivery contracts, and territorial rights. The exclusivity is only valuable if it's recognised in the legal system (and can be enforced if challenged or infringed).

✔ **Intellectual property (IP):** Rights to recognised IP — for example, software copyrights, works of art or patents — build value. Any initiative that asserts or registers IP rights adds value to a company.

✔ **Popularity:** For online start-ups, popularity mostly comes down to the three essential website metrics — number of unique visits, pages per visit and time on site.

✔ **Profitability:** This is a very obvious driver for company value but you need to understand how it can be optimised. In order for a company to be more profitable, it has to increase its revenue without increasing costs to the same degree. Alternatively, the company has to cut costs without affecting revenue (to the same degree). Any initiative that achieves this adds value to the company.

A good way of checking you're also focusing on building strategic value is to create an overview spreadsheet of all projects that are currently being undertaken in the company. The overview should show the project objectives, time frame and status. A monthly review of this spreadsheet typically guarantees that you don't forget about strategic initiatives.

Nurturing your start-up

During this period of becoming an established business, you need to identify opportunities that can further assist your business with rapid growth or market penetration. Many opportunities exist to nurture your start-up, ranging from operational activities (such as search engine optimisation) to strategic initiatives (such as targeting key influencers to join the advisory board — refer to Chapter 3). The following is a discussion of suggested measures to nurture your start-up during this growth phase.

Cash injection

Once you have proven a particular business concept and your start-up is generating revenue or making a profit, evaluate whether you could accelerate business growth by having more financial resources available. This is generally an ideal situation to attract investors because key elements of the business have already been proven. Most investors are keen to see their investment being used for acceleration and scaling rather than proving a concept.

Relocation

Does your current location work as an advantage or disadvantage to the company's business? If you can address significant location-based negative factors by relocation, this phase of the company's growth path may be the time to do so. Factors to consider include availability and cost of qualified staff, access to channel partners or major clients and suppliers, access to investment capital, and availability of office space and the quality of office facilities (in particular, access to the internet and available online services).

Insurance

As your business grows, the dependency on key members of staff typically increases and so does the liability risk for directors and the executive team. Insuring key staff and the executive team is a useful measure to mitigate associated risks to the business.

Many insurance companies in Australia and New Zealand offer director and executive officer insurance as well as insurance packages for other key staff.

The insurance package you choose for key staff should also include crisis and trauma cover to cover the cost for temporary staff in case of accidents, illness or disability.

Business insurances are completely separate to individual life insurances of particular staff members. The aim of business insurance is to protect the company rather than the individual who has experienced an incident such as an accident or illness.

Site optimisation

After several iterations of improving your minimum viable product (refer to Chapter 4 for more on iterating quickly), you also need to optimise your website for usability, performance and search engine indexing. Often small changes can make a big overall difference in how your site is perceived and experienced by customers, competitors, and potential investors and partners.

Certification should also be considered when looking at site optimisation. This involves getting your payment system certified by a certification authority to instil confidence in your customers that your company is offering a professional, secure and trusted payment process. The certification process typically allows you to display a 'trust seal', which clearly identifies your company and the certification authority. Common certifications include Verisign (www.verisign.com.au), Truste (www.truste.com) and BBB (www.bbb.org).

Standardisation

The initial period following the launch can be quite chaotic — many things may be done 'on the fly' and standards may have been made up as you went along. That's perfectly all right and is perhaps unavoidable when starting out. However, once things have settled down a bit (and you have some money available), consider an exercise to consolidate and structure the way you do business.

Typical areas to standardise include

- Document templates for key documents (such as invoices, contracts and sales letters)
- Procedures
- Travel and expense guidelines
- Use of brand collateral (that is, where and how your logo should be displayed)

Seeking to standardise certain areas may trigger a 'clean up' exercise, where you go back over previous documents, contracts and web pages to tidy up any important aspects of your business that no longer fit with the defined standard.

Team composition

When your business takes off, you need to identify any skill gaps or overlaps. Your team and team composition needs to grow with the business. As a result, you may have to update employment contracts, train staff, hire new team members or even make some employees redundant. This is an ongoing process but having an optimal team during this initial growth stage is particularly important.

Also consider what services can be outsourced — for example, book keeping, order fulfilment, server administration or customer service.

Board composition

Just like with staff (refer to preceding section), you need to reflect on the composition of your board of directors as well as the composition of your advisory board (if you have one). You need to determine whether or not different skill sets or areas of expertise are now also required at board level.

You may want to consider potential opportunities to expand the board and bring in skills, contacts or investment — for example, because you're approached by someone who wants to join the board. Alternatively, you may have to actively seek out additional board members. Either way, get into the habit of reviewing the board composition regularly (at least once per year).

If you haven't put together an advisory board for your company, the initial growth stage after launching is certainly a good time to consider doing so. Look for key influencers in your industry or people with extensive business networks and approach them with a suggestion to join your advisory board. In my experience, many established business people don't mind helping out a promising start-up as an advisor (and often without any remuneration). (Refer to Chapter 3 for more on advisory boards.)

Utilising tools to help growth

You may be familiar with the saying 'Work smarter, not harder'. The suggestions in this section are in this category — showing you how to work smarter.

As your start-up grows, you need to constantly look at opportunities to make your (business) life easier and streamline operations. The following are a number of suggestions to consider:

- ✓ **Cloud-based services:** If you haven't started your company using web-based or online software, now may be a good time to tackle this shift. Unless you can identify a specific need to manage a sizable IT infrastructure in-house (which includes managing backups and security), I recommend you shift as much business data and services as possible to a *cloud-based system*. Cloud-based systems use a range of technologies to allow seamless scaling of critical IT resources. Initial aspects you could look to moving onto a cloud-based system include computational power, disk space and network bandwidth. These systems are typically run by third-party suppliers who manage your IT infrastructure for you (usually a range of options are available at reasonable cost). For example, document and file storage can easily be done with Dropbox.

✓ **Customer relationship management (CRM):** Every profitable business has customers and, as the number of customers grows, you need to have tools in place that help you manage your customer base effectively.

If your company is based on subscriptions or online users, you probably already have a system in place to manage them. However, if you operate a retail or B2B model, you may not have a system in place because all your interactions with customers to date have been transaction-based or ad-hoc. So if you now want to send out an email blast to previous customers or look up how much sales you got from a particular client, it may be quite tricky to organise. That's where CRM systems come in, helping you manage all interactions with key clients or even your entire customer base.

Many CRM systems exist but I'd recommend you start with a number of common options, like SugarCRM (free), SalesForce or Zoho. You also need to pick a staff member who's interested in learning how the software works.

✓ **Self-service systems:** Many aspects of looking after your customers and staff require manual intervention (for example, because you have to approve requests or respond to queries). As much as possible, you should try to increase the level of self-service for all aspects of your business. A good example is creating self-managed 'frequently asked questions' (FAQ) on your website. Tools like assistly.com, getsatisfaction.com and zendesk.com can help you achieve a high degree of self-service.

Measuring Your Progress

Running your start-up in the early days may feel like you're actually running around all the time because you always have so much to do.

Lots of activity (and bustle) is good, and is generally easier to deal with than no activity at all. But you want to avoid acting like a headless chicken — running around without any direction.

More importantly, you need to get a sense of whether you're making progress and, if you are, how far you've come with your business.

Think of running your business in the same way you'd run a cross-country marathon — you need a map, a compass and frequent check points that tell you whether or not you're on the right track.

In the following sections, I introduce the business equivalents of a map, compass and check points.

Planning and goal setting for success

One of the most important disciplines to get into in business is adequate planning. I use 'adequate' as a qualifier in this statement because some start-ups have literally planned themselves to death by spending a large portion of their available time on strategising, meeting and budgeting.

For most enterprises in the first few years of business, a quarterly planning cycle is adequate. This frequency represents a useful balance between operational considerations and strategic directions when planning the next business period.

Ideally, planning sessions are synchronised with board meetings so that directors can review achievements and progress over the last quarter and set targets for the next quarter. By using the board meeting to do this, any agreed targets also have an 'official' character and may be integrated into an incentive package for the executive team. This means the business interests are aligned with the interests of the team managing the company.

In most cases, quarterly planning provides a set of high-level targets that can then be translated into more specific initiatives and focus areas.

Useful preparation for planning sessions is to create or update a set of standard documents that can be reviewed by decision-makers (the board of directors). Here's a list of material to include in the preparation documents:

- ✔ Competitor analysis
- ✔ Environmental scan of current market, consumer and technology trends that may affect the business

> ✔ Set of financial accounts over the last quarter (profit and loss statement and balance sheet)
>
> ✔ Strengths, weaknesses, opportunities, threats (SWOT) analysis (see Appendix B for a sample SWOT template)

Other documents than the ones included in the preceding list may be relevant for the planning session (such as key performance indicators). However, no matter what documents you use, the information within them needs to put decision-makers in a position where they can set meaningful targets based on the current business situation and performance against plans.

Once targets have been agreed to (for example, in the board meeting), record these quarterly goals and communicate them to the rest of the company in a meaningful way — such as through a large wall chart or individual team meetings. Use whatever works for your team but make sure all staff are aware of current targets and how they contribute to achieving them. For documentation purposes, I recommend using the one-page business plan — refer to Chapter 3.

Grasping the importance of continued analysis and measurement

Making progress in a start-up (and in most companies) is typically based on a simple plan–execute–measure cycle. Strategic direction and quarterly goals tend to inform business operations and provide guidance on what initiatives to focus on. But then your business operations and the execution of initiatives need to be measured in a way that tells everyone about the status and impact of current activities.

At a strategic level, the measurement of a company's progress is typically done through key performance indicators and tracking of financial parameters (such as sales revenue, liabilities, and operating cost or expenses) against budgets and targets. At a day-to-day operations level, these high-level performance indicators need to be related to operational measurements such as website statistics, sales figures and customer data. Ideally, the various teams also agree on targets for their operational metrics that line up with the overall quarterly business goals.

For example, if a business target is to reduce the customer service cost, this could result in the following initiatives:

- ✔ Increase the reliability, performance and usability of products and services
- ✔ Increase the rate of customer support requests that can be answered through self-service
- ✔ Standardise the response to customers for common issues and requests

In turn, each initiative has a set of distinctive metrics that can be tracked. For example, increasing the reliability, performance and usability of products and services could be measured by looking at the

- ✔ Downtime (the amount of time, per day or per week, access to the product or service was unavailable)
- ✔ Number of logged product or service defects and the number of new defects
- ✔ Performance metrics such as response times (for example, for a page refresh after a button has been pushed)
- ✔ Rate (per day or week) at which defects are remedied
- ✔ Usability indicators such as abandon rates (for example, of a payment process)

Another useful way to simplify reporting and make metrics more meaningful to staff is to use facets (components of a particular business aspect you are trying to affect) and a scoring system (such as, on a scale of 1 to 10). Your facets could be the same measurements mentioned in the preceding list. However, all of these metrics have different units and you have no easy way of assessing whether a particular measure is good, average or bad. That's where the scoring comes in. You can pick two data points of what you believe to be a 'bad' measure and an 'outstanding' measure for a particular metric. For example, having your website unavailable for more than two days a month is 'bad' and this would therefore receive a score of 1. Having your website unavailable for less than one minute a month is 'outstanding', which would receive a score of 10.

You can define the scales and scoring mechanisms for each facet and then add them up to create a total score. For example, if you have five facets and you are using the 'out of 10' scoring system, your maximum score would be 50. These scores are much easier to compare and communicate than complex unit measurements.

You can't improve what you don't measure and so you need to put your business, teams and staff in a position that they can easily see how their actions and contributions affect a particular target. This is also really important for keeping motivation levels up (especially if achieving targets is celebrated appropriately).

To track certain aspects of your business, you may need to get accurate external measurements. For example, it doesn't matter how quickly your homepage loads when you are on your own computer — what matters is how quickly it loads for most of your customers in their respective geographies. Fortunately, many tools exist to achieve this — companies like Gomez.com, Smartbear.com and Alertra.com provide external monitoring and measurement of your site. For qualitative measurements like customer satisfaction, you can use survey tools like SurveyMonkey.com, iContact.com or Zoomerang.com which can provide you with a survey score and trend reporting of how the score changes over time.

Even for a small company, measuring and tracking can become quite a task in itself. That's why I recommend creating simple management *dashboards* (high-level overviews that allow you to quickly access a large number of parameters) right from the beginning. You can usually create these dashboards quite simply in a spreadsheet after collecting metrics from the various teams (or even organising an automatic update process that grabs data from other documents or systems). A good example for a useful dashboard is the Google Analytics dashboard view, which summarises all key metrics of a website on one page (with the ability to drill down into each area). (For more information, see www.google.com/analytics.)

Automation is the key to successful monitoring of metrics. If gathering together key metrics and parameters takes a long time, you're not likely to keep doing it. In an ideal world, however, all the metrics you're tracking pop in to your dashboard or your email inbox. This is entirely achievable because practically all statistics and monitoring systems offer scheduled reporting functionality that automatically generate statistics and send them to you. For example, Google Analytics lets you schedule standard or customised reports that are then sent to you by email. This is an excellent way to track website statistics.

Tracking your market and competitors

An important area to collect information on for strategic meetings (refer to the section 'Planning and goal setting for success' earlier in this chapter) is your market and competitors.

You need to be aware of any recent development in your market and what your competitors are up to at any one time. Having this information readily available allows you to factor it in during strategic decision-making, or when designing or updating tactical marketing campaigns. For example, if one of your competitors has dropped their prices substantially, perhaps you can update your pricing strategy or launch a counteroffer.

As with tracking key performance measurements (refer to the preceding section), the best way to monitor your market and competitive landscape is to utilise automated services as much as possible. Fortunately, this kind of monitoring is really easy to achieve. Google, Alexa and LinkedIn (and many other sites) offer *alert* functionality. This allows you to configure content alerts based on certain keywords or categories (for example, news on a particular technology or industry).

Some suggestions for setting up your own market and competitor radar include the following:

- ✔ **Alerts:** You can set up several Google Alerts that scan general web content as well as news content for any content that matches relevant keywords. Specify the keywords in a way that delivers the most relevant information to you. Alexa offers a toolbar that allows you to track various sites (including competitor sites). And check out LinkedIn, which also offers company alerts.

  Do a number of web searches and whenever you find highly relevant information save the search as an alert. You can then schedule the alert to run once per week (with results usually delivered straight to your inbox).

- ✔ **Bots:** Some websites display traffic or popularity indicators online — for example, auction and retail sites often list the number of items in a particular category as well as pricing information for specific products or services. In some cases, this information can be used for trend analysis to see how a particular category (of products or services) is doing on other sites. To monitor this effectively, you need to set up a *web-scraping bot* (web agent) that finds

> this information for you and downloads it automatically. Popular bots and scraping tools include mozenda.com, ubotstudio.com and automationanywhere.com.
>
> ✔ **Newsletters and feeds:** Sign up to your competitors' newsletters, twitter streams and RSS feeds. That way you can find out what they're up to without having to go to their website regularly. Also look at signing up to newsletters of industry websites or general news sites on technology or online trends (such as mashable.com, reddit.com, Technorati.com or readwriteweb.com).

With all these alerts and reports coming your way, you need to get organised to make sure your inbox isn't clogged up with information that you won't always have time to process as it arrives. If you're using an offline email application (such as MS Outlook or Thunderbird) use folders, tags or rules to organise email. For example, create a folder (or tag) called News&Alerts and classify alert emails that way. In many email applications you can also define rules that do this classification (and organisation in folders) for you automatically.

Take some time to set up rules and folders — do it once and do it properly. After that, you should be able to access any news or alerts quickly without having to dig around in your inbox.

Revisiting your business plan

As your business is taking off and you're learning a lot of things about your market and customers every day, you need to reflect on lessons learnt, and newly gained market and competitor information in your overall business plan.

Your business plan should be updated at least once per year. But you should also update the plan when significant events occur — for example, if you decide to change direction with your company or discover a major opportunity in the market, or your competitive landscape changes considerably.

You may be tempted to view updating your business plan as a low priority because you can never seem to find a good time to do it. However, by capturing essential information for your business in a business plan and checking against that plan regularly, you can really understand how your company's development is unfolding.

Understanding your company's development isn't only useful for decision-making (and making sure you don't repeat mistakes) but it also gives you a sense of your personal and professional growth. When looking back over the last six to twelve months, you're likely to be amazed at what you and your team have achieved.

Having an up-to-date business plan is particularly important when you're considering an investment round, applying for a government grant or bank loan, or when negotiating a strategic partnership with another company.

You're often asked to provide a copy of your business plan during the due diligence phase of these processes. Updating a business plan in a hurry (because you need to send it off the next day) is never a good idea. Having an up-to-date plan readily available makes your company look professional and agile (which is what investors want to see).

Particular areas to focus on when updating your business plan include the following:

- ✔ **Assumptions:** Look at whether any assumptions in your plan are still valid and relevant. Also look at which ones have been proven.

- ✔ **Business development to date:** As part of the executive summary or in the introduction, include a section on major achievements, milestones and decisions to date.

- ✔ **Financials:** The figures used in the business plan should line up with the actual financials of the company.

- ✔ **Ownership structure:** Consider whether any changes to the company's shareholders or equity structure have occurred, and include any changes in the plan.

- ✔ **Product and service description:** As you modify your offering, make sure the descriptions in the business plan are still accurate.

Part III
Growing Up

Glenn Lumsden

'I don't care about the customer anymore... I just want all the search engines to like me.'

In this part ...

After all the excitement of the launch and growing your traffic or customer base, you might have to work even harder to ensure your growth doesn't slow down unnecessarily. Sometimes slowing growth is actually caused by internal bottlenecks, skill shortages or other issues.

In this part, I provide some guidelines on detecting and addressing limiting factors in your business. I also provide practical suggestions for common growth strategies. If the growth of your business has plateaued and the reason is beyond your control, it may well be crunch time for making a decision on whether or not to continue with your current business. In the following chapters I offer some help with making such decisions.

Chapter 6

Recognising Your Limits

· ·

In This Chapter

▶ Identifying growth limits and bottle necks

▶ Evaluating resourcing options to address growth limits

▶ Deciding on product development

▶ Updating your IT systems

▶ Making sure your business can carry on, no matter what

· ·

*O*nce you have 'cracked' the magic formula of your business and your company is growing rapidly, it's time to hang on to your hat and enjoy the ride. This is often a pretty mad phase in the start-up journey — where your little company transforms itself into a 'proper' business.

During this phase, start-ups make the transition from a little venture run by a bunch of entrepreneurs in a shed to a proper company with employees, premises and a corporate identify. This transition is not always easy and so this chapter covers some key changes that tend to occur and provides tips for a smoother ride.

I outline how to keep the growth momentum going and provide a closer look at how entrepreneurs can identify any hold-ups to achieving sustained growth. I also cover guidelines for partnering up, criteria for making strategic technology decisions and, finally, how to ensure your business keeps running, 24 hours per day.

Understanding Why Your Growth May Slow Down

If you're looking at your management dashboard (refer to Chapter 5) and notice that things are slowing down, don't panic (at least not right away ... you can always panic later).

Even if you started out with growth rates of over 100 per cent month on month, maintaining this kind of growth is difficult (and rare). If your growth figures slow down dramatically over a short period, that's a worrying sign. But if your growth rate merely dips from 100 per cent month on month to stabilise somewhere around 70 per cent, that's still pretty good growth.

In the following sections, I cover the factors that cause your growth rate to slow as your business becomes more established, and ways to accelerate growth again.

Overcoming growth problems

The first step in understanding why your growth rates dip at all is to look at factors that influence your growth. A general distinction is between external and internal factors. Internal factors (such as staff shortages, technology problems or product issues) are much easier to address because the issue causing a decline in growth is within your span of control. External factors are harder to tackle but you still have some tried and tested methods for overcoming growth problems at your disposal.

Internal factors

When you suspect the root cause of your growth decline is internal, you then need to look more closely at what's going on inside your company. Check for the following:

- **Quality drop:** Maintaining a consistently high quality output of products and services can be difficult. Sometimes people just get tired, sloppy or fed up. Quality issues should become apparent in your surveys, feedbacks and support requests. If they do arise, talk the situation through with your team and identify suitable options. This may require staff development (see the last bullet in this list), re-focusing, re-energising, re-shuffling (such as a change of roles or swapping team members) or even moving on staff who no longer enjoy a particular role. (Refer to Chapter 4 for more on re-energising staff when it seems like they've run out of steam.)

✔ **Resource limitations:** More often than not, a slowdown in growth during this phase is caused by resource limitations. For example, your IT infrastructure may be maxed out (see the section 'Facing Strategic Technology Decisions' later in this chapter if you think this issue is affecting your growth), your team may be fully utilised or you're about to run out of money. As a general rule, if you have significant available funds, you can use these funds to fix any other resource limitations. Even a severe skill shortage can be solved by you paying more than the next guy or covering relocation costs to attract people from interstate or even overseas (see the section 'Addressing skill shortages: Buying in skills and outsourcing' later in this chapter for more tips). If you have enough money to do what it takes, do it. If not, raise funds — see Chapter 7 for more information on raising capital.

✔ **Slip-ups:** If you've made a mistake (such as in a marketing campaign, a PR opportunity or a software release), you need to own up to it. Admit that an issue exists, hide nothing and be as honest as possible about exactly what happened. Customers can be ruthless with passing judgement but they can also relate to a bunch of decent business people apologising for making a mistake. Offer compensation wherever possible and identify opportunities to tighten up your internal quality checks to prevent another slip-up.

✔ **Staff issues:** Sometimes seemingly small communication issues can blow up into huge problems — especially in start-ups. These flare ups may seem to occur in the heat of the moment but they're often caused by serious underlying problems. Staff issues range from minor motivational hang-ups all the way to highly disgruntled staff, and often become obvious during sustained growth, when cracks begin to appear as the pressure is on to put out high quality work all the time. Skill gaps, team culture or confidence can also be the reason for non-performance.

If you think staff issues are slowing your growth, you need to engage a HR professional (if you don't yet have an HR person in your team). An external HR consultant comes with no 'baggage' around historical problems in the team, and this fresh perspective can often make a big difference, providing easy ways to defuse a situation.

Internal issues can sometimes drag out longer because they may not receive the same attention as external issues (see the following section). However, when you become aware of an internal issue that's affecting the growth path of your company, you should waste no time in addressing it. Leaving any of the factors listed in this section unaddressed can kill your company. So deal with these situations quickly and effectively.

External factors

All other things being equal (that is, all internal aspects of your company are working well — refer to preceding section), you can typically pinpoint a number of 'usual suspects' for your situation, as follows:

- ✔ **Competition:** A competing product may have entered your market or one of your competitors may be running an aggressive marketing campaign. Check your competitive landscape and evaluate your options to respond (options include dropping your price or matching the competitor's offer). If a new superior product has entered your market, it's time to pull out all stops and work on a differentiation strategy to set your product or service apart from your competition.

- ✔ **Disruption:** If new technology is eroding your market, you need to evaluate whether you can switch technologies quickly to take advantage of your market position. Waste no time when this happens — literally every hour counts to make sure your products or services don't become obsolete.

- ✔ **Economic downturn:** If you launched your start-up just before a regional (or global) economic downturn, your main priority must be on surviving the crisis. The good news is that this also typically affects all other companies. However, your focus may need to be on securing finance (or potentially cutting costs) to get through. Historically, many start-ups have used periods of reduced economic output (such as the period directly following the dotcom bust) to update technology, automate processes and re-energise their teams.

- ✔ **Focus shift:** Sometimes the world goes through mega-trends that tend to use up a lot of 'headspace' and get a good share of consumer spend too. A good example recently was global warming. After Al Gore's campaign shown in *An Inconvenient Truth*, it seemed almost every news article and blog post was somehow related to this issue. When this happens, you need to keep your cool and stick to what you know (unless you can see a direct link between whatever is going on and your business).

✔ **Malicious attack:** If another party attacks or hacks your site, congrats! That's usually a good sign that you're onto something truly valuable (hackers are busy people — they don't waste time with small fry). Dealing with the usually inconvenient and annoying facts of an attack (if you're aware of it) requires effort and dedication. For this, you typically need expert help — see the section 'Improving your system security and responding to hacks' later in this chapter for more.

✔ **Market saturation:** This is one of the most dangerous factors. If you've already maxed out most of your market (because you got the market size wrong), you need to act quickly to identify other markets, such as markets in other geographies or industry verticals — see Chapter 7 for more.

Whatever the external factor you identify as potentially slowing down your growth, don't lose sight of what you've already achieved with your start-up. Don't throw in the towel just yet — any of the situations covered in this section are pretty much part of the start-up journey. The key is to focus on your strengths (what got your start-up this far) and use the skills available in your team to tackle the issue head on.

Developing skills and expertise

A great way to support the growth of your company and avoid any hold-ups is to constantly work on your skill base and areas of expertise. Many successful start-ups constantly push the boundaries of their own knowledge and skills to achieve excellence in their core competencies.

Developing skills in your team and company is often a two-way process — not only do you need to respond to requests from staff to develop in a certain area but also highlight areas where team members can take on new responsibilities. But you can also undertake initiatives as a company to keep developmental opportunities open or to create inspirational challenges.

Here are a number of suggestions to help you manage skill development within your start-up:

✔ **Allow some free play:** Take a number of hours out every month and allow people to work on whatever they are interested in or something they want to learn. Google has done this successfully with their Google Friday program. Even if it's only two hours each month, give it a go — seeing how people use that time is worthwhile.

✔ **Organise a staff exchange:** You may be able to organise a short-term placement or secondment for team members with other start-ups. This is quite common and, as long as you have a good network of entrepreneurs, should be easy to set up. Ideally, organise exchanges where staff get an opportunity to work in a different area to pick up some useful skills. Keep in mind that even a week-long placement can be very useful.

✔ **Participate in suitable (and short) competitions:** Many initiatives exist in Australia and NZ to show off your skills or produce something new. Examples include Google's summer of code (code.google.com/soc) and O'Reilly Media's Foo Camp (see baacamp.org for the Kiwi version).

✔ **Present at an international conference:** If you get an opportunity to demonstrate something your company makes or does at an (inter)national event, go for it. In Australia and New Zealand, you have a choice of many suitable events every year (such as WebStock and XMedia Labs, to name but a few).

✔ **Take on an intern:** If one of your staff has an interest in mentoring or managing staff, ask that person to look after an intern. Check with your local university (or even internationally) for placement programs. You may be able to get your hands on some very talented students at a relatively small cost (such as a nominal salary that's then topped up by a supporting organisation).

Other techniques for upskilling, such as attending training courses, seminars or conferences, are also useful. However, start-ups often do things differently so don't be afraid to try out some unconventional ways for your staff to pick up new skills and expertise. When your venture is in transition from a tiny start-up to a recognised (small) business is a perfect time to do this (before your company has gotten too big and your HR policy gets in the way).

Partnering Up Versus Outsourcing

As you're working out how to do things better, faster and cheaper in your start-up, you may want to evaluate to what extent you can partner up with others to further accelerate your growth. The key aspect of partnering is really to work out what you consider a core skill or core asset of your company. In line with that, you need to know what you're good at and where you lack suitable expertise or scale to produce a high quality output, and so may benefit from partnering up.

The following sections cover all you need to know about partnering — working out the best business arrangements with possible partners, determining your core competencies and finding outsourcing opportunities.

Developing win–win business partnerships

Partnering can be a very useful strategy to accelerate growth. However, developing a fruitful business partnership requires careful consideration and planning. When your start-up takes off, you typically get approached by all sorts of companies that want to partner with you (success attracts a lot of attention). Unfortunately, many of these offers are actually useless — they're one-sided (with all of the benefits going to the other partner), become a distraction or end up as a huge drain on your resources without any upside.

Everyone involved needs to understand that partnerships must be based on a win–win relationship, with a clear understanding of contributions expected from each party. In other words, nobody should agree to any partnership unless you have had a chance to fully consider the potential merits and required effort.

Business partnerships aren't typically used to address resource shortages and hence tend to be very different from outsourcing arrangements. Business partnerships generally exist to develop a business opportunity that both partners benefit from, whereas outsourcing is typically used for executing a particular business function as a paid-for service, which may help with addressing resource shortages. (See the section 'Addressing skill shortages: Buying in skills and outsourcing' later in this chapter for more on outsourcing.)

In an ideal partnership, the two partners have complementary competencies or assets that each party can bring to the partnership. So, in order to participate successfully in a fruitful partnership, you need to know what your competencies (and assets) are. Hopefully, you already know this from running your business and understanding what your 'secret sauce' is — that is, what is it that you do differently to other companies that has resulted in the success of your business to date.

Core competencies can be just about every business function in your company. More often than not, core competencies are related to essential skills such as software development, marketing or customer service. Core assets can be your user base, network, product or service and so on.

When partnering with third parties, you need to understand how your core competencies or assets can be successfully combined with those of your potential partner to exploit a given business opportunity. For example, if your core asset is the subscriber base of your blog and someone offers you a partnership opportunity to turn your blog into a smartphone app, it may well be worth considering (especially if you have no skills in developing apps).

Make sure you do the maths on any partnership opportunity and work out the cost to you (and include indirect costs such as the time you need to spend on the partnership) versus the potential revenue opportunity (or other quantifiable benefits such as a brand exposure). Ideally, the potential upside of a partnership outweighs the cost by far. If the contribution of the potential partner can just as easily be achieved by simply buying the equivalent services, you may want to consider that as an alternative to partnering.

Business partnerships can be done in a number of ways — common constructs include joint ventures and co-branded marketing campaigns. (See *Web Marketing For Dummies*, 3rd Edition, by Jan Zimmerman and published by Wiley Publishing, Inc., for more information.)

Don't enter a business partnership without some form of agreement in place. At the very minimum, you need to have a memorandum of understanding when working with another company. The legal paperwork protects you from undesirable outcomes for your business. As usual, the devil's in the detail with partnership agreements, so I highly recommend involving your company lawyer to draft or check any agreements.

When agreeing to business partnerships, make sure you protect your intellectual property (IP) — that is, your hard-earned, validated product–market fit and your core assets. All of these recognised assets need to be mentioned specifically in the partnership agreement, and a mutual clause of respecting copyrights, IP and other assets between the two companies must be part of the agreement.

Addressing skill shortages: Buying in skills and outsourcing

As well as developing skills internally, you may need to consider 'buying in' skills for your start-up. Here are a few suggestions on how to do this:

- **Engage consultants:** A quick and effective solution for addressing skill shortages is to work with consultants or subject matter experts. Since consultants are usually quite expensive, it makes sense to only use these resources for specific tasks over short periods. The following is a list of useful areas of expertise where I believe it makes sense to use consultants for short engagements:

  - Human resources

  - IPO/public listing

Gamifying and interactive products

The concept of gamification or gamifying products or services refers to the use of game theory and game mechanics in otherwise non-game related contexts. Game mechanics include aspects like keeping score, awards and leaderboards. In gamification, these aspects are applied to ordinary (or even mundane) activities associated with a product or service. For example, foursquare.com makes extensive use of rewarding users with badges and social recognition for repeatedly 'checking-in' to venues (like a cafe, park or shopping centre).

A great use of gamification was demonstrated by Volkswagen with their concept site www.funtheory.com. The site challenged people to develop fun activities with social benefits. Perhaps the best-known example to come out of funtheory was the 'piano stairs' where an ordinary subway staircase was turned into a virtual piano keyboard. Piano key sounds would play as people stepped on each stair. As a result, more people chose to use the stairs rather than the escalator, which was situated right next to them.

- IT security

- Media relations (for significant media releases)

- New market entry

- New technology and trends (such as gamification and cloud computing)

- Specific compliance tasks (such as US Food and Drug Administration approval)

- Website or web app performance tuning

✔ **Find additional business partners:** Sometimes the most suitable way to cover a skill shortage is to bring on an additional business partner (such as another director who also buys into the business). However, this is the most complex option — refer to Chapter 2.

✔ **Hire freelancers and contractors:** Working with freelancers and contractors is similar to but generally a bit cheaper (sometimes a lot cheaper) than working with consultants, especially over longer periods. Another benefit when using freelancers is that you can advertise a freelance job on common job boards such as `seek.com.au` and `thebigidea.co.nz`. The job ad also functions as advertising for your company and generally increases traffic and interest. Make sure you put a sound contract in place (use a template — see Appendix B for an example) and be very clear about the contractors' responsibilities and the term of the engagement.

In addition to the options outlined in the preceding list, you can consider *outsourcing*, which usually involves choosing a specific function within your company and outsourcing its management to a third party.

The key differences between buying in skills and outsourcing are responsibility and implications of non-performance. In outsourcing contracts, the provider guarantees the service to a defined service level — if they fail to do so, the contract usually defines the resulting penalties. For example, most hosting contracts include performance agreements for uptime — the website has to be up for 99.9 per cent of the time. For every hour that the website isn't available below this percentage, the hosting provider has to pay a certain amount (as agreed in the contract). In comparison, if you've hired system administrators to run the website server and the website goes down, the administrators do their best to get the site up again but wouldn't have any agreed service levels in the contract and certainly no penalties.

Start-ups can benefit hugely from outsourcing (especially in the early years) if the functions being outsourced are selected correctly and the corresponding outsourcing contracts are suitably structured.

As a general rule, never outsource any part of your core assets or core competencies. This is important because your core assets and related core competencies make all the difference in a company. Typically, core competencies are also hard to copy and so form part of your competitive advantage. For many web-based businesses, development of online applications and platforms is a core competency but hosting a website or web-based application may not be (because it requires expensive IT infrastructure and highly specialised knowledge). That's why many web-based businesses use a hosting provider rather than hosting their websites internally.

Pay close attention to the structure of outsourcing contracts (in general) and, in particular, to any functions that affect external communications such as customer service, media relations and investor relations. I strongly recommend you keep control of these functions even if operational components are outsourced For example, control any media relations by requiring a 'sign off' for any media releases that are put together by an agency, and control customer service by putting in place stringent performance benchmarks (such as issue resolution time, customer feedback scores or telesales revenue).

If you're considering a particular outsourcing service, speak to existing clients of that service and ask about their experiences with the outsourcing provider. Check with them how they structured their contracts to ensure service objectives and performance metrics are met.

Facing Product Development Decisions

You may think new product development is a bottleneck in your business. However, one of the things that start-ups do a lot better than large enterprises (typically) is being able to drive their businesses at a faster pace. That is, start-ups can generally reduce the amount of time it takes to release new software (for example, to offer new features), acquire new users or customers, and respond to new trends or market opportunities.

Large companies (even the ones that used to be start-ups themselves) tend to slow down once they get to a certain size. Frequently, when companies have more than about 250 employees, things tend to slow down because internal processes must be introduced to maintain consistency and control.

You can use this 'corporate inertia' to your advantage and outexecute everyone else in your space, then defend your competitive advantage — by doing everything faster than everyone else. That way you're also at least one step ahead of your competition.

Online products are essentially based on software development, so one way you can stay ahead of your larger competitors is to commit to a certain release cycle — for example, a release of at least one new feature each month. You then need to structure your team around this monthly release cycle.

If you commit to a monthly release cycle with your start-up business, the release date is sacred. Come hell or high water you must release on the release date. This method provides a certain discipline and focus to improve the product quickly.

One way you can ensure you're presenting your customers with the most up-to-date and relevant product is to use the *perpetual prototype* approach. This approach works by offering an existing product and its modified prototype at the same time. (You can do the same with your products by never removing the 'beta' label from your site.) This approach enables start-ups to finetune products and services for a long time, and achieves a number of objectives that help them to remain agile and responsive.

Using a perpetual prototype sends a clear signal to users that you're actively working on the system and inviting them to try out new products or features. In return, you generally get immediate feedback from users, who indicate whether they like the updated prototype or not. Sometimes, you may need to roll back a change because users didn't like it — but that's much easier to do when the change only affected the prototype version of your product.

Use a *Pareto chart* to decide which features of your software to work on for the next release. Pareto charts provide a simple mechanism to determine the likely impact of a particular intervention. You can measure the impact in aspects such as cost, revenue, number of complaints or number of feature requests. Typically, you measure the impact as a relative percentage value compared to the overall problem or opportunity. For example, if your company gets a total of 100 support requests a month and you have categorised them by problem area, you can create a Pareto chart that allows you to identify by what percentage you can reduce your 100 support requests if you address a given problem. This also works for revenue opportunities or feature requests from users. As a general principle, you should always optimise on particular criteria (such as cost, revenue or effort) rather than work on features that your developers like best. (Lots of further information on **Pareto charts** is available online — just enter the term in your search engine.)

Companies like Facebook have demonstrated the perpetual prototype concept successfully by simultaneously offering an existing product and its modified prototype. For example, the Facebook timeline option was made available for several months as a beta product before it was released to all users.

Facing Strategic Technology Decisions

The growth path of your start-up is littered with minor and major hurdles. One potentially major hurdle is the ability for your underlying technology to scale up. Rapidly growing start-ups can go from processing a handful of sales transactions to handling well over 100,000 sales transactions within a couple of years. When you consider these enormous growth rates, it's not surprising that strategic decisions about underlying technology platforms and core applications are required every one to two years (or maybe even more frequently in extreme cases).

Fortunately, scaling up has become easier with the availability of cloud-based platforms but you may still be required to go through redeveloping or replacing your core technology. You may also need to look at how and when you make new software developments available, and whether you should tackle technology problems by building or buying in solutions. Another situation you may be faced with is a malicious attack of your online application or website. The following sections cover all of these aspects.

Redeveloping your core technology

Ideally, you don't want any aspect of technology restricting your business growth. Unfortunately, that's not always possible because technology solutions cost money (one way or another, even when using open source software). As such, starting out with a system that can support the operations of a start-up all the way to an enterprise level corporation may not be possible (no matter what all the IT vendors say). Most likely you need to use different solutions at various stages of your business growth. As a business person you may not understand the exact details of the technology your company is using. However, you need to understand the key parameters of the solutions in place and work out the best timing and scope of technology replacement projects.

I highly recommend developing a proper business case for any redevelopment project you're considering. Beware of making a habit of 'fire fighting' (that is, only reacting to major crises) or 'just doing' (replacing technology on the fly without planning or preparation). Neither of these modes are generally successful for start-ups and, given that you're changing the core technology (and perhaps the core asset) of your business, developing a sound business rationale for the upgrade make sense.

If you have a board of directors, any major technology upgrades or replacements typically have to be signed off by the board, so having a business case and recommendation ready for the next board meeting is a good idea — that way, the matter can be discussed and a decision can be documented.

Scope

So, you've identified that your business growth is hampered by technology and you need to upgrade. But where do you draw the line with upgrading? Do you upgrade your entire technology stack (for example, eCommerce platform, content management system, programming language and all other components)? Or do you just replace a specific element (for example, adding more disk space, buying the enterprise version of an existing application)? It can be tricky to work out which option is the most suitable for your business.

A commonly used technique to make these types of decisions is to use a cost benefit analysis (CBA), which compares a number of scenarios. CBAs generally consider three scenarios: The *status quo* scenario (continuing with the existing technology), the *quick-fix* scenario (adding patches or upgrades to existing technology) and the *new platform* scenario (redevelopment or replacement).

When comparing these options, make sure you have realistic estimates of cost and use your current business data (such as sales volume) to predict future benefits and cost savings. Also consider the following aspects in your CBA:

- ✔ **Downtime cost:** The cost of unavailability of the technology (either due to increased failure rates or while replacing the technology).

- ✔ **Opportunity cost:** The cost of missing out on revenue or growth as a result of not having an unconstrained technology in place.

- ✔ **Switching cost:** The cost of introducing new technology (including cost of installation, training and productivity loss).

 Another useful technique when completing the CBA is to work out a *revenue minute* figure for your website — that is, the total revenue generated from the site per month (including all transactions, subscriptions and advertisements) divided by the number of minutes per month (for example, 31 days × 24 hours × 60 minutes). This gives you an idea of the financial effect of any downtime on your site as a result of performance issues or upgrades.

Timing

Like determining the scope of your upgrades (refer to preceding section), getting the timing right for your technology upgrades or redevelopment option is also not that straightforward. Typically, a good time to do any work on core technology or applications never appears (because the 'show must go on' while you're upgrading).

 Having a solid CBA in place (refer to preceding section) is crucial to ensuring you base your decision on the timing of your technology upgrade on sound business principles. Otherwise, the decision just involves guesswork or intuition, which generally doesn't work out that well. Once you've done your CBA, you can factor in some time-dependent variables such as cash flow (available capital), staff availability, growth predictions, and known events, and work out how your CBA score changes dependent on different dates or periods.

Sometimes you don't even have an option for when you perform your upgrades, because a major technology change is forced upon you (for example, because the software version you're using is no longer supported). However, as a general rule, err on the side of urgency — when you're a start-up, embarking on a technology upgrade or replacement project too early is better than doing so too late. In a rapid growth scenario, you just don't have time to wait around.

You also need to do some serious planning about how gradually you should phase in your upgrades or a new platform. Your business situation typically dictates whether to use a gradual phase-out and phase-in approach or an immediate switch. Sometimes, you can make use of periods when business is slow (such as between Christmas and New Year) to roll out some major upgrades.

 Make sure you consider business factors (such as transaction volume, staff availability, holiday periods, cash flow and anything else that could affect an upgrade) when planning a technology upgrade or replacement.

Making build or buy decisions

Sometimes a quick way to resolve bottle necks or achieve scale is to switch to an enterprise-level product. You may also need to automate a process that up until now you have done manually (for example, order processing). This is a classic scenario for many businesses — and one where you need to decide whether to build a suitable solution from scratch (perhaps even in-house) or to buy an existing solution that is then customised to your needs.

With your start-up, your bias should be towards 'buy' decisions for any solution that's not considered part of your company's core business. This is because time is usually the most critical aspect to consider in start-ups. So being able to buy and implement a solution quickly is worth more than potentially saving a few hundred dollars by building a solution internally. However, the time factor (that is, how quickly a solution can be fully implemented) for buying an existing product typically depends on how well that product fits with all your other systems. In other words, the benefits of buying a readymade product may be reduced by how difficult it is to integrate it with your existing IT infrastructure.

Table 6-1 provides an overview of the pros and cons of creating a custom product versus buying a readymade one.

Table 6-1   Creating a Custom Product Versus Buying a Readymade Solution

Custom Product	*Readymade Product*
Pros	
Easy to integrate with existing systems	Available immediately
Provides best fit with needs or requirements	Problems (bugs) with software are responsibility of vendor
Full access to source code for modifications	Utilise expertise and scale of vendor
Cons	
Development risk is carried internally	Integration risk is carried internally
Requires time to develop (including delays)	Reliance on vendor for software updates and support
Expertise to implement a good solution may not be available in-house	May not fulfil needs and modifications to software may be difficult (or impossible)

Depending on the situation, each approach may provide a cost advantage (sometimes building a system from scratch is cheaper; at other times buying is less expensive). However, for start-ups time is usually the most critical factor and so buying a solution is typically more suitable — especially if you can be flexible with requirements (that is, accept compromises on features and functionality) and so have the solution available quickly.

Improving your system security and responding to hacks

When you're starting out and working through many iterations
of a prototype or beta product, security is typically not an issue.
However, when your company has assets that represent value to
others, it's pretty much 'open season' for anyone wanting a piece
of your business cake. Success and value attract attention — no
matter whether that's a physical asset or a virtual asset like a
website. So you need to prepare yourself for the onslaught of
hackers and take precaution to protect your assets.

Note: The following provides a quick overview of preventing
and responding to online threats. For more detailed information,
see *Hacking For Dummies*, 3rd Edition, by Kevin Beaver, and
Networking All-in-One For Dummies, 4th Edition, by Doug Lowe
(both published by Wiley Publishing, Inc.).

Prevention

While protecting against online threats is a topic that fills books,
you can implement a number of practical measures for a basic
level of protection. If you don't have a technical background, you
can use the following measures to check with your development
and system administration team.

Make sure your IT people are watching for the following:

- ✔ **Automated daily offsite backups of your core
  systems:** These come in handy if your system has been
  compromised and you need to get back to the last stable
  state.

- ✔ **Hosting security in place:** Work with your hosting
  provider to set up firewall protection and other security
  mechanisms. They can usually provide a reasonable level
  of security for little effort and cost.

- ✔ **Intrusion detection:** Many IT systems can be set up
  to monitor any unusual activity and send alerts when
  suspicious activity is detected. Work with your IT team to
  set these up for your core business systems.

- ✔ **Non-standard configuration:** All standard set-ups (such as
  default passwords and address ports) should be changed
  to a non-standard set-up to prevent the risk of automated
  'brute force' attacks.

✔ **Regular patching of all system components:** All components in your system, and especially open source components, need to be updated frequently to avoid security risks as a result of known loopholes (usually referred to as *exploits*)

✔ **SQL injection filters:** One of the most common security threats for websites is a technique called *SQL injection* where hackers enter programming language in the online form fields to try to access information from the site and/or corrupt the site. (Much more information is available online; just type **SQL injection** into your favourite search engine.) Get confirmation from your development team that measures are in place to prevent SQL injection attacks.

✔ **Stringent password policy:** All systems should enforce non-trivial passwords (such as through the mandatory use of special characters in passwords). Don't allow any names or words in the English dictionary as passwords. Again, this is to prevent automated brute force attacks.

✔ **Virus protection.** This is pretty much a no-brainer for all computing equipment based on Windows operating systems. All laptops and PCs used in your company should have a minimum level of protection.

You don't need to spend a huge amount on security. Free virus protection software is available. Some products have limited usage periods — meaning they expire after 30 days or so — but the version offered by Avira (www.avira.com) is free with no expiry date.

✔ **'We'll be right back' page:** Create a simple web page on a completely separate system that displays a short message to customers that the system is temporarily unavailable. If you become aware of an attack, you can simply switch your systems to point to this page while you work on restoring your systems and services.

The preceding list is only a starter list — many more techniques are required to achieve an adequate level of protection. A 100 per cent secure system doesn't exist, and in reality security is a function of cost — that is, the more money you're prepared to spend on security measures, the more secure your system. For start-ups (and, in fact, all companies), the level of security protection they employ is a constant balance between security risk and implications of a security breach on one hand and security-related cost and effort on the other.

Set up a simple risk framework for security threats, where you assess implications of a breach. For example, if your site is down for two days, how much revenue are you likely to lose? How much brand value is likely to be destroyed from negative press about a 'hack'? Once you consider these factors, you can develop a rationale (or a formula) for setting a security budget.

PayPal spends a significant percentage of their revenue on protection against security threats. The company must do that because their entire business is based on ensuring secure financial transactions.

Response

The first rule of responding to a security breach or hack is 'don't panic'. Here's a suggested process you can go through when you become aware of a security breach:

1. **Hold an immediate crisis meeting with key staff to assess the extent of the breach**.

    The main purpose of this meeting is to quickly decide whether the entire system (website) needs to be shut down.

2. **Shut down the affected parts of the system or the entire system immediately.**

    If possible, put up a holding page that displays a message to your users that the system is temporarily unavailable.

3. **Change all system passwords and address ports immediately**

4. **Split your team into three main areas of responsibility: Detecting how the breach happened, restoring services, and dealing with media, customer and user enquiries.**

5. **Attempt to restore services.**

    Only attempt restoration if you can be certain that the loophole that led to the security breach can't be used again to compromise the system.

Once services have been restored and the security loophole has been closed, investigate the extent of the damage caused by the breach. Retrace the steps of the attackers and find out whether they have accessed or stolen any sensitive information (for example, credit card details, personal information, contact details or any other personal details). Compile a comprehensive report of all damages.

If any users or customers are severely affected by the breach (for example, because credit card information was stolen from your system), contact all users immediately to make them aware of the situation. Contact credit card companies and the police.

If users were only affected by the unavailability of your services, prepare a statement to be sent out to all users with a sincere apology, as well as an explanation of what happened, what measures you have put in place to prevent similar issues and a form of adequate compensation for the inconvenience caused.

Following a security breach or attack, you may want to get an external security audit done by a specialist firm. Once your system has been attacked, it's likely to be attacked again in the future. You need to put extra measures in place to protect against future attacks.

Sometimes you can actually contact attackers (for example, through an open request on the site to get in touch) and make them an offer to disclose how they 'got in' and what they were doing in the system. This is somewhat tricky but can be faster and cheaper than doing the detective work yourself. Whether or not this strategy is advisable highly depends on the level of maliciousness displayed by the attacker. If they just did it for fun, working with them is probably feasible. If they're professional hackers who are after valuable data, it may not be feasible.

Let's Talk About Business Continuity

When your company reaches a certain size and level of transactions, you need to make sure that 'the lights don't go out' no matter what happens. For online business, this usually means the online (or mobile) platform is always available. But it also means that the business can continue when minor and major dramas happen internally (for example, a key person gets sick). So you need to think about 'business continuity' and take measures to ensure your business can carry on no matter what.

Here are some suggestions for things to put in place to ensure business continuity:

- ✔ **Define your business processes:** As much as possible, create documents (even little run sheets or reminders can help) that document how to complete any business-critical processes, like fulfilling an order or putting through a credit card charge.

- ✔ **Implement technology enhancements:** Work with your IT team to make use of techniques to increase the availability of your systems (for example, through redundancy, load balancing or failover systems). Same goes for the ability to recover quickly from an outage (through having a robust back-up strategy in place).

- ✔ **Manage your knowledge:** Encourage knowledge transfer as much as possible so that your team spreads key knowledge across multiple people. In case someone is sick or unavailable, you should have someone else who knows how to complete the most critical tasks of the absent person.

- ✔ **Nominate a 'second in charge':** Organise roles and responsibilities in your team in such a way that clear rules are in place to state who can make decisions when the usual decision-maker isn't available. Also consider availability of key staff when planning holidays or other absences.

- ✔ **Plan:** Ensure contact information for staff is constantly shared and up to date. During critical periods, work out an emergency roster system so that someone is always available to make decisions or check systems.

Customers and competitors can be pretty unforgiving when it comes to business downtime. For most online start-ups these days, this means 24-hour availability, 365 days a year. Make sure your business is able to live up to this expectation.

Recognising When to Move On

After your launch and the initial growth period, you may also realise that somehow your company isn't showing any signs of taking off. You've tried numerous combinations of market and customer hypotheses, you've listened attentively to customers and have launched multiple versions of your product or service.

But despite your best efforts, you haven't found the magic formula (yet). At the same time, you realise that your resources and the energy levels in the team are running low.

While you may be just going through another episode of the 'start-up blues' (refer to Chapter 4), it may also be something more serious. (If you've already gone through one or more periods of the start-up blues, you may also be able to tell that this time round the situation is different.) You may need to look seriously at the viability of your company and start-up, or whether or not you personally still want to be involved with it.

Here are some warning signs to look out for that can indicate serious viability issues for your company:

- ✔ **Customer churn:** If customers consistently abandon your product or leave your service (for example, unsubscribe) after they have experienced it, you should be concerned. This is a worry, especially if this happens over long periods and despite making changes to your offering.

- ✔ **Disruption:** This can occur when a strong and well-resourced competitor has emerged and is going head to head with you, or when a new technology or innovation has become widely available that renders your product or service irrelevant.

- ✔ **Inability to charge:** If you offer a popular product or service but all attempts to charge for it (or run it supported by advertising revenue) fail consistently, it's time for a serious re-think.

- ✔ **Mounting debt:** If your company is in financial dire straits and all of your resources are tapped out, you need to stop and think. Investors don't like investing in companies that are almost bankrupt — so if you don't know how to pay your bills or how to meet payroll, suspend operations and evaluate your options.

- ✔ **Personal crises:** If you or someone in your family is going through a serious personal crisis, you may need to put your business on hold (or wind down) and go back to employment with a large company while you sort out the crisis.

Watch out for recurring personal health issues because these can often appear as a result of continued stress and a work–life balance that's out of kilter.

✔ **Website traffic downtrend:** If your website traffic pattern shows a general downwards trend, or your traffic only picks up with expensive advertising but afterwards goes back to pre-campaign levels (or below), it's time to worry.

Most entrepreneurs aren't able to fulfil their dreams with the first, second or third business they start. In some cases, many attempts are required to crack a particular business model and create a wildly successful company. So you should feel no shame in closing down a start-up if you believe you've satisfied yourself that there's no point in carrying on. Winding down the business quickly and cleanly is much better than letting the company die a slow, messy and painful death.

Your reputation as an entrepreneur is in part based on your ability to shut up shop at the right time to focus on your next project. Investors welcome entrepreneurs with this kind of experience — in fact, my company WebFund doesn't usually work with entrepreneurs who haven't experienced business failure before. Letting go of your dream and closing down a company involves something that's highly educating, and the experience gained is extremely useful for the next business you start.

So don't be discouraged to try again or become a bitter entrepreneur angry at the world. This is the stuff that true entrepreneurs are made of — the ability to experience setbacks and pick yourself up again to embrace the next opportunity with the same level of enthusiasm as the last.

When you do decide to close down the business, do yourself a favour and capture key lessons learnt in whatever way makes sense (for example, record a podcast, write a book or organise a debriefing session with your team). Do whatever works to make sure you don't repeat the same mistakes in your next venture.

These days your online footprint is very easy to check and is usually more revealing than any CV you ever write. So don't block out any future opportunities because you left a mess with one of your previous companies. Make sure you close down your business cleanly — honour all liabilities and communicate your decision clearly to staff and customers. Look for options to provide a form of continuation for existing customers — don't just switch off your service and leave them in a pickle.

Typically, you can identify a competitor or alternative service that can take over your customer base and continue servicing your customers. If no suitable options are available for your customers, give them enough notice before shutting down. Same goes for suppliers and business partners.

Once your start-up is closed down properly, have a drink with your team, investors and business partners and go out of business in style.

Don't get too upset, worried or distracted by what other entrepreneurs tell you about their start-ups. In my experience, all entrepreneurs — no matter how famous or well funded — are essentially in the same boat with their start-up. Everyone is trying to create something from nothing, which can be hard! To the outside world, most entrepreneurs paint a rosy picture of their venture — everything is going really well, the product uptake is massive, and investors are queuing up to invest. More often than not, the story on the inside is completely different and these same entrepreneurs have to overcome the same challenges that we all face. While it can be tough to constantly hear from others about how well things are going for them when you are slogging your guts out in your own start-up, also know that a lot of what others tell you is essentially hogwash. Don't let stories from others distract you. Stick to your guns, keep your head down, and keep executing your idea. You might find that your start-up is the one that ends up actually getting bought or starts making real money, while the others are still just talking the talk.

Chapter 7

Growing Strategically

· ·

· ·

*W*hen your company has not only 'cracked the magic formula' but is also generating significant revenue or, even better, making a profit, you have made it through to a very pleasant part of your start-up journey (yes — this is when you typically upgrade your life and put in an order for a ridiculous car).

In this chapter, I cover the aspects that become the main focus of your business as it matures. I look at expansion strategies, attracting capital, maturing your internal processes and structures, and staying ahead of your competitors. A lot of the work ahead of you now lies in effectively preparing your business for the next stage of its journey (which may or may not involve you).

Expansion Strategies

Once you have a profitable company, you may be keen to expand your business by offering additional products or services. Unless the new products or services you wish to offer are just variations of your existing offering (for example, through offering a basic-, premium- and enterprise-level version of an application), this step requires careful consideration. Creating lots of additional products or services (because your existing ones are going well) is tempting, as is immediately seeking to sell into other geographies.

However, keep in mind how you got to where you are now — through lots of testing, adjustments and re-testing. The same process is required when launching new products or entering new markets. The approach you should take when expanding your business is rarely obvious and so in the following sections I share some tips on what to consider when making this move.

When offering variations of existing products or services, make sure you're not creating a risk of *cannibalisation* of your existing customer base (where you're just eating into existing sales). Many airlines experienced this, and had to shut down or sell their 'budget' products because these were cannibalising existing business.

Companies generally use two main strategies to grow their businesses once they reach market saturation or max out their market share, as follows:

- ✔ Same market, complementary (or new) product
- ✔ Same products, different market (typically different geography or different vertical market)

I cover these options in the following sections, as well as ways to enhance your brand.

Following a radical expansion strategy — where, for example, you launch a new product in a different market — is rarely a wise move because with such an approach you're literally starting again from scratch. If you believe you need to expand in this fashion (perhaps because you have another business idea), you may want to consider spinning off a different company to explore other opportunities. That way, if the new business doesn't work out, your existing (profitable) company isn't affected.

Expanding your product or service offering

When considering the launch of another product or service (that's significantly different to your existing offering), ask yourself the following:

- ✔ What knowledge or expertise have you acquired from developing your existing product or service that gives you a distinct advantage over competitors?

✔ What compelling market factors exist that prompt a new product or service launch?

✔ To what extent have you gone through the same process of product–market hypothesis and market testing with the new offering?

✔ Do any economies of scale exist that you can take advantage of with your new product or service (for example, shared development or customer service teams)?

✔ Do you have enough resources (human and financial) to ensure that the new product or service launch doesn't negatively affect your existing operations?

No matter how you organise the launch of a different product or service in your existing market, your existing company structure, processes and operations are going to be affected by it. Here are some suggestions to improve your chances of success when launching new products and services:

✔ **Create a new organisational unit for your new products or services.** This makes resource allocation, tracking and reporting much easier.

✔ **Develop a complete business case for every new product or service launch.** Launching a new product or service is like launching another company in many ways. So make sure you've done your homework on finances, business models, resourcing, and customer and market analyses (refer to Chapters 2 and 3).

✔ **Make your new organisational unit into a 'profit centre' or 'profit and loss' unit.** This usually comes with some accounting complexities but works out in the long run when you need to figure out whether or not the new unit is actually profitable. Also consider how you account for the costs of shared services, such as office space, admin and IT support.

✔ **Put someone in charge of the new products or services.** You need someone who's responsible (and accountable) for making your new offering successful. Work with this person to create a management structure (including responsibility for staff and finances) that enables clear accountabilities for the new products or services.

Looking at upstream and downstream expansion

Upstream and downstream expansion offer some interesting ways to expand your start-up business. *Upstream* expansion is where you go from offering a specific product or service to creating a platform (of products and services). A good example is companies that sell website ads. An upstream expansion would be selling ads for other companies on the same site or creating a system that allows other companies to sell and purchase advertising slots and advertising collateral.

Downstream expansion is where you go from selling products to selling accessories or complementary services around the product. A successful product is the seed of a portfolio of other products and services. On an app or game this might be status, electronic goods or expansion packs — and the game Angry Birds, which started as an app and has since expanded into versions of the game being created for personal computers and gaming consoles, and merchandise being sold based on its characters, is a fantastic example of this strategy.

When considering new products or services, you should also consider your brand and whether or not it could use some finessing. See the section 'Enhancing your brand' later in the chapter for more on this.

Exploring other geographies

When looking to grow the business, perhaps an even more common approach than launching an entirely new product or service (refer to preceding section) is geographic expansion.

Most MBA students have to study business cases of failed geographical expansions, because this kind of move is often not well-considered or planned out. Many entrepreneurs assume because they have been successful in one territory, they know how to sell their product or service in another, but this is often not the case.

The implications for your business when considering an entry into another market are similar to the factors listed in the preceding section. However, you also need to consider a few additional factors and the following is a list of the most common mistakes start-ups make when launching in other geographies:

- ✔ **Having no knowledge of the local market und culture.** The world is a diverse place and 'doing business' typically varies a lot from one country to another. Even among English-speaking countries, significant differences in language and culture exist. A common mistake is to assume that the same market rules, consumer behaviour and buying preferences exist in another market.

  Avoid having to learn expensive lessons yourself on local domain knowledge. Hire local experts or work with advisors who are experienced in the market you intend to expand to.

- ✔ **Only offering a straight translation of your software, website, or product or service descriptions.** Simply translating your offerings often leads to embarrassing or inadequate presentations of products or services because cultural factors are often not sufficiently considered. A better approach is to *transcreate* content or descriptions, where you translate but also create new aspects. Ideally, all content should be written by locals who can work with your team to explain how to position products and services in a way that fits with the local culture.

- ✔ **Servicing other geographies remotely.** Many start-ups don't consider the operational implications of servicing other geographies adequately. A big problem is managing operations when dealing with different time zones (especially when offering customer service or support remotely). Make sure you think about resourcing your business support processes in a way that makes it feasible for customers in other markets to deal with your company (in the same way your customers deal with local companies). The risk is that your products or services get a bad reputation — in the same way that overseas call centres have gotten a bad reputation in Australia and New Zealand.

For start-ups in Australia and New Zealand, launching in the United States or the United Kingdom seems an obvious expansion. However, many entrepreneurs underestimate the differences that exist between our region and these two markets. Doing business in the United States especially, but also in the United Kingdom, is very different. On top of the cultural (and language differences), you're likely to experience differences in aspects such as the sales processes, contracting and consumer laws. Familiarise yourself with all these aspects before launching in either of these two regions. Work with ex-pats or local teams to create a suitable offering in these markets.

Developing other markets

Expanding into other markets doesn't necessarily mean a geographic diversification; you can also offer the same product in a different *vertical* market (a market of all new customers within your existing geography).

 A good example of developing into vertical markets is Facebook, which originally only targeted the college and university student market (and a student ID was required to register). Over time, Facebook opened up more and more markets including the corporate market (such as through allowing companies to have a Facebook page). The essential product and features of Facebook stayed the same throughout this expansion into other markets.

Compared to expanding your business through offering new products or services or through moving into new geographies (see preceding sections), expanding vertically is perhaps the simplest and least risky way to grow your business. Still, you need to consider any expansion well so that you don't waste efforts on something that doesn't create any returns. Writing a business case for the planned expansion provides a useful discipline to make sure your business doesn't rush into this initiative.

Enhancing your brand

Your company's brand deserves a closer look when considering a new product or service, or a new geography or market. When considering these expansion strategies, companies generally use two approaches:

- ✓ **Branded house:** This usually refers to a diverse collection of products and services under a common label (usually displaying a particular characteristic of the main brand, such as agility or thriftiness). Prime examples of these types of brands include Virgin, the Easy Group or even Apple. Frequently the organisation that underlies a branded house is a group of organisation units (or even separate companies), which all operate independently. However, the overall brand of the group is prominently displayed and strict rules about brand usage are enforced across all products and services.

✔ **House of brands:** This is where a company manages a portfolio of products or services that all have separate, independent brands. Companies in the fast-moving consumer goods (FMCG) sector are often organised in this way. Examples include Proctor & Gamble, Toyota or Coca-Cola. In this case, the brand of the individual products or services dominates and the brand of the company that makes these is of secondary importance.

As soon as you have two products that aren't directly related and address different markets, you need to figure out which branding strategy you want to pursue. My recommendation is to initially launch the new product or service under a separate brand (but perhaps with a by-line like 'powered by [your company name]'). If your new product or service doesn't do well, you can simply cut your losses and focus on your main product. If the new product or service does well, you can consider creating a branded house at a later stage.

Even if you're not expanding your product range or markets, consider how well your current brand fits with your products and services. In many cases, start-ups create their brands in a bit of a hurry and on a limited budget. When your company has grown significantly and is profitable, you can further add value to your company by enhancing your brand.

Here are some suggestions for ways to enhance your brand:

✔ **Definition:** You may not actually need to change your brand but you may need to define it properly, which can add value to your company. By defining your brand in detail, you can ensure that the brand is used consistently and correctly at each interaction with your customers. For example, the use of images in your advertising collateral or even the style of writing ads are all highly influenced by your brand and should be consistent. Inconsistencies in presentation or messaging confuse customers, which can lead to missed sales opportunities. You can also better align your internal corporate culture with brand values and the brand essence.

✔ **Rebranding:** Sometimes the best way to deal with a brand is to replace it (perhaps because it no longer represents a suitable image for your products, services or company).

A rebranding exercise isn't trivial. You need to work with experienced professionals who have done similar projects before. Ideally, you're able to test new brands with existing customers on a small scale before committing to a complete rebrand.

✔ **Refinement:** The halfway house between defining your brand and rebranding is to refine it. Refinement also includes defining your brand properly but typically includes a form of modification as well, such as a colour scheme change, logo change or update, change of fonts or tone of voice. If you search online for the historical use of logos for many consumer products, you can see how they have been refined or refreshed over time. (Some brands to start your search with include Holiday Inn, British Airways or Shell.)

The best way to define your brand properly, and ensure it's used consistently and correctly, is to hire an agency or brand specialist.

Attracting Capital to Accelerate Growth

At various stages of your start-up journey, you may need to consider raising capital to fund the various initiatives you have planned for your business. During the early stages, most entrepreneurs need funds to get a product or service out the door. During later stages of the evolution, funds are typically required for the survival of the company or to finance business growth. Whatever the situation, fundraising is an interesting and often complex process that all successful entrepreneurs understand (and do well). The following sections cover options for fundraising, what to do (and not to do) when approaching potential investors and how investment affects your existing company structure. (These sections cover raising funds from private investors or investment firms — the process for public listings differs from the other forms of attracting capital and I describe this in Chapter 9.)

Raising capital: Your options and preparation

In Chapter 2, I list the main options for attracting capital into your business. During the later stages of your start-up journey, some of these options may no longer apply — for example, friends or family may not have the kind of funds your business needs. Once the business has been established and is generating revenue (or profit), most start-ups rely on attracting capital from business angels, private investors, venture capitalists (VCs) or through a public listing.

Your source of funding typically determines the process you follow for attracting capital. When applying to business angels and VCs, they generally outline what you need to do to be considered for funding (refer to Chapter 2 for more details). Working with private investors is often less structured but you can still follow similar principles. In all cases, you can go through an internal process that helps achieve a successful outcome.

Here's a suggestion of an internal process to follow when raising capital:

1. **Identify the investment opportunity and clearly quantify the capital requirement to fund your business.**

2. **Determine the planned return on investment and document assumptions and projections.**

3. **Put together a high-level document that outlines the opportunity for external investors.**

   Include all terms of the investment deal — most importantly, share price, equity stake and other key parameters, what the investment is used for, and how and what kind of return can be expected (and over what period).

4. **Create an informal and high-level investment deck.**

   The *investment deck* is a set of slides that describes your business, the investment opportunity (the key terms of the investment deal, as outlined in Step 3), as well as what the investment funds are to be used for. These slides can be distributed among potential investors. ***Note:*** Keep the deck short — no more than 10 slides.

5. **Test the investment deck with friendly investors or advisors to improve and refine.**

6. **Craft a short investment pitch that you can deliver when an opportunity to speak to an investor presents itself.**

   Aim for your pitch to describe the opportunity but only be about 30 to 90 seconds long. Write the pitch down, edit it to perfection and learn to deliver it with impact. These short pitches are usually referred to as *elevator pitches* and you need to have one readily available for your business if you want to get serious about raising capital. The purpose of a an elevator pitch is to get an interested party to want to know more about the opportunity.

7. **Identify suitable sources of funding and research them.**

   Learn about the potential investment sources' processes, previous investments, current investment interests and how to best approach them (and whether or not you can engineer an introduction).

Once you have completed the preparation tasks outlined in the preceding list, you can start approaching investors. A lot about successful fundraising depends on how well you are prepared.

Entrepreneurs make many mistakes when trying to raise funds. Here's a list of the more common ones:

- ✔ **Being desperate:** Ironically, the best position to raise capital from is when you don't need any money. Investors don't like investing in companies that are financially distressed or, if they do, they generally dictate the terms.

- ✔ **Not being able to tell a convincing story:** Many entrepreneurs with highly successful companies and promising ideas fail to attract investment because they can't articulate themselves or they present an unconvincing proposition to investors. (Refer to Chapter 2.)

- ✔ **Not having a cornerstone investor:** Investment deals are often done through *syndication* (where many parties and individuals come together to invest in a business). Problem is, someone has to be the first one to invest so others can follow (investors can be a bit like lemmings). This person or party is usually referred to as the *cornerstone* investor, or lead investor, and having someone in place is a crucial step in successful funding rounds. Sometimes you're better off deferring funding rounds (if possible) until you can confirm a cornerstone investor.

✔ **Not having your records in order:** Once investors are interested, they generally want to have a look at your books (and in some cases follow a *due diligence* process, where you disclose all relevant information to the investor). Often, an investment deal fails at this stage because the necessary information is either not available at all or not in a useful state (for example, all records are kept in a shoe box).

✔ **Not knowing what to do with the money:** You may be surprised to find out how many entrepreneurs struggle to answer a simple and common question: 'What are you going to do with the (investment) money?' Anyone raising any capital needs to be able to answer this question automatically. Another common question to prepare for is the following: 'What would you do if we gave you double the money you're asking for?' Investors use this question to gauge the size of the opportunity they've been presented.

✔ **Overvaluing:** Unfortunately, most entrepreneurs significantly overvalue their companies and are inflexible when it comes to agreeing on a fair value. An external valuation is often a good way to get a reality check on the company's most likely value and provides a useful mechanism to progress on negotiations with investors. See valuecruncher.com for more.

✔ **Starting too late:** Successful fundraising requires a 'warming up' of investors over several months (sometimes years). This is an informal process (and usually involves having coffee with people and talking about the business) that happens casually over time. However, these informal chats are often the key to closing a funding round because investors already know about you and your business when it comes to the official pitch.

In almost all cases, a start-up is much better off with an investor on board even if the investment deal goes through at a lower share price than expected.

Unfortunately, a lot of deals also fall through because of the inflexibility of founders and existing investors around shareholdings and control — see the following section.

Get into the habit of doing informal catch-ups with investors over coffee or drinks. Even if you don't get any investment out of it right away, keeping in contact gives you an idea of how investors think, what they want to see and what their investment interests are. A lot of the 'intel' you get from these meetings can be very helpful when pitching your business to any investor.

Understanding dilution and control

When investors invest in a company, they typically get a shareholding in return for putting money into the company. In other words, the new investor buys a number of shares that the company issues. As a result, the company's shareholdings change, which can have an impact on the board composition or voting rights.

The new investment also means that the previous set of shareholders get *diluted* (their percentage shareholding is reduced). For example, if your company has 1,000 shares on issue and a new investor buys 500 new shares the company issues, all existing investors get diluted by one-third. So if you own 500 shares (50 per cent of the company), after the investment deal goes through and the new shares are issued you own 33 per cent of the company (500 of the 1,500 shares on issue).

Although most entrepreneurs are keen to attract additional capital into the company, they're also worried about losing control of their business or 'giving away' a shareholding that could represent a lot of money when the company is sold or goes public.

 You need to separate fact from fiction when it comes to concerns about dilution and losing control when taking on new investors. In reality, many of these concerns turn out to be non-issues for entrepreneurs.

Here's a list of common concerns raised in my discussions with entrepreneurs, and my responses:

✔ **I don't want someone telling me what to do with my own company.** During the early stages of a company, investors typically acquire large shareholdings and request a seat on the board. The reason for this is that early-stage companies are high-risk investments and investors want to make sure their interests are represented. However, the representative on the board doesn't want to run the company. More often than not, investors add a lot of value to board meetings.

Investors lose all of their investment if the company doesn't go well. So supporting the existing team as best as possible is in the interest of every investor. Any concerns about control (such as veto rights on strategic decisions or major transactions) can be negotiated and specifically covered in the shareholder agreement. Investors fully understand the importance and value the existing team brings to the table — the last thing an investor wants to do is change that (and risk losing their investment).

✔ **I don't want to give up a percentage shareholding because this could represent millions of dollars when I sell my company.** Giving up shareholding is often hard for first-time entrepreneurs because of the theoretical value the shares represent and the concern about ownership. Unfortunately, the value of a company remains theoretical until someone is willing to pull out a cheque book and pay something for it, and many entrepreneurs are under the illusion that their company is worth far more than it actually is.

Ask for an external valuation to get a real understanding of the value of your company.

Some entrepreneurs also fight tooth and nail over very small percentages (such as 1 per cent shareholdings or fractions thereof). This shows a narrow-minded attitude and isn't helpful — and is likely to turn investors away.

You're aiming to have a wildly successful company so minor differences in percentage really don't matter in the greater scheme of things. If you end up selling your company for $100 million and personally end up with $20 million, does it really matter whether you get $19.9 million or $20.1 million? Don't sweat the small stuff.

✔ **Investors just want to push me to sell my company.** Investors are primarily interested in getting a good return on their investment but they don't typically do this at the expense of the future of the company.

Investors may push for a sale when the timing is right and an offer is on the table. However, any trade sale of the entire company needs to be agreed by the board (which an investor can't force upon the other shareholders unless the investor owns almost all the shares).

Investors may push for a public listing if they believe the company is able to attract significant capital through the listing process. Again, this would have to be agreed by the board and typically if the company is in such a good shape to warrant a sale or listing, all shareholders are going to significantly benefit from it.

Get to know your investors before they invest and make sure interests are aligned. Talk openly about their intentions and expectations under a number of scenarios (for example, subsequent funding rounds, a trade sale or public listing). The most important thing when dealing with investors and different shareholders is to make sure the interests of all parties are as closely aligned as possible. As long as that's the case, original founders are unlikely to feel disadvantaged by any major decisions taken at board level.

Get your lawyer to explain the significance of *major transactions*, *tag and drag* clauses and *non-dilution* clauses to you when negotiating with investors. These are often sticky points during the last stage of closing an investment deal. Have a look at the section 'Hiring a good lawyer' for more details.

Investment — timing is everything

A lot in life is about timing and so it is with investment. The easiest way to get investment is when you don't actually need the money — your company is profitable and growth is funded through cash flow. For many entrepreneurs, that's not possible because large upfront investment is required to build a product, or the initial sales and marketing effort is capital intensive. So you need to attract investment — you don't want to do this when you've got nothing to offer or you're about to run out of money.

Traditionally, start-ups have three points in time when they require funding: At the seed stage, during the initial growth stage and during the acceleration stage. I cover funding during the seed stage in Chapter 2, and growth and acceleration stages in the following sections.

Growth stage

To attract further capital after the initial seed funding round you need to have added a lot more value to your business — otherwise, you don't have an attractive investment proposition.

Let's say you started a business and were able to raise seed capital of $100,000 at a $250,000 *pre-money* valuation (what your company was valued at before this investment). This means immediately after investment your company is worth $350,000. If you need to raise further funds but the value of your company is still around $350,000 (or, heaven forbid, less than $350,000), an investor interprets this as a stagnant company.

At the very least, you need to double the value of your company from one investment round to the next to keep investors interested. Continuing with the preceding example, a realistic scenario to attract funding from an angel investor in the next funding round is a valuation of $1 million.

Perhaps you have built a minimum viable product and have managed to sell it to a number of customers. You can now justify to investors why your company is worth a lot more than at the last funding round, and so can ask for a significant amount of money — for example, $250,000 at a $1 million valuation.

Acceleration stage

After the growth stage (see preceding section), the next time you want to raise money for your company is ideally in the acceleration stage. This means the business is making money and is either approaching break-even or is already profitable. The money at this stage is ideally used to accelerate growth (not for the survival of the company).

Again, you need to demonstrate that the value of the company has gone up significantly since the last funding round. At this stage, investors typically want to see a valuation that's based on external reference points, revenue (profit) or massive growth. Ideally, you have a sizable customer base and revenue to show to investors to push up your valuation. Most deals at this stage are done on valuations of $5 million or above.

Table 7-1 shows a typical investment path for a company that starts with a seed-stage valuation of $250,000 and grows successfully from there.

Table 7-1 Typical Investment Path for a Growing Company

	Idea Stage	Seed Stage (Pre-money)	Seed Stage (Post-money)	Angel Stage (Pre-money)	Angel Stage (Post-money)	VC Stage (Pre-money)	VC Stage (Post-money)
Company value	$0	$250,000	$350,000	$1,000,000	1,250,000	$5,000,000	$6,000,000
Investment		$100,000		$250,000		$1,000,000	
Shareholding:							
Founder	100%	100%	60%	60%	45%	45%	36%
Seed capital investor			40%	40%	30%	30%	24%
Angel investor					25%	25%	20%
VC							20%

Only approach investors when you can demonstrate a significant value increase from the previous round. Check Chapters 4, 5 and 6 to see what you can do to add value to your company between rounds.

Keep a constant eye on your remaining 'runway' (refer to Chapter 2). Investment rounds take a long time and the more money involved the longer they take. Angel rounds typically take around three months (from approaching an angel investor to having the money in the bank). VC rounds can take up to six months because of the elaborate due diligence process.

If the story of your company's growth doesn't unfold as in the example shown in Table 7-1, you may have to accept significant discounts to your ideal valuation to keep your company going.

Investors are generally quite good at gauging the state of your company and growth path. If your growth is much slower than expected, investors interpret this as a riskier investment and consequently demand a *risk premium* when investing in your company. In other words, they apply a discount to your valuation and offer to invest at a lower share price.

In most cases, entrepreneurs accept the lower valuation to keep going with their companies (because doing so is still better than having to shut down altogether) but considering a shutdown may actually be the best option.

Your current idea may not be the one that takes you all the way to a successful exit. Sometimes, you're better off cutting your losses and moving on to the next idea.

Know your *walk-away price* before you approach investors. Get together with your team and look realistically at your company. Define a valuation at which point you'd rather shut down the company than accept investment. Most importantly, check how much longer you can keep going with the resources you've got. If you're days away from not being able to pay the bills, you're too late for attracting investment anyway.

Hiring a good lawyer

Having access to a good lawyer during fundraising rounds is absolutely essential. Ideally, you already have a relationship with a good lawyer in place — if not, it's a good idea to spread your feelers and find one before starting a funding round.

Here are some tips on finding a good lawyer:

- ✔ Reach out to your network of entrepreneurs, mentors and advisors and ask if anyone can recommend a good option.

- ✔ Do an online search for lawyers in your area using specific key words like 'shareholder agreements', 'term sheet' and 'investment'.

Once you've got a list of names, contact the lawyers and ask them whether they have worked with start-ups and have been involved in funding rounds. Do a reference check on any companies they mention.

You need to work with a lawyer who knows the Companies Act for your country well, understands the particular needs of start-ups, and all the 'tricky bits' of the investment process.

Some lawyers specialise on working with start-ups and investors, which can be useful for attracting capital. They often have deals available that give start-ups access to reduced rates (usually in return for a bonus payment on closing a successful funding round) and can also help with the fundraising process itself — for example, they organise introductions to investors.

Whoever you chose in the end, make sure you have someone you trust on your side when negotiating investment terms. Whenever more than one party is involved in an investment round (for example, because the round is a syndicated deal) the drafting of a revised shareholder agreement can get tricky because all parties are aiming to have their interests recognised in the document. Clauses in the shareholder agreement can get very complicated and you may get lost in the legal mumbo jumbo. Your lawyer's primary role is to explain to you in plain English what certain clauses mean and how they impact on your business and shareholding.

Making Changes as Your Company Matures

When your start-up reaches the stage where it has become a fully sustainable business (and perhaps even generating profits), you need to pay attention to a few internal factors that may not have been relevant before (because everyone was so busy trying to get to where you are now).

At some point in your start-up journey, the internal dynamics of your team start changing. Initially, most start-ups tend to have a relatively flat organisational structure where all team members share risks and rewards. Over time, this changes to a hierarchy and more of the 'employer–employee structure' typically displayed in established companies. This shift might happen in small steps over long periods but you need to recognise this change because it typically comes with a number of decisions that need to be made and expectations that need to be addressed.

The following sections cover the impact this change has on the company culture, organisational structure and remuneration scheme of your staff (or team).

Managing changes in company culture

Start-up life in the early days can feel a bit like the Wild West of business. Many entrepreneurs who have left the corporate world to start a company often have a desire to do things differently in their own business. And nothing is wrong with that.

I've seen start-up spaces where music videos were being played nonstop on large video screens at an incredible volume. Others have assembled an entire server park in their bedroom and I've had to step over layers of cables and equipment to get to the kitchen table to have a meeting with the founders. Being able to run the company in whichever way you want is one of the fantastic perks of running a start-up. This unconventional approach often attracts others who want to become part of the team.

Initially, the shared vision of creating a successful company and excitement around a product or technology often replaces the need for a solid salary package. At this point, team members also tend to be quite forgiving if things don't always go according to plan (such as salary payments being made late).

However, over time and as the company matures, this attitude tends to change. And, as your company grows, you often have to bring on additional staff who weren't there at the beginning and as a result have different expectations from a company they want to work for.

The initial start-up culture inevitably gives way to a more traditional corporate culture, which often includes a standard office space and working conditions (playing loud music isn't really helpful for getting work done), office hours and perhaps even a dress code. Often these changes to the company culture are born out of necessity because simply not enough space is available to accommodate everyone or because you need to frequently hold meetings with external parties (such as clients or investors).

Most investors are quite used to dealing with alternative office spaces and company cultures but over time also want to see a shift towards a professional and presentable corporate image. This doesn't mean your start-up office needs to look like a bank. You can use creativity to display an alternative approach to doing business but still portray an air of professionalism whenever visitors come in for a meeting.

Accepting changes in company culture can be tricky for members of the initial team because the new, more corporate culture can feel like something they wanted to leave behind in their old jobs. A good way to deal with this situation is to create different spaces within an office environment (if possible). For example, many start-ups end up having a games room or a 'chill-out room' where some of the previous culture is still kept alive but in a way that doesn't impact on the rest of the office. Also write down some aspects of the company culture so all staff members are aware of them — for example, articulate company values, aspirations and unacceptable behaviour.

Looking at recruiting and organisational design

Often the initial team of a start-up is loosely organised and may not have employment contracts in place because all of the team members are founders and are compensated through shareholding. Also the company typically doesn't make any money so a lot of founders sustain themselves through tapping into personal funds. Sometimes additional team members are hired on a casual basis or are compensated through small equity stakes (often referred to as *sweat equity*).

Recruiting in start-ups is a critical task because each recruitment decision has a significant impact on the company (especially during the early stages). Don't take a casual approach to bringing on staff — even early on. This is likely to lead to complications down the line (for example, when the company is profitable and initial casual arrangements have to be converted into proper employment contracts and stock options). While it may seem like an unnecessary administrative overhead, drawing up proper employment contracts for all staff (including founders) as early as possible is actually easier.

Having proper employment contracts in place is not only good business practice but is also a matter of compliance with the law. In Australia and New Zealand, strict legislation is in place to protect employees from being taken advantage of and the last thing your start-up needs on its journey is to have to deal with the employment court.

In addition to the actual employment contract, you need to have a job or role description in place that clearly outlines the tasks and areas of responsibility (or accountability) for a given job. For management positions, this needs to include budgets, staff management responsibilities and delegated financial authorities.

As well as the contractual side of recruitment, you also have to consider how to structure your company. As you hire more staff, you need to think about how you manage new staff members and how they can best contribute to achieving the company's goals. A good way of thinking about potential structures of the company is to create a future organisational chart.

Think about how you would organise your company in three years' time when you have three times as many staff as today. Once you have come up with a suitable structure for a future scenario, you can relate this structure back to your current situation and put in place pathways for strategic recruitment — for example, hiring staff with the potential to head up a particular area of your business.

When deciding on your organisation structure, also consider how the structure helps to align staff with the overall objectives of your company. Small companies typically follow a *top–down* planning approach, where organisational goals (such as customer acquisition and increased customer retention) can be broken down into targets that are set for teams (or even individual staff). The organisational structure and goal setting need to be transparent enough to enable (and empower) staff to achieve their team goals and thereby achieve the company's overall goals.

Deciding on stock options and incentive schemes

As well as staffing and staff structures (refer to preceding section), another aspect that tends to become increasingly important when managing a growing business is how to provide incentive for staff to achieve the company's goals and how to build loyalty to prevent high staff attrition rates. Most start-ups do this through a combination of cash bonuses and commissions, non-monetary incentives and perks, and stock options.

The following is a description of these incentive methods and how to use them:

- **Cash bonuses and commissions:** Cash incentives work best for short-term results. Most typically, these are used for KPIs that are directly related to the current growth stage — for example, number of users, sales transactions or website traffic. Do some maths before agreeing on cash incentives based on a number of scenarios (cover average results, good results and outstanding results). Make sure you can actually pay the bonuses under all scenarios. (Nothing is worse than getting everyone fired up about a bonus and then not being able to pay it!)

- **Equity:** Many start-ups distribute small portions of equity to staff in the form of an employee share ownership plan (ESOP). If the company is publicly listed, this is usually done through stock options. Typically, this type of compensation is used to encourage loyalty and tenure with the company. Commonly, ESOPs are structured so that the value of the shares can only be realised at some point in the future or upon reaching certain milestones. Any of these plans need to be set up with the help of an HR consultant and lawyer.

- **Non-monetary incentives:** These work really well to lift motivation and to accelerate the team-building process (especially when the company is growing fast and new staff are frequently joining).

  You can use a whole range of non-monetary incentives — here's a list of some common treats:

  - Food or alcohol — perhaps a nice bottle of champagne

- 'Money can't buy' experiences (often related to the nature of the business — for example, representing the company at an invite-only event)

- Special awards or recognition

- Tickets for a sporting or arts event

- Time off

You may want to reserve a portion of equity when structuring shareholder agreements. Many start-ups reserve between 1 and 10 per cent of their overall equity for employees (including the CEO). The equity shares are usually made available to employees in small increments over long periods.

Dealing with Threats to Your Business

By the time your start-up is generating revenue, you're typically not able to keep your success a secret, especially not if you're achieving rapid growth with a consumer product or service.

At some stage, you probably need to deal with a competitive response (for example, from an incumbent player) or with another company that aims to copy what you have achieved. Although it may be unsettling to deal with serious competitors, you can also see this as another validation of what you have achieved. It means your company is being taken seriously — you have arrived on the world stage of business.

The following sections cover the various types of competitive threats to your business and provide simple guidelines on how to deal with a threat.

Responding to direct competition

In Chapter 5 I highlight the need to have alerts in place that help you scan your business environment, track trends and keep an eye on the market in general. Ideally, one of these alerts notifies you right away when a new competitor appears on the scene or when an established company decides to go head-to-head with your company (through launching a very similar product or service at a lower price).

When direct competition occurs, don't panic or make any rash decisions on pricing or product and service positioning. Instead, follow these tips:

- ✔ Purchase your competitor's products or services (ideally via someone who can't be linked to your company) and find out as much as you can about the offering. Experience the products or services and find out how your own products or services differ.

- ✔ Get an understanding about how well the competitor is doing in the market and, most importantly, at what rate its market share is growing. This can be easily accomplished through market surveys — for example, create an independent survey and ask potential customers what product or service appeals to them (by brand), what they consider buying or have bought already. You can repeat this survey every month to see how your company or brand compares to your competitors.

- ✔ Find out about the company that's behind the competitive threat. What is their business position? What resources do they have available to them? Have they recently been acquired or raised significant funds? Direct competition can be a serious threat to your business if a well-resourced incumbent is trying to take you out of business. However, more commonly, competitive threats come from companies that are actually in trouble or simply want to copy what you're doing to gain market share quickly. Doing a bit of company research helps you decide on your response to the competitive threat.

Once you've done your research, you have a number of ways you can respond, and I outline the most common in the following list. *Note:* The options I outline aren't infallible — the most suitable response highly depends on your business situation. A discussion of these responses to competitive threats has been included to illustrate some options and their implications.

Ways to respond to a competitive threat include

- ✔ **Outexecuting, outperforming, outinnovating:** Doing things better and faster than your competition is always a good strategy, and this tactic should be the predominant response to direct competition. Large companies typically struggle to keep up with innovation and trends. Small, agile start-ups are almost always in a better position to implement new features or technology quickly. By demonstrating that your company can do that, you become a primary acquisition target for larger players — which is exactly what you want. Ideally, you want to be a pain in the neck for established players so they feel they don't have any other option than to buy you (and, as a result, you can command a good price for your company).

✔ **Undercutting:** If you find out from your customers that the price point is really important to them and your competitor offers a comparable service at much lower rates, you may want to consider dropping your prices. Before you do that you need to analyse your cost structure and work out what the reduced revenue does to your cash flow. Ultimately, you need to be in a situation where you can sustain the reduced prices indefinitely.

Dropping prices is a dangerous play because consumers can get used to price cutting and may soon expect to pay even less for the same product or service. In some industries, this has led to a 'race to zero' (and wireless internet service is a good example of this — free wifi is becoming available everywhere). As soon as you realise this is happening you need to modify your product or service to find another market segment where margins are still high enough to sustain your business.

✔ **Ignoring:** Sometimes the most suitable response to a competitive threat is to not react at all. You can easily get distracted and worry about competitors all day — companies start out in similar fields all the time. So accept it as part of doing business and don't waste energy on working out what to do about a competing offer — stick to your guns and carry on with the good work you have done so far.

✔ **Releasing a marketing campaign:** A well-targeted marketing campaign can also be a good response to a competitive threat. In order to execute the campaign well, you need to know what your point of difference (to your competitor) is and emphasise that in the campaign.

✔ **Specialising:** When you realise you're about to enter a losing battle with a strong competitor, focusing on a particular niche (segment, geography or a particular demographic) may be the best option. When Apple realised they weren't going to win against Windows-based computers, they specialised very successfully in the personal computer market, focusing on making computers that particularly suit the media, creative and arts segment. (Then Apple innovated and introduced the iPod — and the rest is history.)

Handling imitation

Imitation is a common problem for many companies (especially well-known consumer brands). As the barriers to entry in many markets and industries have become very low other companies can more easily copy your products and services.

If you have rights or patents that you can enforce, you can explore your legal options. However, in many cases, that is not possible because the imitators operate from other geographies (with different legislation) or the procedure is simply too expensive (or time-consuming).

When dealing with potential rights and patent infringements, check your options with a lawyer. Sometimes simply sending a 'cease and desist' letter is enough to intimidate an imitator into backing off.

Aside from legal action, another course of action is to strengthen your brand and to highlight the importance of using the correct URL and brand names. You can even alert customers to be aware of imitations. Make sure you work with search engine optimisation companies to attract traffic away from imitators. If you're doing online, keyword-based advertising (such as the options available through Google, Facebook or StumbleUpon) work with the media owner to ensure that the imitators can't buy keywords that are related to your product. (Google, for example, has a team that investigates fraudulent or inappropriate use of keywords.)

Ideally, you already have a trademark in place for your brand (company name) as well as your product and service names. If not, do so right away because the time of filing for a trademark has legal implications (that is, the first to register generally gets the trademark). Fortunately, you don't need to wait until registration is complete to indicate to the world that you're intending to protect your brand or product. You can use the trademark symbol TM to indicate your intention to register and protect a trademark and use ® once the registration is complete.

Addressing online community projects

One of the trickiest competitive threats to deal with is when an online community decides to create a very similar product or service to yours and then offer it free of charge. (A well-known example of this is Wikipedia, which is threatening the business of traditional encyclopaedia publishers.)

Reacting to community projects (and practically all open-source software projects) can be tricky because these projects are *crowd-sourced* (created by a crowd of volunteers) and the initiatives are generally not run by a commercial entity. Ownership of products is handled under creative commons agreements (where a legal framework of fair use licenses allows the sharing of intellectual property). However, one of the most promising responses to such a threat seems to be to partner up with the project.

Often these community-based projects still need a limited amount of funding (for example, to pay for servers or network bandwidth). As a result, they are reliant on contribution or sponsorship. If you become aware of a crowd-sourced or open-source project that's threatening to undermine your business, work out the benefits of sponsoring the project and agreeing on cooperation with the community.

Often such sponsorships develop into a business model where the system is available as open source but also under a commercial license. The open source database MySQL is a good example of such a model (originally sponsored by MYSQL AB, then bought by Sun Microsystems and at the time of writing owned by Oracle). The system is still available as a free version as well as an 'enterprise' version sold through Oracle.

Sometimes, community projects end up running out of steam and closing down by themselves. So don't over-react, look at your options.

Getting sued

Having to deal with lawsuits can be a real distraction for start-ups and, in some cases, can mean the end of the journey for the company.

The first thing to do when receiving a letter from a lawyer or company that threatens a lawsuit or notifies you of litigation is to check its authenticity and validity. Is the company that's threatening you with a lawsuit (or suing you) real and could their claim be in any way valid? You may come across fraudulent companies who send out letters that look like legitimate claims but turn out to be completely made up.

If the letter has passed the initial authenticity and validity test, you need to speak to your lawyer and get a legal opinion on the matter. If your lawyer advises that the threat or claim is real, you need to discuss your options.

As a general rule, if the matter can be settled for less than $1,000 (or $10,000 if you're cashed up), your best option is to pay up and move on. That way you're not wasting valuable time on the lawsuit (and burning your hard-earned cash on lawyer and court fees). If significantly more money is involved or your entire business is at risk, you need to get on top of the situation quickly.

Sometimes you can seek resolution outside of the legal system by requesting a meeting with the other party. If that's not possible, you need to fully understand why you're being sued and what can be done about it. If you want to avoid litigation, you may have to change your business practices or business model — but this may still be cheaper or more viable than going to court.

Opportunity costs and energy drain on you and your company are probably the biggest threats to your business.

Sometimes, no other option exists — you have to go through with the entire legal process and take your chances in court (assuming you're not knowingly involved in illegal business practices, in which case your business is over anyway). If this is the case, you need to follow any temporary court orders (such as injunctions) and prepare for the trial with your lawyer. During this time you need to instil confidence in your team that you are handling the situation and that the business is going to continue.

While you can't do much about it if someone wants to sue you, I certainly wouldn't recommend devoting a lot of time and effort on suing other businesses. Spending time in courtrooms isn't a great way to run a company and isn't where you want to be as a successful entrepreneur (despite what you might have seen from famous entrepreneurs). Ideally, you want to spend your time where you add most value — at the helm of your company, in front of a computer or in the lab.

Part IV

Chasing the Pot of Gold: The Reason Your Start-Up Exists

Glenn Lumsden

'Mr "Yahoo", or whatever you like to call yourself, will you stop making these prank calls about buying my son's business? And the same goes for your friend Mr "Google"!'

In this part ...

*T*he last part of your start-up journey may seem comparatively easy — your company is making money, you've optimised your operations and business life is sweet. However, don't forget your investors who may get a bit impatient now to 'cash in' on their investment. So in this part I look at what's involved in making it possible for investors (and yourself) to cash in, starting with ensuring your business is in the best possible state for a potential sale or public listing. You may also need to work hard to position your business for a potential sale or acquisition by a competitor, and I show you how.

In this part, I also cover everything you need to know about preparing your business for a public listing on the stock exchange, taking you through the listing process and how to prepare for it.

Chapter 8

Starting to Make Money: The Post-Profit Stage

*1*n the post-profit stage of a venture, start-up life is sweet. This is the stuff dreams are made of and you can thoroughly enjoy a few business luxuries (like paying for professional services and not having to ask for favours all the time).

However, this stage is also quite risky — and your biggest risk is that your business becomes 'fat, dumb and happy'. In other words, you stop paying attention to the details that created the success in your business, such as listening to customers and checking on competitors or market trends.

To help you avoid that, this chapter discusses what you need to do to keep your feet on the ground as a founder and how to further increase the value of your business. I also talk about getting into a position where leaving your company at some point is possible (should you wish to), and provide a quick look at what you can do to give back to your long-term supporters.

Keeping Focused and Grounded

The post-profit stage is generally far less risky than previous growth phases because your product or service is well established in a sizeable market. But it's not without risk. In the following sections, I cover these risks and show how you can avoid them and keep your feet on the ground, paying particular attention to customer feedback and not falling into the trap of the 'founder syndrome'.

Avoiding internal risks during the post-profit stage

Many of the common risks start-ups face during the post-profit stage are internally focused, as follows:

- **Diversifying the business unnecessarily:** The success with the business can lead founders and executives to a mindset of 'we're good at everything' and, as a result, expensive and unnecessary products and services can be generated.

- **Lacking attention to detail:** Getting complacent when you're very successful and profitable can happen easily. Suddenly customer requests or complaints aren't taken seriously anymore, and general sloppiness can creep into business operations and decision-making. (See the following section for more on customer feedback.)

- **Losing motivation:** Founders may suddenly be seen on golf courses a lot when they reach the post-profit stage. Some lose motivation altogether or are already focused on their next idea.

- **Over-spending on non-essential initiatives:** This can include expensive media campaigns, celebrations or new product ideas.

- **Taking out too much money to pay dividends:** Some start-ups distribute a lot of money to founders or shareholders once they become profitable. This is highly risky because the business situation and financial position of the venture can change rapidly.

Although investors and shareholders may put pressure on you to provide dividends, you need to demonstrate sound financial management skills by outlining a strategy on how you suggest the company should use the profits. Investors and shareholders are generally keen to receive information relating to dividends or use of profits so, ideally, you should already have something in place before they ask.

The best strategy to adopt during this stage of the start-up journey is to continue exactly as before (that is, while the company was struggling to make money). Any profits should be invested in improving current products and services (refer to Chapter 7) or should be retained as financial reserves (check with your advisory board or accountant for the percentage of retained profits that's right for your specific business).

For more on continuing to improve your company, see the section 'Making a Great Business Excellent' later in this chapter.

Understanding the importance of customer feedback

How external parties perceive the company is a critical aspect of keeping your feet on the ground during the post-profit stage. Most importantly, you need to look at how you treat customers and how they experience your product and services now that the company is profitable (and perhaps highly profitable).

Although most start-ups have to work really hard to attract customers, losing them is comparatively easy. Customers have the habit of voting with their feet — in other words, if they don't like something, they go somewhere else.

Having customers complain is actually a blessing because at least you find out that they're not happy and you have an opportunity to do something about it. More often than not, customers simply find a different provider who better meets their needs or expectations (and you never hear from them again).

MySpace is a prime example of ignoring customers and paying a high price for it (through massive loss of company value). After the initial rapid growth phase, MySpace became very popular with bands and artists who used the site for profiling, promoting their creative work and managing bookings. However, MySpace wanted to remain a general social network and so didn't provide any specific 'killer features' for artists (while letting the site design get out of control). At the same time, MySpace didn't pay enough attention to emerging popular features displayed by Facebook. And so MySpace ended up in a position where they didn't offer popular features that mainstream social networking users wanted and didn't offer specific features for their own most loyal customer group of artists and bands.

Dealing with customers and listening to their requests and suggestions can require a lot of effort and you may find it tedious at times, but it's an absolute necessity at all stages of your venture, and particularly during the post-profit stage. Good customer service is a great way of keeping your customers loyal to your brand, even as competitors try to move in on your market share. Putting specific measures in place to make sure good customer service happens and you incentivised staff to continue their good work pays dividends.

Try using a *call-recording system* (where you can record and monitor incoming calls and perhaps use them later for training) when customers contact the company about enquiries, complaints or other customer service-related matters. Sometimes just switching on such a system can prompt staff to give customers the attention they deserve.

For more on training your staff to provide great customer service, see *Customer Service For Dummies*, 3rd Edition, by Karen Leland and Keith Bailey (publishing by Wiley Publishing Inc.).

Keeping product-related conversations going with your customers has other benefits for your start-up. A lot of innovation and ideas typically come from the people who use your products and services in the real world.

Use specific measures to facilitate the customer feedback process at your start-up, such as the following:

- **Conduct surveys:** Many start-ups (as well as established companies) frequently survey their customer base on specific aspects of the business (such as satisfaction with the product, price and performance).

   When customers take the time to fill out a survey on your start-up or its products or services, showing your appreciation is important. Make sure you reward customers for taking part in the survey.

- **Establish product forums or product-user groups:** Many established software companies have dedicated a part of their website to ongoing discussions about the company's products and services. Usually these forums require registration but are available to all customers (for example, with a valid customer ID).

- **Organise user conventions and seminars:** You can periodically organise an event at a central location (where most of your customers can easily get to) to demonstrate product use, present case studies or new features and open the floor for any questions your customers may have.

✔ **Use Twitter for facilitated discussions:** Many companies tend to use Twitter as a marketing mechanism but I think Twitter is more powerful as a customer service tool. Encourage customers to share their experiences with your product (good and bad) via Twitter. Make sure to respond to every tweet with honesty, integrity and a practical solution. The history of these tweets creates a powerful public testimonial of your customer service.

Air New Zealand uses a Twitter handle for communications with frequent flyers and anyone following them. The Twitter team responds to individual posts and questions with specific details. This is a great example of using social media well to improve services and manage customer expectations.

✔ **Visit customers:** Visiting loyal customers is always a good idea. Some companies have started sending their CEOs or senior management to sit with customers and listen to them. Most customers really appreciate getting attention from key staff and being able to offload anything they're not happy with.

With all of the techniques outlined in the preceding list, make sure that you have a follow-up process in place so that customers who make a suggestion or complaint receive feedback about the outcome of their interaction.

Overcoming the founder syndrome

Investors use the term *founder syndrome* to describe a situation where founders are unwilling to let go of certain aspects of their business, even when they're clearly no longer able to perform them. This attitude of founders creates a major risk to the future success of the company. As a result, business operations or growth suffers and the performance of the company is below optimal.

Holding on to all aspects of your business is fine when you own 100 per cent of the company. However, when investors are involved this gets trickier (refer to Chapter 2 and Chapter 7 for information about getting investors involved in your business). Investors want a maximum return for their investment, which generally means the company has to operate at its optimal performance at all times. If this isn't possible because of the founder's skill or competency gaps, investors are likely to push for a resolution. Unfortunately, this process can get very unpleasant for everyone involved and has led to the complete collapse of some companies.

In this section, I cover the main issues that can lead to disagreements, and how to overcome them.

Dealing with different perceptions

The most difficult aspect of founder's syndrome to deal with is when a discrepancy exists between your own perception of performance and shareholder or investor perception. In other words, you believe you're doing absolutely fine on a particular task (such as sales) whereas the shareholders believe you're underperforming.

The easiest way to deal with a discrepancy between perceptions is to get an external party involved to provide an independent opinion. Just make sure you all agree on the contracted third party before the review is done.

As an entrepreneur, you need to look at yourself and your own performance honestly. If you're performing activities that you don't enjoy or feel 'out of depth' on, look for alternatives. Consider whether someone else is really better placed to perform these activities. Yes, you might lose a bit of control but that's an inevitable process of your company's growth.

Overcoming different opinions

A disagreement over the company's direction or growth strategy between founders and investors or shareholders isn't easily resolved and can be the source of ongoing tension at board meetings.

You can try external parties to address this situation (such as a business strategy consultant or mediator) or take some time out at a management and board retreat to resolve fundamental issues. If the issues are irreconcilable, you can investigate to what extent the business could be split, such as spinning off a business unit and making it into a separate company (assuming this addresses the fundamental disagreement over the direction of the company). If nothing works you're faced with the dilemma of a situation you find unsatisfactory.

As with any unsatisfactory situation, you generally only have three options:

- ✔ Put up with the situation
- ✔ Change it
- ✔ Leave

If disagreements between you and your board are continuing, seriously consider leaving. Yes, leaving a business you've built up from the ground is hard. But as a true entrepreneur you're always going to have another idea and another business. In many cases, an exit out of an unsatisfactory situation with the board can be financially lucrative and altogether freeing (as suddenly a large amount of pressure is lifted). In Chapter 1, I emphasise the importance of defining success — perhaps you've already achieved success beyond your wildest dreams when your start-up was just an idea! So why hold on to your business when you can cash in now and move on?

Resolving issues between multiple founders

In start-ups with multiple founders, irreconcilable disagreements over the company strategy can also emerge at the post-profit stage.

You may be able to find a way to resolve this situation through the use of external help (such as a mediator or consultant — refer to preceding section). However, if the issues can't be resolved, splitting the business may be the only viable option.

Numerous examples exist of bitter rivalry between founders (and sometimes family members) that could only be resolved by splitting the company. A famous example is the brothers Adolf and Rudolf Dassler, who founded a sports shoe company. In the 1950s they decided to split the company: Adolf continued with the company, which eventually became Adidas, whereas his brother started Puma Sportswear. Both companies have done really well (obviously) so a split doesn't always lead to a disastrous result for the company and founders involved. In fact, more often than not, the seemingly more radical option of a split represents a more viable outcome for the business than a drawn-out dispute.

See the sidebar 'Getting a business divorce' for more on splitting a company or removing a founder from the board.

Getting a business divorce

Splitting a company or removing a founder from the board of directors is a bit like divorcing a spouse — typically lawyers are required at some stage. Seeking legal advice should be your first step in these 'divorce' proceedings. Your lawyer can remind you of the meaning of relevant clauses in your shareholder agreement and advise how these clauses apply to your current situation. As with all negotiations, be clear about your own positions and your 'walk away' options (that is, any terms that aren't agreeable to you), which your lawyer can help you develop.

To help you prepare for meetings (with your lawyer or with other parties), the following list summarises typical 'sticky' points (aspects of terms that parties often find difficult to agree on) during a business divorce:

✔ **Company value:** The most efficient way to resolve any disagreements over the current value of the company is to get an external valuation done.

✔ **Conditions of an exit:** You may find that particular conditions of an exit are difficult to agree on such, as a *non-compete period* (which prevents exiting parties from setting up a new company offering the same products or services in the same market) or the wording of a media release announcing the departure of a founder. Work with a mediator

or professional negotiators to resolve these issues.

✔ **Intellectual property:** This aspect is perhaps the most difficult to resolve because identifying in retrospect any specific parts of intellectual property that can be attributed to a person or group can be really difficult. Most likely, a value of the company and all of its intellectual property needs to be agreed on. The exiting party is then compensated for relinquishing any claims to intellectual property developed during active years in the company.

✔ **Performance or behaviour of a director (founder):** Assessing performance and behaviour of directors is difficult and typically based on examples or incidents that expose the company to unnecessary risk or reduced financial performance. Having clear role descriptions, delegated authorities and targets in place (all set by the board) helps to assess behaviour and performance.

✔ **Shareholding:** Disagreement may arise over exact shareholdings because of a lack of documentation, use of verbal agreements or uncertainty over specific conditions that would trigger allocation of shares (for example, maturing of share options). Ultimately, only documented agreements and transactions have legal bearing — that's why making minutes during board meetings and recording all decisions relating to shareholding is so important.

Negotiation and conflict resolution are highly specialised skills that many entrepreneurs have not been exposed to — so in the interest of time and an amicable outcome getting help from professionals may be the easiest option. Consider involving a professional mediator or negotiator (in addition to the legal team) to assist with the process of agreeing terms for your business divorce.

Making a Great Business Excellent

As part of preparing for an exit (which may not be that far off now that your company is profitable), you need to think about how you can keep adding value to your company to extract the maximum amount of money (return on investment) when you sell the company or your shares.

The following sections discuss ways to add value to your company by using the principles of lean management and business continuity planning. (Refer to Chapter 7 for other techniques to mature your business, such as expanding your product or service offering or expanding into other markets and territories.)

Optimising your processes

In the manufacturing world, lean management and optimisation techniques such as *Six Sigma* (which focuses on finding out where errors occur and trying to remove these errors and any variability in processes and outcomes), have been used for over two decades to create more efficient processes (and thus a more profitable product or service). Many of these principles can also be applied outside the manufacturing industry.

The central idea of lean management is the elimination of process waste, where *waste* is defined as any activity (or process step) that doesn't add direct value to the end customer. Keeping overheads and waste at a minimum is the primary goal.

Although process optimisation techniques can be applied at any stage of a start-up, the post-profit stage may be the first time you get a chance to actually look at exactly how you're doing a number of key tasks and processes in your business.

You're likely to have certain aspects of your start-up where the same processes happen hundreds of times on a given business day. So if significant process waste exists in any of these processes, this waste can have a substantial impact on your bottom line.

Processes where waste may exist in your start-up include the following:

✔ Change and release management (for example, when undertaking constant software development)

✔ Customer sign up and customer invoicing

✔ Customer support and customer service, including complaint handling

✔ Decision-making

✔ Expenses and corporate travel

✔ Management reporting at various levels of the organisation including board reporting

✔ Procurement and purchasing

✔ Product or service development

All of these processes can go through *process optimisation*, where areas of waste and potential for improvement are identified. The steps in this approach are as follows:

1. **Pick the most frequently used processes and describe how they're currently performed.**

   Customer sign-up, order processing or invoicing are typically performed frequently in a profitable business.

   Describing and 'mapping' processes is best done by an external business process analysis expert. The task requires a lot of experience to capture processes at the right level of detail and gauge where process waste occurs.

2. **Analyse current processes with the aim to streamline the overall task.**

   In order to do this well you need to capture process data along the way. Key things to capture are:

   - Name and position of the person performing a particular process step

   - Tools used to perform a process step (or, if automated, what system is performing the process step)

   - How long each process step takes

   - What the delays between individual process steps are

   - What resources are required to complete a process goal

   This is also called *current state* analysis.

3. **Analyse the results.**

   Use a specialist for this task, who can help you identify process waste based on the data you've collected. An experienced process analyst can quickly identify key areas of wasted effort and suggest ways to improve the process.

4. **Define *a future state* process map and process description.**

   Based on the process analysis you can now streamline the process in question and come up with a better way of doing things that reduces time or costs.

A crucial aspect that's often forgotten when doing process optimisation is capturing the 'voice of the customer'. This is where you interview or survey your customers and ask them about how well the process is performed. This step is incredibly important (and often revealing) because customers may have a completely different perception of the importance or quality of a particular process step. Asking your customers for feedback always leads to a useful outcome (if done respectfully), but it's even more crucial when doing process optimisation work.

Look out how your attitude to waste in your company affects the mindset of your staff (especially those who recently joined). I know of a few founders of highly profitable companies who refuse to upgrade their premises so as not to send out the wrong message to staff (that is, our company has lots of money, so let's splash out). This frugal mindset can then be reflected in all business decisions (from incurring expenses while on a business trip to confirming marketing budgets for the next financial year).

The basic approach to process optimisation as outlined in this section can be applied to just about all business processes. The analysis is incredibly powerful and most process analysts work on the basis of being able to achieve a 40 per cent reduction of costs or time and often this reduction filters through directly to your bottom line.

For a much more detailed discussion of lean management, see *Lean For Dummies*, 2nd Edition, by Natalie J. Sayer and Bruce Williams (published by Wiley Publishing Inc.).

Restructuring your operations

The initial focus of most start-ups has to be on agile product and service development (rapid iterations of product or service variations to achieve product or market fit quickly). When you reach the post-profit stage with your start-up business, operations tend to change.

Once the product–market fit has been verified, the company typically focuses on scaling up to expand reach and generate revenue. Once profitability has been achieved with a particular product or service and the need to scale constantly slows down, you can change how the business is organised and move profitable products and services into an optimised Business As Usual operation.

Established companies tend to work on a portfolio of products or services at various stages in their product life cycle. Figure 8-1 shows the typical life cycle.

The general idea in the product life cycle context is that the development and launch of new products is financed from income generated by cash cow products. (Out to pasture products are former cash cow products that have reached the end of their life span and are eventually shut down when the operating cost exceeds the income generated.)

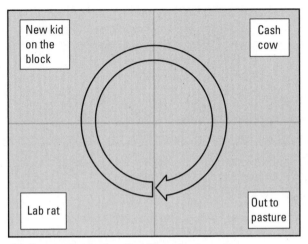

Figure 8-1: Four quadrants of product life cycle.

Even if you're not planning on developing separate products or services (and so may think you don't need to have a cash cow to finance them), you still need to have a clear understanding of how you're managing the costs associated with your product or service.

The following is an overview of the costs typically involved with a product or service and how much each cost should represent of gross revenue:

- ✔ **Product maintenance:** Includes staff and resource costs for continuous improvement (minor development) and fixes. As a general rule, spending should be approximately 10 to 15 per cent of gross revenue for established products.

- ✔ **Product operations (commercial):** Includes transactional cost such as credit card charges, invoicing and credit risk (from customers who default on their payments or are late with payments of invoices). This cost should be below 5 per cent and ideally below 1 per cent of gross product revenue.

- ✔ **Product operations (technical):** Includes the cost of all resources required to provide the product to customers (for example, server cost, network cost and license cost). This should be as low as possible — the exact percentage you're able to achieve in this category highly depends on the nature of your product or service.

✔ **Product support:** Includes staff and resource cost
for customer, quality control and product support.
Ideally, this cost should be below 20 per cent of gross
product revenue.

✔ **Sales and marketing:** Includes all marketing and
advertising spend, commissions and related sales cost
(for example, sales staff). For established (mature)
products, the cost of sale should be around 10 per cent
of gross product revenue.

Understanding how these components affect the overall
profitability of your product or service allows you to optimise
operations. Some companies manage to create highly
profitable products or services that have 25 per cent or less
overhead costs. If you manage to get your overhead cost
below 50 per cent during the post-profit stage you're still
doing well.

Succession Planning

Ironically, making yourself redundant in a profitable company
actually adds value to the company. Many potential buyers
are most interested in buying a well-oiled machine — in other
words, a profitable company that requires little attention. If the
company doesn't need you to operate well, this represents a
reduction of risk to buyers (because you could get hit by a bus
any day).

You also need to consider the following scenario: What would
happen to your company if you weren't able to come to work
for a long time? Unless you've been working hard to plan for this
scenario, your company may struggle or collapse altogether if
you're no longer available.

To address this situation and to make your company more
attractive for a trade sale you need to think about succession
planning of key staff — and predominantly the founders
(including yourself).

Here's a quick step-by-step on how to go about succession
planning:

1. **Identify key staff or founders who have expressed an
   interest or are at risk of leaving the company in the
   medium term.**

2. **Ensure that the role description for people identified in step 1 is up-to-date and reflects what they're currently doing.**

3. **Develop a strategy for sharing responsibilities with other staff (leave the most critical functions for last).**

   Your strategy may involve identifying internal (or external) candidates who can take on additional responsibilities from key staff identified in step 1, and developing a training plan to bridge skill gaps and provide a support structure for staff taking on additional tasks.

4. **Over time, gradually reduce the direct operational involvement of key staff and replace with projects that are more strategic in nature. At the same time, fully hand over responsibility for tasks to trained-up staff.**

A period of three to six months generally allows enough time to hand over most operational responsibilities to other staff and ensure that tasks are carried out to the level required.

Once a task is handed over to another member of staff, avoid meddling or still carrying out aspects of the task. An all or nothing approach works best in terms of who is responsible for executing a given task or function. That's not to say that you can't support the other person but, ultimately, that person needs to be able to perform this function without your help.

Succession planning and the handover of responsibilities can also be used as a motivator for eager staff who demonstrate great potential.

Recognising Your Responsibilities as a Growing Business

The success of your venture is generally a combination of effort, determination, support and luck. While celebrating your successes (and failures) is important, this section covers what I call *business karma* — the idea that anything you do for others (including other businesses) comes back to you (and your business).

In a practical sense this comes down to two main activities:

✔ Helping (young) entrepreneurs in the same way that you received help when you started out with your business.

✔ Recognising and rewarding your long-term supporters — be it your very first customers, your mentors and business advisors or your early stage investors (refer to Chapter 2).

Giving back to others is a final step in turning a somewhat chaotic start-up into a well-rounded, respected and sustainable company that you can be proud of.

Helping others succeed

Just about all well-known entrepreneurs and business figures are actively supporting the next generation of business leaders and entrepreneurs. Many of them share their advice free of charge through their blogs, websites or Twitter streams. As such, doing the same thing now that your business is profitable is a good idea.

Here are some ideas for what you can do to help others (ideally free of charge):

✔ **Actively support your local start-up ecosystem.** Give talks at relevant events or organise meet-ups to share ideas. A great example is to organise or contribute to a local 'Start-up Weekend' (see startupweekend.org).

✔ **Contribute to community-based projects.** If you've used any open source software along the way, think about contributing back to some of the projects you've benefitted from. For example, if you're using an open source content management system for your website and have modified a particular aspect that might be useful for others, dedicate a few hours or days of one of your developer's time to contributing the code back to the project.

✔ **Meet with entrepreneurs who contact you and ask for some advice.** Decide how much time you can dedicate to this (perhaps one hour per month) and arrange meetings. Think back to the early days when you just started out — how did it feel when you suddenly got the attention of a well-known entrepreneur who gave you some time?

✓ **Start a blog/website/publication and share your insights and lessons learnt.** Highlight what it was that made your venture succeed and the advice you would now like to give others starting out.

✓ **Start an intern or trainee program at your company.** Many young entrepreneurs (sometimes ones still in high school) are keen to get real-world experience in the corporate or start-up world — give them a chance!

You may experience a slightly selfish aspect to these activities — helping others makes you feel good. So you even get some immediate reward when doing these things!

Giving back to your long-term supporters

Giving back to your long-term supporters is another important aspect of recognising who and what has contributed to your company's success over the years. Most businesses have three external stakeholder groups that should be recognised or rewarded at this stage (refer to Chapter 7 for suggestions on how to reward your internal stakeholders — your employees).

The three external stakeholder groups are as follows:

✓ **Business advisors and mentors:** You may want to express your gratitude to advisors and mentors who have helped you along the way. A common way to do this is to pay advisors and mentors a handsome sum of money (once you have cashed out on your business) or to give them share parcels at favourable conditions (as a gift).

✓ **First customers:** These are the people who took a real risk on your company in the early days of your business — before things were working properly and when you had just launched your product or service. Imagine how many issues these guys had to put up with as you refined your products over time. So recognising their patience and loyalty (if you haven't done so along the way) makes perfect sense.

A good way to reward initial customers is to pick a meaningful number of customers (perhaps 50 or 100) and reward them with a special gesture. This could be a personal letter, a small personalised gift, a visit or special treat. The monetary value of the gift isn't as important as the appropriateness and meaning of the reward and the effort that has gone into creating or presenting the recognition. Another form of recognition of your initial customers is to use a public profile element to show which customers were some of the first members or customers of your business — for example, a member number (like 00001) or status name (such as 'elder').

✔ **Non-institutional seed investors:** These are most likely friends, family members or other early stage investors who took a punt on you. Many of these people are likely to be dear to your heart anyway and perhaps you have already recognised their contributions (by paying back a loan or giving them share parcels). If not, you really need to do so now that your company is profitable. In addition to fulfilling the financial obligations you may have to them, the same principle applies as described in the preceding bullet for your customers — you should recognise and reward their contributions with meaningful gifts.

Don't forget to give back to your family who have (most likely) had to put up with many late nights or business trips while you were building your business.

Chapter 9

Achieving Your Start-Up Vision and Cashing Out

* *

In This Chapter

▶ Putting your exit strategy into action

▶ Understanding the requirements for acquisitions and trade sales

▶ Assessing offers and finalising the deal

▶ Preparing for an initial public offering

▶ Experiencing business life after major equity events

* *

*F*or most entrepreneurs, achieving their start-up vision means that they have either created a profitable company that they like to work in (for the rest of their lives) or have sold their interest at a good price to provide financial independence. While exiting your company (after receiving an offer too good to refuse) sounds like a wonderful part of the start-up journey, this stage is still filled with traps and potholes.

To help you steer clear of any obstacles to achieving your start-up vision, this chapter discusses the three principle options for 'cashing out' of your business: Selling your interest, trade sales and acquisitions, and floating your company on a stock exchange. I look at trade sales and floats in more detail, covering exactly what you need to know about handling offers you may receive from interested parties to buy your business, and how you prepare your start-up for an initial public offering. Finally, I have a quick look at how your life may be after any of these events.

Selling Your Interests

If achieving your start-up vision involves a big cheque for you personally, selling your interest in the business you started is perhaps the shortest path to a big pay out (assuming that your company is profitable and valued at an interesting price for you — see the section 'Getting your company valued' for more).

In theory, the process of selling your interests is relatively straightforward — as a founder, you own a certain percentage of shares in your company. You can then apply this percentage to a recent valuation of your start-up to determine a monetary value that you can seek to realise by selling your shares to someone else. Sounds easy right?

Well, in reality, this process can become quite complicated if you don't plan for all aspects of the sale and its aftermath. Most of the complexities can arise because of your motivation to sell, what happens to the company after you've sold your interest and, most importantly, who you sell your shares to. The following sections cover these issues to give you a better understanding of the possible complexities.

Checking your motivation to sell

You need to be careful about what you say is behind your interest to sell your shares (especially if you want to sell all your shares and effectively exit the business) when talking with your fellow founders, directors, investors and members of the board. Any indication you're keen to sell generally triggers immediate questions around your motivations.

The main concern with selling your interest is that you may know something about the business or market that the other stakeholders don't know (yet). So having a credible reason for selling your interest is absolutely crucial.

The following are all likely to be considered credible:

- ✔ Change in life circumstances (for example, move to another country for family reasons)
- ✔ Change of business interests (such as a desire to pursue a different idea)

✔ Fundamental disagreement with the adopted company strategy (for example, as a result of a board decision that you opposed)

✔ Health reasons, especially long-term health issues

Planning for your start-up without you

As the founder, or even as one of the founders, other stakeholders in the business see you as essential to the success of your business. Not having you around is a concern to them because they need to figure out how to run and grow this business without your input.

When you announce your intention to sell your interest in the business, you need to have something in place to alleviate the fears of other stakeholders. Succession planning is a great way to do so. Ideally, you've groomed a replacement candidate over the last few months who's ready to take over for you. (Refer to Chapter 8 for more on succession planning.)

If you don't have a succession plan in place, you may want to suggest the following measures to address the concerns of your business stakeholders:

✔ You sell only a portion of your shares (rather than your entire shareholding) and remain involved in a board or advisory capacity.

✔ You stagger the sale of your shares over a specified period and participate actively in the recruitment and handover to a suitable candidate.

✔ You sell your interest but agree to continue as an employee of the company for a fixed period.

Considering your buyer

The best tactic for lining up a possible buyer for your shares in your start-up is to pay attention to the motivation of other shareholders (in the first instance). It may well be that some of your existing shareholders are interested in increasing their holdings. In that case, you can approach them directly and in confidence to discuss potential options.

Your second option is likely to come from an external party. Either you or the company may be approached by a potential buyer and you need to analyse the benefits of all aspects of this offer and how these benefits can then be communicated to other shareholders (see the section 'Handling Purchase Offers' later in this chapter).

Pursuing external buyers for your shareholding can be risky if word gets back to your other stakeholders. Ensure any discussions are strictly in confidence.

Your last option is probably looking to an institutional or private investor who you have a relationship with and are able to discuss the deal confidentially.

Ideally, you can disclose your intentions to the board, co-founders or other stakeholders openly and honestly in a way that doesn't put your company's future at risk. If that's not possible, you need to carefully plan for the sale and line up a potential buyer, and then plan your announcement and how you can address shareholder concerns.

While the prospect of getting your hands on quite a bit of cash may be appealing, don't lose sight of the fact that this is your business. You started it or were involved in its inception, so you don't want to see it collapse after you leave, right? Bear this in mind when you evaluate your options and work with your co-founders and other stakeholders to create a viable solution for you to exit the business. Timing is often a key factor — the more time you allow yourself for this process, the better the outcome is likely to be.

Preparing for a Trade Sale

An exit option for yourself can suddenly appear when someone who wants to buy your business approaches you. However, many of the acquisition deals we hear about in the business news don't just happen. In most cases, you have to engineer your business into a position where your company is either extremely attractive to others or where you leave other companies no choice but to buy you (to protect their market share).

Acquisition deals tend to be the result of a long-term strategic plan that the management team of the acquired party has executed (precisely for the purpose of being acquired). The purpose of an acquisition strategy is to create *leverage* in the business (some form of pressure on other companies or potential buyers), which puts the company in a good bargaining position for negotiations with potential buyers. How do you do that? The first and most important step is to dedicate time and energy to preparing for an acquisition.

Not all entrepreneurs position their businesses adequately (or not at all) for a trade sale or acquisition and, as a result, they miss out on having viable options for selling their businesses.

The following sections provide a sequence of steps you should go through (over a few months) to prepare your business for an acquisition or trade sale.

Getting your company valued

In Chapter 5, I provide a general overview of common valuation techniques and value drivers that add value to a business. When you're at the point of selling your company (or even selling your interest in the company or listing your company at a stock exchange), you need to understand how your company is valued in detail.

In most cases, you need to get an external valuation done before you can sell your interests in the company or before proceeding with a trade sale or acquisition. You need to provide details about your business to the valuation expert who then estimates the value of your company.

Working closely with the people providing the valuation of your start-up pays off, because they base part of the valuation on their understanding of your business. In particular, you need to ensure assets such as 'goodwill' and intangible assets are represented well.

A good way to prepare for a valuation is to look at a sample valuation report and go through it with your accountant or someone who can explain it to you (if you're not familiar with financial terminology and valuation methods). Have a look at the following sample report: valuecruncher.com/downloads/ExampleReport.pdf.

After you understand the key sections and value drivers of a valuation report, get your business ready for valuation by optimising key parameters or preparing information relevant to the valuation. That way, the valuation process can be completed quickly and in a way that presents your company in the best possible light.

For more on valuing your company, see *Business Valuations For Dummies*, by Lisa Holton and Jim Bates (published by Wiley Publishing, Inc.).

Ensuring your books are in order

While you're positioning your company for a trade sale or acquisition, you really need to get on top of your paperwork. As part of any sale (or investment), your company has to go through a *due diligence* process once the general terms of the deal have been agreed. The purpose of the due diligence process is to allow a potential buyer to validate claims you have made during the initial stages of the acquisition or sale.

Due diligence is generally split into a number of areas of interest, such as financial, legal, assets, production/operation, tax/compliance, governance, IT and staff. Depending on the type of company and business transaction, all of these (and others) or only some areas may be looked at during the due diligence phase.

Here are a few suggestions to help you prepare for audits in the various categories most likely to be focused on during the due diligence process:

- ✔ **Assets:** Ideally, you've already got an asset register in place — if not, create one. An asset register is a simple table (often an Excel spreadsheet) that lists all assets of significant value in your start-up. Include the purchase/creation date, initial value, current value, depreciation, location and a short description of the asset.

- ✔ **Financial:** This may well be the most important and most extensive due diligence area, so focus on tidying up this area first. Make sure all your financial records (especially year-end accounts) are in order and easily accessible. Brief your accountants and internal finance staff about a potential due diligence process so they can prepare for a voluntary audit of financial records.

- ✔ **Governance:** Of particular importance in this category are minutes of all board meetings, management meetings, AGMs and other important meetings considered relevant. Make sure all minutes are readily available in one place.

- ✔ **HR/staff:** Have a list of key HR policies, templates, standard contracts and organisational charts easily available. Ideally, also have a folder with CVs and profiles of all staff or key staff available for review.

- ✔ **Legal:** Ensure all legal documents are in one place and easy to access. For example, create a folder containing all legal documents, starting with the company registration certificate, company constitution and shareholder agreement. After that, create an additional section for amendments to the shareholder agreement and share issues, trademarks and copyrights, patents (if you have any) and all important contracts. If your company has been in lawsuits, make sure you have summary documentation of proceedings (and references to detail documentation) available.

- ✔ **Production/operation and IT:** For online ventures, production/operation is typically combined with IT because most of the operational elements of the business are of an IT nature. Create a folder with high-level information about the hardware and software components of the company's IT infrastructure, as well as an overview of current and historical projects.

- ✔ **Tax/compliance:** This area may be done as part of the financial audit, but it's useful to have all tax- and compliance-related information readily available.

Note: The suggestions in the preceding list are only intended as general tasks to prepare a due diligence process. Each due diligence team is likely to ask for specific documents in specific formats.

If you're concerned about past issues that your company has gone through (for example, if your company had a nasty dispute with a shareholder or a legal battle over copyrights), think about how to present these issues to the due diligence team. As a general rule, you're usually much better off disclosing any potential areas of concern up-front rather than trying to hide them. If the due diligence team finds a substantial issue that wasn't disclosed earlier, they may well decide to abandon the acquisition or sales process.

Identifying and analysing potential buyers

In most cases, your likely buyers are your competitors, industry or market aggregators, or global powerhouses like Facebook (recently acquired Instagram), Microsoft (recently acquired Skype) or Google (recently acquired DailyDeal). You may have several options, depending on how you present your business — map them all out and draw up a list of potential buyers.

For each of the buyers you identify, you then need to analyse their current business situation, competitive threats and opportunities, and acquisition history. Consider the following suggested tasks to complete this step:

- ✔ Get your hands on annual reports and check the media releases on the buyer's website.

- ✔ Find out about the ownership structure — in Australia and New Zealand, you can simply go to the ASIC and Companies Office websites, respectively. Most other countries have a similar business registry website that you can use.

- ✔ Develop a comparative SWOT (strengths, weaknesses, opportunities, threats) document for your company and the potential buyers. You need to fully understand how the two companies can potentially complement each other. This exercise reveals which areas of your business are most interesting for a potential acquisition.

Your company needs something that either poses a competitive threat or represents an advantage to the potential buyer.

- ✔ Search the web for news on the potential buyer, looking particularly for past acquisition or mergers. If a company has a history of frequent acquisitions, they're likely to be acquiring more companies in the future.

- ✔ Use your existing network (such as board members, advisors, business partners) to find out about the financial position and appetite for acquisition of your potential buyer. If they're 'cashed up' (for example, have recently closed a large fundraising round), they may be looking to buy market share or expertise.

Developing tactics to get acquired

After you have all the background information on each buyer, decide on a plan to make your company attractive to one (or a number of) potential buyers by strengthening the areas that pose a competitive threat or represent an advantage to others.

You can try a number of tactical initiatives to increase your chances of getting acquired, as follows:

- ✔ Put together an aggressive marketing campaign that specifically targets a weakness of a competitor (and potential buyer) or is designed to draw attention from certain interest groups (for example, traffic aggregators).

- ✔ Team up with other players in a particular market to create a strong partnership (or potential merger) that seriously threatens the market leadership of a competitor.

- ✔ Design a public relations strategy involving media releases and (hopefully) articles in business publications highlighting your advantageous business position (for being acquired). You may need the help of a friendly journalist for this initiative.

Spreading the word

If you're particularly keen to sell your business quickly, you may want to consider directly approaching a competitor or potential buyer. While this puts you in a slightly less advantageous bargaining position for negotiations, it may well speed up the acquisition or trade sale process for your business so it's worth considering.

Before approaching competitors or potential buyers for your start-up, consider your approach carefully. You need full commitment from the board, your co-founders and staff. After word gets out that you're looking to get acquired, maintaining the status quo becomes difficult. Whatever you do, have a Plan B in place to continue with your business, just in case your potential buyers aren't interested (either because they don't see a compelling reason to buy or because they're holding out for a bargain).

One of the best ways to 'force' a sale is by delivering awesome
financial results and out-executing or out-innovating all other
players in the market. Excellent result performance or innovation
rarely goes unnoticed in the business world.

Handling Purchase Offers

Perhaps one of the biggest risks when exiting from or selling
your start-up is accepting an offer to purchase your business
too quickly and without thinking it through. If you act too
quickly, you may end up selling out too early or under
unfavourable conditions.

In some cases, the offers can be substantial (compared to
what you set your eyes on when you started out) and you
may consider anything over a certain amount (for example,
$10 million) a great offer. However, unless you do your
homework on the offer (and especially the conditions of the
offer) you can't really say whether it's a good offer or not.

When your venture reaches profitability and perhaps a certain
level of public exposure, you may start to receive offers to
purchase your company. When this happens, you need to keep
a cool head and deal with the offers rationally instead of giving
in to an emotional response to sell straightaway. If the offer is
time-bound and you don't feel you have enough time to fully
work through it, simply ask for an extension on the deadline.
If the potential buyers are truly interested, they're very likely
to agree to this (if not, they probably weren't that serious to
begin with).

In the following sections, I cover analysing the details of the
deal, involving a professional negotiator and finalising the deal
before you all sign on the dotted line.

Knowing if a deal is worthwhile

As a starting point for deciding whether a purchase offer is
worth considering, you need to have a full understanding of
the value of your company (refer to the section 'Getting your
company valued' for more detail).

Your up-to-date reference point for what your company is worth can either be a recent independent valuation you had done, a recent investment round or an internal valuation done by your finance team. You can then use this reference point as a basis for comparing the current value of your company to the offer.

 Have your company valued by someone you trust and who specialises in company valuations. Yes, valuations cost money but they're very useful — even if you don't go ahead with a sale just now. Unfortunately most companies doing valuations try to sell valuation work at inflated rates and they prey on financially naïve start-up entrepreneurs. As a rule of thumb the valuation should cost you about 1/10 of a per cent of the value of the company. For example if your company is worth $1m you should pay around $1k for the valuation.

Aside from the actual value of the offer, you need to pay very close attention to its terms and conditions. The list of conditions that could be included as part of an offer is infinite, and so get legal advice on the implications of these conditions. Some of them may place restrictions on you as a business person (for example, non-compete agreements, which mean you can't offer similar products or services in certain markets for a specified time, or the requirement for you to remain in the business for a certain period).

You also need to fully understand the financial terms of the agreement (that is, the proposed settlement process and the proposed compensation methods). Offers often include a mix of cash, stock options and shares in another legal entity. So also work through what these aspects mean for you personally and for your business.

Dealing with purchase offers can be quite distracting and so you need to make a judgement call as to how much time you want to spend on research every time you receive an offer.

 You also need to do research on the buyer before making any decisions about the offer. If the potential buyer is a well-known and respected company or business person, spending a decent amount of time on working through the proposed deal is probably a good idea (even if you don't go ahead).

You never know — you may be dealing with this person or organisation again in the future. If it's an offer from an unknown or dubious party (do some quick background checks via an online search or your business network) don't waste a lot of time on it. If the offer sounds dodgy or too good to be true, it probably is. In most cases you're best off to dismiss dubious offers quickly.

When evaluating purchase offers, also consider the future of your company and any implications on staff. If you're selling all your interest in the company, you may find having any influence on what happens after you sell hard, but asking about the buyer's intentions certainly doesn't hurt. Many deals include specific clauses on what happens with staff, business units or special provisions for projects the company is involved in (such as sponsorship deals, charitable donations or community projects). So don't be afraid to bring these aspects up in negotiations as well.

Hiring a professional

Depending on the size of the deal, you may benefit from hiring a professional negotiator. Negotiating the sale of a business is typically a complex process and you may not have the necessary skills to get the best possible outcome. It's really a bit like hiring a tax lawyer — yes, most likely you can do your tax declarations yourself but how long does it take and can you be sure you haven't missed any opportunities for refunds or items you needed to declare?

If the offer on your start-up is above $5 million, you're almost always better off with a professional negotiator. Often, you can make part of the fee dependent on the outcome the negotiator can get for you. Get the negotiator involved as early in the process as possible to avoid unknowingly disclosing (or giving away) points your negotiator may be able to negotiate on.

Don't rush into a sales process or agree to an offer too soon. In most cases, you don't need to rush (and especially not when you know that the buyer is artificially creating the timing pressure). Take your time; you may receive a better offer soon.

Sealing the deal

After you've analysed the potential buyer and perhaps hired a negotiator (refer to preceding section), you're ready to negotiate on common sticky points of a company purchase offer. These include the following:

- ✔ **Management contracts:** Covers the terms and conditions placed on key staff after the acquisition or sale. Explore all available options around remuneration, performance targets and period of the agreement to get to a satisfactory outcome.

- ✔ **Operations:** Make sure you consider the interests of all stakeholders of your company (including customers, staff and shareholders) to get an agreeable deal. For example, if you have to abandon a product as part of the acquisition, consider what happens to existing customers and staff.

- ✔ **Valuation and company value:** Perhaps the most essential point to negotiate during an acquisition or trade sale. Make a case for a particular valuation method to be used and involve comparative data to validate assumptions.

Refer to the section 'Knowing if a deal is worthwhile' earlier in this chapter for more aspects worth negotiating.

You need to work through the various pros and cons of an offer with your fellow directors or members of the board and then provide a recommendation to shareholders. Be prepared to deal with your investors, who may be keen to sell when you prefer to decline an offer. The best method for resolving internal differences in opinion is to base a decision on a rational evaluation of the offer (if need be by an independent advisor). Often a useful way to resolve a deadlock is to devise a counteroffer that includes terms that all stakeholders of your business can agree on. It is then up to the potential buyer to deal with the counteroffer.

After the terms of a deal have been agreed in principle and the specific points have been confirmed during the due diligence process (refer to the section 'Ensuring your books are in order' earlier in this chapter), you need to work on the execution and communication of the agreement. This may include a number of legal and governance-related processes (such as putting the deal to shareholders or clearing the deal with authorities). Communicating the agreement is usually done through media releases or press conferences and is sometimes accompanied by marketing campaigns (for example, if consumer brands and rebranding is involved). Typically, you do all this with the new owner of the company to ensure that a beneficial story is communicated to all stakeholders (and the public).

Always work in the interest of all stakeholders — nothing is worse than being seen to simply cash out on a deal and leave behind a mess (or without consideration for the interests of other key stakeholders).

Going Public: Offering Shares

Perhaps one of the most exciting parts of the start-up journey is listing your company on a public stock exchange. Investors usually refer to this process as *floating* or *listing* a company, *going public* or *doing an IPO* (initial public offering).

The reason this step is very exciting has to do with the options it presents to investors, shareholders and staff. After your company is publicly listed, all shares can be traded easily at the stock exchange. While IPOs are typically done to raise capital for the start-up, the nature of the process also allows the realisation of investments. In other words, investors and founders are able to sell (some of) their shares on the stock market and thus create a financial return on their investment.

Using New Zealand's Unlisted exchange

If you operate in New Zealand, you can also list your company on The Unlisted exchange (unlisted.co.nz). Unlisted is a trading facility for small- to medium-sized businesses not registered on a stock exchange under the Securities Markets Act. The Unlisted facility has different rules to stock exchanges and potential investors in companies using Unlisted aren't protected to the same levels that investors in publicly listed companies are (by the Securities Markets Act). Make sure you fully understand the terms and conditions involved when using Unlisted before considering it as a viable option to listing on a regulated stock exchange.

In the following sections, I cover the benefits and process involved with this option, including a breakdown of the listing process and how you prepare for going public.

Understanding the listing process

While you can potentially perform the acquisition and sales process for your company (or the process when selling your personal interest) yourself, you can't usually complete a listing process all by yourself (that is, without external advisors and specialists).

The listing process is generally quite complex due to the need to comply with stringent legislation that's based on providing investment opportunities for general investors (as opposed to specialised or sophisticated investors). Every country has legislation in place that provides a legal framework for how investment in companies and the trading of interests (shares) is to be conducted.

Most entrepreneurs and company directors aren't familiar with the details of the listing process and as such need to rely on the expertise of external advisors. However, being familiar with the general process of an IPO helps you understand what's required from you and your fellow directors or co-founders when the time comes to go through with a public listing.

Note: The following is a somewhat generalised version of the actual listing processes used by the Australian Security Exchange (ASX) and the New Zealand Security Exchange (NZX). For details, please read the two excellent listing guides available from the ASX (www.asx.com.au/documents/resources/asx_ipo_brochure.pdf) or the NZX (www.nzx.com/files/assets/NZX_Guide_to_listing.pdf).

Here are the basic steps you go through during an IPO:

1. **Consider the IPO.**

   The first step in every listing process is the internal consideration. This is usually initiated by the management team, the board or an investor. The following motivations are generally listed as the main reasons for considering a public listing:

   • The company requires additional capital for growth that can't be sourced from existing investors or through private equity investments.

- The company wants greater access to capital markets and exposure to a wider range of investors.

- Founders and existing investors want a flexible option for realising their investment.

As part of the consideration stage, companies typically contact the relevant stock exchange and listing specialists (advisors) to scope out and evaluate the potential for a successful listing. The consideration process finishes with a decision to list (or not).

2. Appoint advisors.

After a decision has been made to proceed with a public listing, the company needs to appoint a number of advisors (or an external listing team through one provider). The listing team or team of advisors is typically composed of lawyers, accountants, underwriters and stockbrokers, and other experts as required (such as valuation specialists). The company also needs to decide on other resources required to contribute to internal expertise and staffing during the listing process.

3. Discuss the listing with a stock exchange.

Both the ASX and the NZX emphasise their consultative responsibilities during the listing process. Teams at the stock exchanges should meet with company representatives and advisors early in the process to discuss the planned listing. Typically, various regulatory and compliance issues are discussed.

Consulting with the stock exchange your company is going to be listed on is a very useful step. It's in the interest of all parties to be aware of listing requirements as early as possible. During this step, you can also work out which exchange to list on because the stock exchanges usually run a number of exchanges.

4. Prepare the prospectus.

One of the key deliverables that need to be produced during the listing process is the investment *prospectus* (sometimes referred to as the *offer document* or *investment statement* in New Zealand). This document is a mandatory requirement to listing on the Australian and New Zealand stock exchanges, and its purpose is to inform potential investors about the investment opportunity and provide a detailed description of the company, the business situation and any other information that investors need to be aware of to make an informed decision about participating in the IPO.

An external auditor usually prepares the prospectus, and this company has a legal obligation to disclose any and all information related to the listing and investment opportunity presented to potential investors.

5. **Apply for a listing.**

The *listing participant* (the company doing the IPO) officially applies for a listing at the stock exchange and lodges the prospectus. In Australia, the prospectus needs to be lodged with ASIC; in New Zealand, the offer documents need to be lodged with the Companies Office. During this step, companies are also typically required to provide declarations from directors and pay listing fees and bonds.

6. **Go through the review and offer period.**

After the official application, a review period usually occurs, where the stock exchange and other relevant authorities review the offer documentation. After the review, you may need to update your application, prospectus or other documentation. Once all material is finalised, the offer is made available to the public.

During review period, companies generally advertise heavily to draw attention to the public offer and draw subscriptions.

7. **Proceed with the listing.**

When the offer period closes, your company needs to have raised the minimum capital required (as stated in the prospectus) to proceed with the public listing. After this step, your company gets included in the official list of companies trading on the stock exchange.

8. **Commence trading.**

Finally, trading commences for your newly listed company and shares can now be traded on the stock exchange.

Getting prepared for going public

In most cases, the listing process takes about six months and involves a large number of interrelated tasks that need to be coordinated. Most companies appoint a project manager to drive the listing process and develop an overall project plan that can be shared with key stakeholders.

Aside from the process outlined in the preceding section, companies intending to go public need to consider many other activities that need to be prepared well to get the best possible outcome of the listing process.

The following are some of the additional aspects companies preparing for an IPO need to consider:

- ✔ **Branding:** Some companies use the listing process as an opportunity for a general image revamp. This can send a signal to potential investors that the company is getting serious about the big opportunities ahead. Rebranding can also help you shed the start-up image and become an established company with sophisticated branding.

- ✔ **External communications and media:** IPOs typically draw attention from business, industry or general media. So a plan needs to be in place for how to handle enquiries and manage the release of information about the listing. Most companies use a communication plan to manage these activities. The plan needs to be inclusive of all external stakeholders — and existing customers and suppliers in particular.

- ✔ **Internal communications:** Doing a public listing is likely to be big news among staff, but strict guidelines should exist on what information can be released at what point. All staff who know about the intended listing need to sign a strict confidentiality agreement, and an internal communication needs to be developed that specifies at what point (and how) other staff find out about the listing. If preferential options for staff are part of the listing process, this needs to be communicated at the right time as well.

- ✔ **Marketing:** The main goal for marketing activities during the listing process is to present the company and the investment opportunity in its best possible light. Ideally, the shares available during the IPO will be fully subscribed or, even better, oversubscribed. This means the company has received at least as many offers to buy shares as shares are on issue. Some companies represent such compelling investment opportunities that IPO share allocations need to be decided by a ballot system (Google's IPO is a good example of this) because so much interest in buying shares exists. Most companies, however, have to boost their subscriptions through marketing activities.

↙ **Staff options:** Many companies want their staff to benefit from the IPO as well. So the management team needs to decide on what options are made available to staff as part of the listing process.

While the listing activity is going on, your company still needs to continue with business as usual. The last thing you want during the listing process is to show any sign of weakness on the business front, so making sure the listing related activities don't interfere with business operations (to the extent possible) should also be part of your planning process.

Life After a Sale or IPO

I have been lucky enough to experience the journey of a number of entrepreneurs who've realised their start-up vision. Many of them sold their company (or interest) at a price that allows them to be fully financially independent for the rest of their lives (assuming they don't blow their capital on the next start-up). It is truly inspiring to witness this process and see the transformation that happens to people's lives (and life styles). What amazes me is that almost everyone I know in this category became extremely interested in helping other entrepreneurs succeed. Many have started a charitable trust or are otherwise involved in philanthropic enterprises. Most of them took some time out and then went straight back into their next venture.

I have been very impressed with the high degree of professionalism I have witnessed in entrepreneurs who just completed an IPO or trade sale. After a massive party and perhaps a few days off, they all attended to matters at hand. Many of them turned up again at 9 am the next Monday to continue their job under the new owner (if that was part of the deal) or helped the new staff get settled in.

I have observed that most entrepreneurs after a trade sale and IPO pay particular attention to any form of share transfer. If they still had shares in the company, they had to observe particular clauses when selling or transferring their shares. This is usually done to protect the interest of all other share holders. In publicly traded companies, specific restrictions apply to share sales of directors or senior managers anyway. If you end up with a publicly listed company, make sure you understand the specific rules around share transactions of directors and staff.

Another aspect that really impressed me with highly successful entrepreneurs is that they generally followed the same approach to starting new businesses. The fact that they had already cashed out on a previous business didn't mean they could ignore the techniques and strategies outlined in this book. In a way it's nice to know that the Mark Zuckerbergs and Kevin Systroms of this world are still subject to the same underlying principles of early stage ventures. So many highly successful entrepreneurs use the same process of preparing product–market hypotheses, testing them, and then adapting their products and services accordingly. My observation has been that no 'magic bullet' exists for start-up success — all entrepreneurs have to work through the same challenges no matter whether they've had a hugely successful exit or not.

Part V
The Part of Tens

Glenn Lumsden

*'The figures look solid, but frankly,
as investors, we'd feel more comfortable
if you were a 20-year-old computer
geek with no social skills.'*

In this part ...

In this part, I provide essential business knowledge in summarised form — bookmark these pages and refer to them often! I outline the 11 mistakes entrepreneurs commonly make that end up killing their start-ups. I then provide ten ways to boost your start-up resources and, lastly, I disclose the ten things investors are looking for in your start-up.

Chapter 10

Ten (Plus One!) Mistakes That Cause Start-Ups to Fail

I often see entrepreneurs making the same mistakes (sometimes repeatedly with several of their ventures), and some of these mistakes can cause a start-up to falter or fail. In this chapter, I list the common mistakes frequently made by entrepreneurs and how to avoid making them.

Rushing In

Many entrepreneurs (myself included) have a tendency to rush in when it comes to setting up new businesses, usually because they're so excited about a future business and the possibility of creating something from scratch. Most entrepreneurs (again, myself included) are also dreamers — in their minds, any future business is always perfect and a sure way to ultimate success. The reality, of course, tends to be quite different.

So, entrepreneurs who want to beat the odds (and become radically successful) need to do something that's almost against their nature — hold off and reflect.

Let several days pass after the conception of an idea (as hard as that may be). If it still feels great after a few days, then you can sit down and write up all assumptions, hypotheses, target markets or segments, and develop some simple use cases for the product or service you are trying to create. This cooling-off period can prevent you from wasting time and money on ideas that seem silly after a few days.

Religiously follow the steps I outline in Chapter 2 on validating assumptions and achieving a product–market fit. And bear in mind that you're likely to have enough opportunities (or a need) to rush things along through the rest of your start-up journey.

Getting Too Far Ahead (Or Too Far Behind) Everyone Else

Timing is a funny thing when it comes to start-ups. Being too early to market with an idea or concept is just as bad as being too late.

In 2006, I was involved in the production of a web-based idea where the designers envisaged that visitors to the website could update text fields on the website by simply clicking into the text. While this is a common feature these days, at the time our users found the concept really confusing. Everyone wanted an Edit and an OK or Submit button when it came to editing texts. In the end we had to ditch the idea and revert back to a more standard editing functionality that most other sites used at the time.

Make sure you're not too far ahead or behind of what's currently accepted as common practice. If you're too late, you're competing in a crowded marketplace. But if you're too early, your business has to spend a lot of money (and time) on educating users.

Running Out of Resources

A common issue that results in start-ups going out of business is simply running out of resources (usually money or people willing to contribute time to the venture). Make sure you understand the concept of a runway (refer to Chapter 7 for more detail) and keep your finger on the pulse with your co-founders and core team members. You need to be able to tell when a resource disaster is coming your way (at least by a few months out).

Controlling a financial runway is relatively simple — look at how much money you've got right now and keep track of your incoming and outgoing funds. Understand that raising capital from external investors takes at least two to three months. So plan your investment rounds early when you still have plenty of runway left.

Avoiding running out of your staff resources is a little bit trickier — predicting what your co-founders and team members are going to do can be difficult. But it's your job as founder to keep everyone motivated and excited about what you're trying to achieve. (Refer to Chapter 7 for ways to keep staff motivated.)

Lacking Focus

For some reason, many entrepreneurs believe that having plenty of options is somehow much better than having only one. Investors are much more worried about entrepreneurs losing focus (by pursuing too many options in parallel) than by them not having enough options to diversify or extend the business.

When presenting to investors, focus on one idea or concept only — and strengthen that one option with as much data and validations as possible. Even if you've identified many ways to extend your idea, resist the urge to tell investors about them.

Once your business is up and running, keep that focus and check every option that comes your way against a plan or targets. Any deviation from your written business plan or goals needs to be as a result of something you have learnt about your product or target market.

Not Validating Core Assumptions

Lots of ventures fail in the early stages of their start-up journey because the founders have built a product or service that nobody needs or buys. This situation is a direct result of not validating core assumptions.

The beginning of every successful venture involves testing, testing and testing. Testing is the only way to find out what customers want and whether your assumptions about market size, uptake, competition and other core parameters are valid.

Ignoring Feedback

Ignoring customer feedback is just as dangerous as not testing assumptions. Ignoring feedback typically happens at two stages of a start-up venture — at the beginning and once the business has achieved product–market fit and product or service uptake is happening. It really doesn't matter how successful (financially) your company is — ignoring customer feedback is never a good idea.

Digg is a good reminder of the importance of listening to feedback. A large portion of the user base at Digg left when the company decided to redesign their site — because these users felt the company was ignoring feedback and didn't give them the functionality they really wanted.

Make an extra and constant effort to understand (in detail) what your customers want. Most importantly, thank them if they're giving you feedback — even if the feedback comes in the form of an unpleasant complaint.

Holding On for Too Long

Knowing when it's time to move on is a great skill to have. Unfortunately, many entrepreneurs aren't blessed with this skill and so hold on to their businesses or positions for too long — meaning their businesses suffer or perish.

Having all the skills required to take a business from an idea to a multimillion or multibillion dollar enterprise is extremely rare. Yes, a number of individuals, like Mark Zuckerberg or Bill Gates, have done it — but these are exceptions rather than the rule. In many cases, founders are actually much better off handing over a business or functions of that business to individuals with the required experience in getting to the next stage of growth or improvements.

Check in with yourself regularly on whether you feel out of your depth in a particular area and to what extent you have achieved your start-up vision. Another idea or project is likely to come along, so evaluate your options. No need to die in your business or with your business.

Ignoring Lessons Learnt

Experiencing problems, issues or disasters as an entrepreneur is a gift. It may not seem like that at the time but, annoyingly, most of the really valuable lessons are all associated with painful experiences of some sort. Entrepreneurs have an obligation to learn from these experiences to help them get to ultimate success with their businesses.

Unfortunately, I come across a lot of entrepreneurs who keep making the same mistakes over and over again. So when you have a challenging experience in your business, take some time to analyse what led to the situation and ask others (such as your advisors) what they think contributed to it. Understand the reasons in detail and try to identify warning signals that you can use in the future to spot the situation before you make the same mistake again.

All of these lessons learnt form part of your business experience, which is highly valuable — unless you choose to ignore them.

Picking the Wrong Partners

The start-up journey is generally a long one and often lasts for a decade or more. So being in business with others is really a bit like a marriage or long-term relationship — staying together 'for better or worse' is challenging.

Many business failures are ultimately the result of disputes between founders. Clarity and transparency from day one helps avoid misunderstandings that can lead to disputes. For example, having a clear shareholder agreement in place (with documented shareholdings and responsibilities) is a great start to manage the relationship between founders. (Refer to Chapter 3 for more on shareholder agreements.)

The same principles apply to strategic business decisions, areas of responsibilities, performance and expense policies (to name a few areas that frequently lead to disagreement between business partners).

Agreeing on a resolution path up-front (before an issue arises that needs resolving) is also a really good idea to make sure you can stay together as a team. Disagreement is a natural and important part of running a business — it is a matter of managing these well so that the business can continue.

Avoid going into business with complete strangers or people you know little about. However, being in business with spouses, friends or relatives can be equally challenging — unless you're absolutely convinced you can work through any conflicts that arise. Go on a ten-day business trip or holiday with someone who you want to be in business with, and see how you get along.

Ignoring the Lawyers (For Too Long)

Dealing with lawyers can be a double-edged sword for entrepreneurs. On the one hand, lawyers are absolutely essential for putting together agreements that hold up in front of courts (if worse comes to worst). On the other hand, lawyers are paranoid by nature and a simple agreement can turn into a 20-page document that's impossible to read for anyone without a law degree (and consequently is useless for customers, potential business partners or investors).

However, lawyers generally have to act in the best interests of their clients and so their job is to make you aware of any and all potential legal risks involved with a business idea. Entrepreneurs have a tendency to ignore these risks in order to proceed with their idea. Sometimes that works out but, in many cases, the legal risk ultimately catches up with the venture and leads to the collapse of the business (as was the case with Napster or MegaUpload).

Seek a number of opinions (from independent parties) on legal matters that relate directly to the potential collapse of your business.

Being Caught Out by Bad Luck

As much as I hate to admit it, unfortunately a lot of good and bad luck is involved in being in business. Nobody in the start-up world likes to talk about good and bad luck because it is, of course, outside of their control. However, it can be a factor and can mean entrepreneurs experience failure despite having done everything right. Be aware that things can happen to even the best laid plans — if this happens to you, pick yourself up to start your next venture.

Knowing what truly motivates you and gives you an energy boost is valuable when you're somewhat depressed about your current business outlook. If you have been caught out by bad luck, you need to lift your spirits again so that you don't drag a lot of baggage around with you, especially into your next venture! Some entrepreneurs use travel, charity work, family (kids) or retreats to pick themselves up after a business collapse. These days, you can even use another start-up 'Pinterest' to creat a dream board or mood board to capture what motivates you.

Chapter 11

Ten Ways to Boost Your Start-Up Resources

*T*his chapter is all about how to identify and utilise resources for your business. Being an entrepreneurship is an art form that requires you to find ways to get something done without using conventional methods (such as paying for it). As an entrepreneur you need to be innovative in all aspects of your business — not only in the products and services you offer.

Presenting to High-Net-Worth Individuals

Presenting your business or business idea to high-net-worth individuals can be a useful way to extend your resources. They may or may not invest, but even if they don't invest but like the idea, they may be able to connect you to other parties who can help with your business.

The key to connecting with high-net-worth individuals is relationships. If you don't know anyone in that category, you probably need to invest some time in networking (refer to Chapter 4) and connecting with high-net-worth individuals is part of that activity. An easy way to extend your network is to get involved (or introduced) into business networks or clubs. Another option is to simply approach a particular individual directly.

When you approach potential investors for the first time, don't pitch to them straightaway. Get to know them, and understand their current interests and motivation in life. Sometimes, you may have to be creative and use other angles (other than business) to get closer to these investors. I have used the 'father' angle (if I know the investor has kids), a common hobby and volunteering (charity work) to meet influential people who ended up helping me a lot with my businesses.

Raising Capital from Institutional Investors

Having sufficient money in the bank is almost always the best option when it comes to funding your venture (although some examples do exist of start-ups that probably had too much money to play with for their own good — ferrit.co.nz is a good one).

However, boosting your resources through *institutional* investors (companies, individuals or organisations with a primary business of investing in other companies) is often the next best option. This money does come with conditions — typically strategic input at board level — but this is a good thing.

Make sure you read the do's and don'ts of pitching to investors in Chapter 7 before approaching institutional investors — you generally only get one chance to speak to them so you need to get your pitch right the first time.

Entering Start-Up Competitions

Start-up (or business plan) competitions can be a useful way to boost your resources — especially during the very first months of starting a new business. Competition prizes can include anything from free mentoring or products and services, to actual cash.

However, entering competitions can come with a downside — the competition itself can be a significant distraction as you need to fill in forms, present or follow the competition requirements. All of this takes time and time is a valuable asset when starting a business.

 Carefully weigh up the benefits of entering competitions versus the downsides. Calculate how much time you're likely to spend on the competition (until the end), add up your hours and multiply by $100. Now look at the value of the prizes and compare. Another option is to only consider start-up competitions before you've actually started your company (that is, while you're still in the conceptual stage). During this stage, you can use the competition as a testing and validation tool for your assumptions. Since competitions involve evaluations and presentations to experts, the judges or mentors test your assumptions — and they can point out where your assumptions are weak or not realistic.

Applying for Grants

Applying for grants is similar to entering start-up competitions (see preceding section) in that the 'prize' (the grant) can be a useful boost but it also requires considerable effort. Most grant schemes involve a vast amount of form filling and (if you receive the grant) reporting. Many grants also come with a long list of conditions your company needs to comply with in order to be eligible for funding.

 I nearly killed one of my businesses with a grant we had applied for (and received). The grant was a matching grant (50 per cent of a particular type of expenses were paid by the grant body). However, a minimum level of eligible expenses was required ($80,000) and this really stretched our resources. Unfortunately, the three-year grant was then shut down after the first year. So we'd started on an aggressive expansion strategy (incurring the necessary level of expenses) with no way to claim 50 per cent of these expenses back in future years. We managed to get through but this was a huge lesson for me to never base any strategy or business on grant funding.

Participating in Incubator and Accelerator Programs

Incubator and accelerator programs are a great way to boost your business resources. Most of these programs offer a significant amount of general business education, mentoring, access to industry experts and, in some cases, access to shared resources (such as a shared office space). Incubators and accelerators take a relatively small amount of equity (such as 5 to 10 per cent) in return for the services you receive.

For entrepreneurs starting their first start-up, these programs are really a no-brainer, and I strongly recommend applying to a suitable program. Aside from all the tangible resources they provide, the most important aspect of these programs is that they provide structure — a particular method for getting the business off the ground. This is hugely valuable in the early stages of a business because young entrepreneurs often find it hard to figure out what to do next or which of the hundreds of things they could be doing adds the most value to their business

Incurring Debt

Adding financial resources to your business by incurring debt is usually only a feasible option for entrepreneurs who either have an asset that can be used to secure the debt (such as a house) or where the business is at a stage that it has tangible assets (or future cash flow such as a confirmed sale).

Traditional lending institutions (such as banks) are very cautious about lending money to businesses following the global financial crisis in 2007. As a result, most entrepreneurs struggle to get a loan that's simply based on presenting a good business plan to the bank manager. And, of course, a significant risk exists that you lose the asset (for example, your house) you used to secure the debt if you can't repay the debt as per the agreed payment schedule. So consider this option carefully. I certainly don't encourage entrepreneurs to incur a lot of debt (not more than you can pay off in about three months in your day job) before they have validated core assumptions and have made some sales.

However, incurring debt is a very attractive option for start-ups once you're more certain you're on to a 'sure thing' with your business — that is, you've validated all assumptions, have achieved product–market fit and sales are beginning to happen. In this case, you simply use the debt to finance the period till you reach profitability.

The big advantage with debt compared to external investment is that the company ownership structure doesn't change as a result of the debt. You don't need to change your shareholder agreement or board composition — when you pay the debt off, your obligation to the lender ends.

Working with Interns and Volunteers

Getting an intern even during the early stages of a start-up is a great way to boost your resources. Especially in the online world, you can easily find a use for a bright student who can program or develop websites. But interns can also add a lot of value in other areas of the business, such as marketing or operations.

Make sure you go through the same selection process for interns as when hiring an employee (or teaming up with a business partner). In other words, don't just say yes to anyone who asks for an internship. Also be very clear about what you expect from the intern and what you provide in return (such as a small salary, work experience and reimbursement of expenses).

Volunteers are in a similar category to interns — but are typically easier to organise and manage. When you launch your online business, you almost inevitably come across people who want to volunteer their services to be part of your business. Commonly, people want to write articles on the company blog, moderate a forum or manage blog comments.

Working with volunteers can really boost the amount of hours you have available for other activities in your business that only you can do. The same rules apply, though, for working with volunteers — be very clear about what their responsibilities are, what you expect from them and how (if at all) they're to be compensated for any work they do.

Make sure you've got a way to terminate any relationship with interns or volunteers immediately or within a short period in case things don't work out. Have a simple contract in place (even with volunteers) that sets out the key parameters of the work.

Sharing Resources

In many cities in Australia and New Zealand, you can now find shared office spaces that are particularly geared towards start-ups. Many places offer a desk with IT infrastructure (such as internet access and printers), admin support (reception or accounting services) as well as shared spaces (meeting rooms). Prices for a desk start from about $100 a week, which is typically a lot cheaper and easier to organise than finding and equipping your own premises. The additional benefit is networking opportunities and being part of a start-up environment. So using such a facility is definitely worth considering.

In a wider sense, I always encourage entrepreneurs to see how they can share resources or use shared resources — including open-source software, staff, transport or expensive equipment. Think creatively about how you can make use of something you need without paying outright for it. Maybe you already know someone who has what you need and it's just a matter of working out how you can share a particular resource. Either way, sharing resources is an easy and effective way to boost the resources available to your business.

Asking Friends and Family to Help Out

Occasionally, your start-up may get close to the brink of collapse because all of your resources are just stretched to breaking point. This is where your friends and family may need to lend a helping hand. Hopefully, they're all aware of your start-up anyway and so asking them to help out is easy.

Asking friends and family to help out is probably a bit of a last resort action — I wouldn't recommend doing this on an ongoing basis or even counting your friends and family as staff. But in my experience friends and family can be a fantastic way to solve a short-term crisis. The operative words here are *short term*.

Funding Your Business Through Cash Flow

Strictly speaking this option is not actually about ways to boost your resources. However, if you can plan and set up your business in a way that you don't need investment or debt, you're on very solid ground with your business.

The ability to fund your business (and its expansion) through cash flow may even be a deciding criterion right at the beginning when you're considering starting a business. If you don't have access to substantial cash resources, you may decide not to execute a business that relies on significant upfront investment. Perhaps you can execute another idea first that's able to attract revenue from day one. Many successful entrepreneurs have started out in this way by creating a (small) cash flow positive business before executing their 'big hairy audacious' idea.

Chapter 12

Ten Things Investors Look for in Your Start-Up

*I*n this chapter, I unashamedly disclose all the secret things investors look for when they listen to pitches from entrepreneurs. Find out what you need to do to prepare your pitch, what information needs to be included in your pitch and how to really impress investors on the day.

What's Your Edge?

A fundamental question that you need to be able to answer when presenting to investors is: How is your start-up concept different from all the other ideas and businesses already servicing your target market? In other words, what's your (competitive) edge? When you plan for a pitch, make sure you prepare a really compelling answer to this question. If you can't answer this question convincingly, you may want to revisit your idea.

A few answers I've heard that are unlikely to impress investors are

✔ **'Our business is like Facebook, just better.'** *Better* is a subjective judgement that's unproven. Ever since the famous VHS vs Beta Max business case, the world knows that a better implementation or technology doesn't mean a better (more viable) business.

✔ **'We provide all the services that Facebook, Twitter, Pinterest and Google provide but on one platform.'** Convergence of existing services is never a great idea unless you have a unique position in the market to be the only player to implement an aggregation of fragmented services (and a need exists for a one-stop-shop solution).

✔ **'Nobody else is doing this.'** 'Unlikely' is what investors usually respond when they hear this sentence. Someone else is always out there who's doing what you're proposing or something similar. Secondly, even if nobody can be found who's doing exactly what you're proposing, it doesn't mean that someone won't be doing it in three months' time.

Validation

More than anything, investors want to see that you've done your homework (in detail) and can pull out impressive or interesting stats about your idea; for example, that you've already run a test using a mock-up site and had 367 people sign up for a service or product (which doesn't exist yet). Even better is if you can provide additional stats around the cost of getting those 367 people to sign-up. (Refer to Chapter 3 for more information on product or service testing and mock-up sites.)

I recently ran a test for a new app to help people remember names. We used Google Adwords to drive traffic to a landing page that briefly explained the concept and asked people to sign up for a free trial. We spent $125 on Google Adwords, received around 1,200 unique visits to our mock-up site and collected 247 email addresses. This means our conversion rate (from visitor to signed-up user) was roughly about 20 per cent and the cost per email address collected was $0.50. This is great data to use when presenting to investors because it means we've validated that at least some level of interest exists and that the acquisition cost of new users for the app may be around $0.50. We were able to complete the entire exercise in about two weeks — so you have no excuses for not having done a similar test when presenting to investors.

A Winning Team

Similar to an edge (refer to the section 'What's Your Edge?' earlier in this chapter), investors want to see that you've assembled a winning team. Investors are likely to ask why you think that you (and your team) are best placed to execute a particular idea. They're looking for you to outline the skills, experience, networks or other resources that you can bring into the business that gives you a distinct advantage over similar teams executing the same idea. You need to prepare a good answer for this question. Make sure you work out what speciality each team member has that uniquely improves your chances of success with the start-up concept.

A Total Market Size of $1 Billion+

In Chapter 2, I discuss the concept of the total market size and total addressable market (TAM). These calculations are really the starting point of every business because they give you a very rough indication of whether a particular concept is even worth pursuing (as a venture that can be highly profitable on a large scale).

Investors typically want to see a total market size or, better still, a TAM of at least $1 billion because they know that most start-ups only manage to acquire a fraction of the TAM. During the course of implementing your start-up idea, you typically discover a lot of facets about the market size that you didn't know beforehand. As a result, the market size or addressable market size may end up being a lot smaller than originally thought.

Investors have seen this many times over and have concluded that unless a new business concept is able to address a market of at least $1 billion at the outset, it's pointless to pursue the idea because the resulting business may simply be too small to be (financially) interesting to investors. So make sure you pick and define a suitable market size when presenting to investors.

An Unfair Advantage

An 'unfair' advantage is something that other start-ups in a similar situation or market don't have. You need to create this unfair advantage by attracting people with unique skills, developing a proprietary component of your service or product, acquiring patents or trademarks, or signing exclusive deals with business partners. You can pretty much have all of these options in place before you present to investors and, as a result, many investors expect you to have an unfair advantage when you present to them.

De-risking

Investors understand risks and rewards really well — they constantly compare investment options in terms of those two parameters. Banks and government bonds typically serve as a benchmark for being the lowest risk investment option possible. The return on these types of investments is virtually guaranteed (unless the bank or government defaults, which is rare or used to be rare — fingers crossed for Greece, Italy, Spain, Portugal and Ireland). However, the returns aren't very attractive to investors (you're lucky to get a 5 per cent return on these types of investment).

As a result, investors look for higher returns and, to get those returns, are willing to accept a certain amount of risk that they may lose some or all of their invested money. Investing in start-ups typically presents the highest risk investment option but also offers the highest rewards. So, if you can significantly reduce the risk of a start-up investment, investors look favourably on your business as an investment opportunity.

As an entrepreneur, you have many ways to de-risk your business. These options include validation and market test results, confirmed sales or a strong sales pipeline, strong sustainable growth, demonstrated ability to scale, a significant market share and all the factors that create an unfair advantage (see preceding section).

When you present to investors make a point of showing what you have done (specifically) to lower the risk involved with your business. A good way of showing this is by identifying all possible risks at the outset and what you have done to address, mitigate or eliminate them.

Proven Ability to Execute Well

Your proven ability to execute an idea or implement a plan is something that investors want to see. So make sure you can point to examples in your career where you executed a project according to a pre-determined plan. You also need to prepare examples of how you handled any deviations from the plan or responded to unforeseen challenges and issues.

You basically need to give investors a lot of confidence that, no matter what happens, you're able to deal with obstacles and find a way to complete a task or achieve a given target. If you want to emphasise your ability to do this, find referees from past projects who can speak up for you.

Boundless Energy

If you don't get an adrenaline rush naturally when presenting to investors, make sure you get a few extra espresso shots in before you pitch. Investors love high-energy pitches (as long as you don't appear outrageously nervous) and are attracted to an abundance of energy. From an investor's perspective, your team is like an innovation engine and everyone wants to see the engine go faster constantly. So appearing to be 'full of beans' is a great way to present.

You also need to demonstrate your enthusiasm and passion for your idea — pitching is really like performing on stage. So get in lots of dress rehearsals with feedback from others to make sure you do well on the day. If you don't have anyone who can listen to a practice pitch, record yourself on video and watch yourself (it's painful to do but extremely useful for improving presentations).

A Solid Revenue Model

The strongest position you can have when pitching to investors is to present a solid revenue model (one that's not based on advertising revenue alone). A strong revenue model is based on product or service sales, commissions, subscriptions or license fees.

In the absence of revenue, only one other aspect of a business generally interests investors and that's massive growth (as evidenced by Instagram's and Pinterest's start-up journey).

If you've already launched a prototype and can point to incredible growth figures (like growth rates of several 100-per-cent month on month and a significant size of users or traffic, such as 100,000 users or unique visitors), you can probably get away with a weaker revenue model such as one based on advertising.

Have a look at Chapter 3 to find out more about revenue generation options.

A Clear Exit Strategy

Last but not least (literally), you need to have a feasible and convincing exit strategy to impress investors. One of the main concerns for investors when investing in your business is how they can capitalise on their investment. In other words, how can they realise the return they're hoping to achieve by investing in your start-up.

Funnily enough, not many options exist to realise investments — companies can pay out dividends to investors (shareholders), complete a trade sale or acquisition, or go public. The only other option investors have to cash in on your investment is by selling their shares to another investor. While your company isn't listed on a stock exchange, selling shares may be tricky (especially if your company is still in the pre-revenue or pre-profit stage). So you need to think carefully about what options you can present to investors that outlines how they can make money with their investment and how the returns are realised.

For example, if you aim to be acquired by Google (which I tend to hear a lot from entrepreneurs), you need to understand exactly under which circumstances Google acquires other businesses and at what stage, price and valuation. The investors you present to probably know details of Google's acquisition strategy so make sure you don't get caught out when asked about your exit strategy.

Appendix A

Finding Support for Your Start-Up

*W*hen you're starting your own venture, you need all the help you can get. To make the process of finding suitable people to help easier, I've included a list here of organisations in Australia and New Zealand you can check out to see if they meet your start-up needs. The lists include all the usual suspects of start-up assistance, like incubators, angel investors and entrepreneur networks. Don't be afraid to contact any of these organisations to see how they can help.

Accessing Support in Australia

Plenty of support for entrepreneurs is available in Australia, especially if you're looking to get your start-up running as quickly as possible. In the following sections, I provide details for Australian incubator and accelerator programs, as well as angel investors, co-working office spaces and organisations to help and inspire you.

Incubators

The following incubator programs are available in Australia:

- Blue Chilli, Sydney and Melbourne — bluechilli.com
- Green Lane Digital, Sydney — greenlanedigital.com.au
- Push Start, Sydney — pushstart.com.au

Accelerators

Only one accelerator program is available in Australia: Push Start Accelerator, Sydney (pushstart.com.au).

Angel investors

The following groups or associations of angel investors are available in Australia:

- ✔ Australian Association of Angel Investors — www.aaai.net.au
- ✔ Business Angels — businessangels.com.au
- ✔ Future Capital (Development Fund), Sydney — futurecapital.com.au
- ✔ Innovation Bay, Sydney — innovationbay.com
- ✔ SA Angels — saangels.com.au

Co-working spaces

Co-working spaces not only offer a cheaper alternative to renting your own premises or office, but also provide avenues for networking with and gaining input from other entrepreneurs. In Australia, two co-working spaces in particular are worth checking for these reasons: Fishburners in Sydney (fishburners.org) and Space Cubed (spacecubed.org) in Perth.

Further help

For accessing further help and useful resources, the open wiki run by Startup Australia (www.startup-australia.org) is great. The site lists blogs, upcoming events and important people, and offers podcasts.

Nosing Out Help in New Zealand

Not to be left behind in the start-up stakes, New Zealand offers lots of support for budding kiwi entrepreneurs. In the following sections, I provide details for New Zealand incubator and accelerator programs, as well as angel investors, co-working office spaces and organisations to help and inspire you.

Incubators

The following incubator programs are available in New Zealand:

- ✔ AUT Auckland University Business Innovation Centre — bic.aut.ac.nz
- ✔ CreativeHQ, Wellington — creativehq.co.nz
- ✔ eCentre Massey, NZ wide — ecentre.org.nz
- ✔ Powerhouse and IIC, Christchurch — www.iic.co.nz
- ✔ The BCC, Hamilton — thebcc.co.nz
- ✔ The Icehouse, Auckland — theicehouse.co.nz
- ✔ Upstart, Dunedin — upstart.org.nz
- ✔ WebFund, Wellington — www.webfund.co.nz

Accelerators

Only one accelerator program is offered in New Zealand: Hyperstart in Wellington (hyperstart.co.nz).

Angel investors

The following angel investor groups or associations are available in New Zealand:

- ✔ Angel Association — angelassociation.co.nz
- ✔ Angel HQ — angelhq.co.nz
- ✔ Sparkbox — sparkbox.co.nz

Co-working space

Co-working spaces in New Zealand that also provide opportunities for networking and increasing your motivation are offered by BizDojo in Auckland and Wellington (bizdojo.co.nz).

Further help

For further inspiration, information and possibilities for networking, check out the following:

- ✔ Startup Weekends — startupweekend.org, wellington.startupweekend.org and auckland.startupweekend.org
- ✔ Unlimited Potential — up.org.nz

Appendix B

Templates

· ·

*I*n this appendix, I provide a number of templates to help you through your start-up journey. The templates can not only save you time, but can also help you cover all of the important components of a particular document.

The templates included here are the following:

- ✔ Memorandum of understanding (MOU — Figure B-1)
- ✔ One-page business plan (Figure B-2)
- ✔ Cash flow sample (Figure B-3)
- ✔ Brand definition (Figure B-4)
- ✔ Media release (Figure B-5)
- ✔ SWOT analysis (Figure B-6)
- ✔ Sample contract for freelancers (Figure B-7)
- ✔ Cash benefit analysis (CBA — Figure B-8)

Another general tip for any other types of documents you need to write is to do an online search for the document name plus the word 'template' or 'sample'. Don't reinvent the wheel — use what others have done before, and adapt accordingly. In most cases, you can find useful sample documents or templates online (free of charge or for a small fee).

Memorandum of Understanding

Between:

NAME A, NAME B, and so on. ('The Founders')

All parties agree to the following:

The Founders agree to form a company ('The Company') for the purpose of _____

The following has been agreed relating to the creation of the new company:

1. Equity in the company is split as follows:
   a. NAME A: _____%
   b. NAME B: _____%
   c. *Continue as required*

2. The Founders have agreed to invest up to $_____ in total into The Company (payable pro rata as per equity split) until further agreement. The initial investment covers business expenses and operations for the first _____ months.

The initial phase of business operations will focus on _____. This phase is expected to last for [*3/6/12*] months. During this phase the roles of the Founders are defined as follows:

1. Name A: _____
2. Name B: _____
3. *Continue as required*

The founders agree to commit to a total contribution of _____ hours per month for the first [*3/6/12*] months (each founder contributes time pro rata as per the equity split). The following targets have been defined for the end of the initial phase:

1. Target 1
2. Target 2
3. *Continue as required*

Following the initial phase, a review period will occur to check progress and decide on next steps. It is the current understanding of the Founders that at this point, additional resources and/or additional capital will be required as well as a need to agree on a comprehensive shareholder agreement.

The Founders agree to make best efforts to keep each other informed about any business-related information at all times. There will be weekly meetings or conference calls and other communication as required.

Other agreements:

- Voting: each founder has one equal vote, major decisions require a unanimous vote

- *Continue as required*

These agreements are indicative in nature and for the purpose of establishing a common understanding among the Founders. If a change to any of the above is required, this will be done in agreement with all Founders.

Signature / Date / Witnesses for all parties on this agreement

Figure B-1: Memorandum of understanding template.

Company logo

Last update date:
Org. name:

Vision / Core Values

Vision Statement

1) Value 1

2) Value 2

3) Value 3

4) Value 4

5) Value 5

Core Competencies

Purpose / Strategy

Purpose

Purpose statement

How do you live purpose / values?

1	Action / Method / Standard 1
2	Action / Method / Standard 2
3	Action / Method / Standard 3
4	Action / Method / Standard 4
5	Action / Method / Standard 5

Strengths

Opportunities

Exit

Future Date	
Revenues	
Profit	
Valuation	

What does success look like?

Success statement

Strategic priorities

1	Priority 1
2	Priority 2
3	Priority 3
4	Priority 4
5	Priority 5

Weaknesses

Threats

Medium term goals (1 year max)

Date (YE)	
Revenues	
Profit	
Headcount	
KPI1	
KPI2	
KPI3	
KPI4	
KPI5	
etc.	

Priorities over next 12 months

1	Priority 1
2	Priority 2
3	Priority 3
4	Priority 4
5	Priority 5

Quarterly goals (3 months)

Quarter #	
Revenues	
Profit	
Headcount	
KPI1	
KPI2	
KPI3	
KPI4	
KPI5	

Rocks this quarter (must achieve) — Who

1	Action / Initiative 1	
2	Action / Initiative 2	
3	Action / Initiative 3	
4	Action / Initiative 4	
5	Action / Initiative 5	

Market

1 Segment / size
2 Segment / size
3 Segment / size

Customer personas

1
2
3

Special Projects (monthly / quarterly)

Deadline:

Measurable Target/Critical #

Objective

Deadline:

Measurable Target/Critical #

Objective

Proven Hypothesis

Validated Assumptions

Figure B-2: One-page business plan template.

Sales/Revenue	Probability	Income/Cost	January	February	March	April	May	June	July	August	September	October	November	December
Clients	100%	Income	$ 3,500.00	$ 2,000.00	$ 3,000.00	$ 4,000.00	$ 5,000.00	$ 5,000.00	$ 7,500.00	$ 7,500.00	$ 3,500.00	$ 2,166.00	$ 166.00	$ -
Products	100%	Income	$ 2,345.00	$ 1,340.00	$ 2,010.00	$ 2,680.00	$ 3,350.00	$ 3,350.00	$ 5,025.00	$ 5,025.00	$ 2,345.00	$ 1,451.00	$ 111.00	$ -
Subscriptions	100%	Income	$ 1,155.00	$ 660.00	$ 990.00	$ 1,320.00	$ 1,650.00	$ 1,650.00	$ 2,475.00	$ 2,475.00	$ 1,155.00	$ 714.78	$ 55.00	$ -
License	100%	Income	$ 1,000.00	$ 1,000.00	$ 1,000.00	$ 1,000.00	$ 1,000.00	$ 1,000.00	$ 1,000.00	$ 1,000.00	$ 1,000.00	$ 1,000.00	$ 1,000.00	$ 1,000.00
Other	25%	Income	$ 500.00	$ 500.00	$ 500.00	$ 500.00	$ 500.00	$ 500.00	$ 500.00	$ 500.00	$ 500.00	$ 500.00	$ 500.00	$ 500.00
Projects														
Project 1	100%	Income	$ 200.00	$ 100.00	$ -	$ -	$ 100.00	$ -	$ -	$ -	$ -	$ -	$ -	$ -
Project 2	100%	Income	$ -	$ 500.00	$ 1,000.00	$ -	$ -	$ -	$ -	$ -	$ -	$ -	$ -	$ -
Project 3	100%	Cost	$ -	$-12,000.00	$ -120.00	$ -120.00	$ -500.00	$ -	$ -	$ -	$ -	$ -	$ -	$ -
Business Expenses														
Salaries	100%	Cost	$ 5,000.00	$ 5,000.00	$ 5,000.00	$ 5,000.00	$ 5,000.00	$ 5,000.00	$ 5,000.00	$ 5,000.00	$ 5,000.00	$ 5,000.00	$ 5,000.00	$ 5,000.00
Marketing/Sales	100%	Cost	$ 700.00	$ 700.00	$ 700.00	$ 700.00	$ 700.00	$ 700.00	$ 700.00	$ 700.00	$ 700.00	$ 700.00	$ 700.00	$ 700.00
Business Dev	100%	Cost	$ 250.00	$ 250.00	$ 250.00	$ 250.00	$ 250.00	$ 250.00	$ 250.00	$ 250.00	$ 250.00	$ 250.00	$ 250.00	$ 250.00
Operations	100%	Cost	$ 170.00	$ 170.00	$ 170.00	$ 170.00	$ 170.00	$ 170.00	$ 170.00	$ 170.00	$ 170.00	$ 170.00	$ 170.00	$ 170.00
Travel	100%	Cost	$ 500.00	$ 500.00	$ 500.00	$ 500.00	$ 500.00	$ 500.00	$ 500.00	$ 500.00	$ 500.00	$ 500.00	$ 500.00	$ 500.00
Legal/Insurance	100%	Cost	$ 900.00	$ -	$ -	$ -	$ -	$ 600.00	$ -	$ -	$ -	$ -	$ -	$ -
Fees	100%	Cost	$ 100.00	$ 100.00	$ 100.00	$ 100.00	$ 100.00	$ 100.00	$ 100.00	$ 100.00	$ 100.00	$ 100.00	$ 100.00	$ 100.00
Other	100%	Cost												
Total			$ 1,080.00	$-12,620.00	1660.00	$ 2,660.00	$ 4,380.00	$ 4,180.00	$ 9,780.00	$ 9,780.00	$ 1,780.00	$ -888.22	$-4,888.00	$-5,220.00
Cumulative			$ 1,080.00	$-11,540.00	$ -9,880.00	$-7,220.00	$-2,840.00	$ 1,340.00	$11,120.00	$20,900.00	$22,680.00	$21,791.78	$16,903.78	$11,683.78

Figure B-3: Cash flow sample template.

Company or brand _____

Organisation vision: How we want the world to be when we, and others working towards the same vision, succeed

_____

_____

_____

Organisation mission: Our fundamental purpose — why does this company or brand exist? What will we do to achieve our vision?

_____

_____

_____

Brand values: Beliefs that we share about our organisation and the brand that should help us achieve our vision. Values that support our brand culture.

_____

_____

_____

Brand essence: Attributes of our brand (adjectives) — what does our brand feel like? How we describe the soul of our brand?

_____

_____

_____

Logo: What our logo represents — colours, symbols that are important to us.

_____

_____

_____

Comparison: If our brand were a car/computer/drink/sports shoe/ celebrity, what would it be?

_____

_____

_____

Figure B-4: Brand definition template.

Media Release Title: Photo / logo

FOR IMMEDIATE RELEASE/EMBARGOED TILL [*DATE*]

FIRST SENTENCE: Must include the most important information, following the format 'local, blood, man bites dog'. That is, local relevance by providing place names, cities, countries (such as Sydney-based); 'blood' represents the attention grabber, like a significant statistics (such as over 1 million views in the first three days); 'Man bites dog' represents an unusual element (such as an app that allows people to see in the dark).

FIRST PARAGRAPH: substantiating the first sentence with additional information

SECOND PARAGRAPH: description of what is being communicated

THIRD PARAGRAPH: statements from key individuals (such as the CEO or a public figure)

Ends

CONTACT INFORMATION:

For more information please contact

NAME, TEL #, MOBILE #, EMAIL ADDRESS

Figure B-5: Media release template.

[STRENGTHS]	[WEAKNESSES]
List of key strengths — these are typically internally focused (such as skills or assets). Example: • Strong keyword marketing skills (one of our founders was the top grossing keyword marketer in Australia in 2012). • • • •	List of weaknesses — these are typically internally focused. Example: • No experience in-house with running a call centre. • • • •
Opportunities are externally focused. Example: • Upcoming legislation change in New Zealand allows selling our product into the NZ marektOpp. • • • • [OPPORTUNITIES]	Threats are externally focused. Example: • Google announced the launch of a very similar product to ours. • • • • [THREATS]

Figure B-6: SWOT analysis template.

THIS AGREEMENT IS MADE BETWEEN:

> **COMPANY NAME**
>
> Address
>
> **('the Principal')**
>
> **AND**

NAME

> Address
>
> **('the Contractor')**

NATURE AND INTENTION OF PARTIES

> Short description of the nature of the contract and the objective of the contract.

SCOPE AND SCHEDULING OF SERVICES

> Description of scope (areas that the contract needs to address) and when they will be addressed. Ideally should include a list of deliverables and when they are completed by.

FEES, EXPENSES AND PAYMENT TERMS

> Remuneration (for example, $20 per hour), to what extent expenses are covered (and which expenses) and what the Contractor is expected to provide themselves. Also include payment terms (for example, on the 20th day of the following month).

PERIOD OF PERFORMANCE

> How long is the contracted period (start date to end date).

INTELLECTUAL PROPERTY (IP)

> Any IP that the Company or the Contractor specifically want to list as protected. Any clauses that bind either party to respect IP of the other party, and how any IP or copyrights are managed that arise from the work the Contractor is doing.

CONTRACTOR RESONSIBILITIES

> List of tasks and responsibilities the Contractor is expected to perform under this agreement.

Figure B-7: Sample contract for freelancers template. (page 1 of 2)

COMPANY RESONSIBILITIES

List of tasks and responsibilities the Company is expected to perform under this agreement.

CONFIDENTIALITY

All confidentiality clauses relating to this agreement and the nature of the work performed under this agreement.

LIMITATION OF LIABILITY

Statements that protect the Company (and Contractor) from any potential damage caused as a result of performing work under this agreement.

INDEMNIFICATION

Statements that require the Contractor to indemnify the Company from all claims, demands, proceedings and associated damages, charges or costs from the Contractor or from third parties where arising out of or in consequence of the provision of the services.

CONFLICT OF INTEREST

Specific statements about conflict of interest that may arise during or after the contract period.

GENERAL, JURISDICTION AND TERMINATION

Any other clauses and definition of the jurisdiction (laws of Australia, laws of New Zealand). Definition of how and when the contract can be terminated (or specification that contract terminates automatically unless renewed).

SIGNATURE AND DATE OF ALL PARTIES TO THE AGREEMENT

Figure B-7: continued (page 2 of 2).

Options*	Weight*	COST			BENEFIT					Score
		Worst case Cost*	Most likely case Cost*	Best case Cost*	Stakeholder 1	Stakeholder 2	Stakeholder 3	Stakeholder 4	Stakeholder 5	
Option 1		$ 3,500.00	$ 2,000.00	$ 3,000.00						
Evaluation Criteria 1 (0.0 - 1.0)					Rating * Weight	Rating * Weight	Rating * Weight	Rating * Weight	Rating * Weight	Sum of scores for criteria 1
Evaluation Criteria 2 (0.0 - 1.0)					Rating * Weight	Rating * Weight	Rating * Weight	Rating * Weight	Rating * Weight	Sum of scores for criteria 2
Evaluation Criteria 3 (0.0 - 1.0)					Rating * Weight	Rating * Weight	Rating * Weight	Rating * Weight	Rating * Weight	Sum of scores for criteria 3
Evaluation Criteria 4 (0.0 - 1.0)					Rating * Weight	Rating * Weight	Rating * Weight	Rating * Weight	Rating * Weight	Sum of scores for criteria 4
Evaluation Criteria 5 (0.0 - 1.0)					Rating * Weight	Rating * Weight	Rating * Weight	Rating * Weight	Rating * Weight	Sum of scores for criteria 5
										Total benefit score - option 1
Option 2		$ 3,500.00	$ 2,000.00	$ 3,000.00						
Evaluation Criteria 1 (0.0 - 1.0)					Rating * Weight	Rating * Weight	Rating * Weight	Rating * Weight	Rating * Weight	Sum of scores for criteria 1
Evaluation Criteria 2 (0.0 - 1.0)					Rating * Weight	Rating * Weight	Rating * Weight	Rating * Weight	Rating * Weight	Sum of scores for criteria 2
Evaluation Criteria 3 (0.0 - 1.0)					Rating * Weight	Rating * Weight	Rating * Weight	Rating * Weight	Rating * Weight	Sum of scores for criteria 3
Evaluation Criteria 4 (0.0 - 1.0)					Rating * Weight	Rating * Weight	Rating * Weight	Rating * Weight	Rating * Weight	Sum of scores for criteria 4
Evaluation Criteria 5 (0.0 - 1.0)					Rating * Weight	Rating * Weight	Rating * Weight	Rating * Weight	Rating * Weight	Sum of scores for criteria 5
										Total benefit score - option 1
Option 3		$ 3,500.00	$ 2,000.00	$ 3,000.00						
Evaluation Criteria 1 (0.0 - 1.0)					Rating * Weight	Rating * Weight	Rating * Weight	Rating * Weight	Rating * Weight	Sum of scores for criteria 1
Evaluation Criteria 2 (0.0 - 1.0)					Rating * Weight	Rating * Weight	Rating * Weight	Rating * Weight	Rating * Weight	Sum of scores for criteria 2
Evaluation Criteria 3 (0.0 - 1.0)					Rating * Weight	Rating * Weight	Rating * Weight	Rating * Weight	Rating * Weight	Sum of scores for criteria 3
Evaluation Criteria 4 (0.0 - 1.0)					Rating * Weight	Rating * Weight	Rating * Weight	Rating * Weight	Rating * Weight	Sum of scores for criteria 4
Evaluation Criteria 5 (0.0 - 1.0)					Rating * Weight	Rating * Weight	Rating * Weight	Rating * Weight	Rating * Weight	Sum of scores for criteria 5
										Total benefit score - option 1

Figure B-8: Cash benefit analysis template.

Notes for Figure B-8:

- ✔ **Options:** All options must be clearly defined and provide real and viable alternatives to achieving the same outcome

- ✔ **Criteria:** Definition of criteria must be clearly documented and can include any kind of evaluation factor other than cost (for example, implementation time)

- ✔ **Weight:** Criteria can be weighted in terms of their importance (priority); you need to agree on the weighting *before* stakeholders score each option

- ✔ **Cost:** The cost for each option needs to represent the 'total cost' over a given period (for example, three years) and needs to include set-up, material, labour as well as ongoing operational cost (including fees, licenses or maintenance costs). If evaluating business options, cost can be replaced with 'profit/loss', which can be a positive or negative figure and can include any revenue generated by a given option.

Glossary

angel investors: Early stage investors looking to create returns on their investment but accepting a high risk. Generally more willing to contribute time and expertise in addition to money

angel round: Capital raised with *angel investors*

backing the jockey not the horse: Investors trusting the ability of the founders or entrepreneurs (to create a successful business) rather than the concept or business idea itself

bandwidth: Time available to perform a task well (bandwidth = time available). To say, 'I have no bandwidth' means to say, 'I don't have time to take on any additional tasks'

big hairy audacious goal (BIHAG): A huge undertaking that may deeply satisfy someone or change the world

bricks and mortar: Traditional business (as opposed to online businesses that don't have a 'shop front' in the physical world)

burn rate: Amount of money spent in a given period (typically a month) by a start-up

capitalisation table: A spreadsheet or table that shows ownership

stakes in a company and changes to equity over time (for example, as a result of a funding round)

CEO: Chief executive officer

CFO: Chief financial officer

CIO: Chief information officer

COO: Chief operating officer

crowdfunding: Raising small amounts of money from a large number of people rather than a significant sum of money from one investor or a handful of investors

crowdsourcing: Achieving a task by allocating it to a large number of people

down round: A funding round done at a lower valuation than the previous funding round

drill down: Detailed view of summary information (for example, budget or website statistics)

due diligence: Detailed analysis of company records, financial status and performance

elevator pitch: A very short sales statement to a potential investor, business partner or customer (for example, made during a short time spent with someone in an elevator); also known as a 30-second pitch

equity event: Any event that affects the allocation of equity in a company (for example, issuing shares, share transfers, *floating a company*)

floating a company: Listing a company at the stock exchange; also known as going public

freemium: A business model that offers certain aspects of a product or service free of charge with a 'premium' component that is charged for

game changer: An idea, concept or aspect that makes a business project worthwhile or not worth doing at all

half-baked: An idea that's not very well thought through

investment deck: Set of presentation slides (typically used for presenting to investors); also known as deck or slide deck

lipstick: The extra flair that makes an idea, concept, prototype or presentation look visually more appealing

liquidity event: Trade sale or *floating* (which allows investors to 'cash in' on their investment)

magic bullet: The perfect solution to a given business problem (typically doesn't exist and the phrase is used to point this out)

market capitalisation (MCAP): The total value of the tradable shares in a publicly traded company; also known as market cap

milk: To take advantage of a well-performing product or situation to gain financial rewards

mom and pop shop: A small-time operation (in investment terms 'not worth investing')

monetise (traffic): To make money from something (for example, from website traffic through advertising)

'nice to have': A product feature or product that's not essential for the functioning or success of a product or business

non-disclosure agreement (NDA): A confidentiality agreement (often requested by entrepreneurs when speaking about their idea or business to investors)

organic growth: Growth of a company with no intervention (for example, as a result of a marketing campaign)

pitch: The presentation of a business idea or concept to an investor

pivot: Change of direction in company strategy (or fundamental change of product or market)

post-profit: When a company is profitable

post-revenue/pre-profit: When a company is generating revenue/income but isn't profitable yet

pre-revenue: When a company doesn't generate any revenue or income

Q1, 2, 3, 4: Financial quarters relative to the beginning of the financial year (which isn't usually the same as the calendar year). In Australia and New Zealand, many organisations start their financial year on 1 April or 1 July

return on investment (ROI): How much money a project generates for a given sum invested. Some investors use this term slightly cynically when they use it to describe a situation where a company isn't doing well and the investor just wants their money back

runway: Period of time before the company runs out of money (or resources)

'secret sauce': A defendable competitive advantage in a business idea (for example, a proprietary algorithm or trade secret)

'selling the sizzle not only the steak': The need to evoke an emotive response when selling an idea, not just talk about facts and figures

series A round: Typically used for the first significant round of funding (usually with institutional investors at several million dollars)

show stopper: An event or situation that prevents proceeding with a given task (for example, launching a website)

sweat equity: Equity gained in return for hourly contributions (for example, receiving x number of shares per y number of hours worked for the company)

upside: Potentially positive financial outcome; the financial reward of a situation

value proposition: The promise of delivering something valuable (to customers); also known as value prop

value uplift: A project or situation that results in an increased valuation (usually used in relation to company valuation)

vaporware: Software or system that's sold to customers but doesn't actually exist

wash-out round: A finance round done at a particular valuation or in a particular manner to remove certain shareholders from a controlling interest or financial benefit

Index

• *W* •

Notes

Notes

Want to learn more about starting your own online business?

Get your ideas off the ground and on the Web — easily and cost effectively

Starting an Online Business FOR DUMMIES

Australian & New Zealand Edition

A Reference for the Rest of Us!

Drive traffic to your Web business using the latest online tools

Melissa Norfolk
Internet expert and founder,
Norfolk Internet Group

Greg Holden

In the book, you'll find:

- How to promote your business through blogging

- The best ways to make the most of Google's search engine tools

- Tips on how to keep your business secure and legal

- Strategies to help you clearly identify your key market

Order today! Contact your Wiley sales representative.

Available in print and e-book formats.

Business & Investing

978-1-11822-291-1
$24.95

978-1-74216-971-2
$39.95

978-1-74216-853-1
$39.95

978-1-74216-852-4
$39.95

978-1-74216-977-4
$29.95

978-1-74216-998-9
$45.00

978-0-73037-807-5
$29.95

978-1-74216-962-0
$19.95

Reference

978-1-118-30525-6
$19.95

978-1-118-30521-8
$12.95

978-1-74216-963-7
$45.00

978-0-73037-699-6
$39.95

Making everything easier!™